Mastering Entity Frar 2.0

Dive into entities, relationships, querying, performance optimization, and more, to learn efficient data-driven development

Prabhakaran Anbazhagan

BIRMINGHAM - MUMBAI

Mastering Entity Framework Core 2.0

First published: December 2017

Production reference: 1141217

Published by Packt Publishing Ltd.
Livery Place
35 Livery Street
Birmingham
B3 2PB, UK.

ISBN 978-1-78829-413-3

www.packtpub.com

Credits

Author
Prabhakaran Anbazhagan

Reviewers
Jason De Oliveira
Alvin Ashcraft

Commissioning Editor
Merint Mathew

Acquisition Editor
Chaitanya Nair

Content Development Editor
Lawrence Veigas

Technical Editor
Tiksha Sarang

Copy Editor
Safis Editing

Project Coordinator
Prajakta Naik

Proofreader
Safis Editing

Indexer
Francy Puthiry

Graphics
Jason Monteiro

Production Coordinator
Deepika Naik

About the Author

Prabhakaran Anbazhagan is a Microsoft Solution Architect living in Chennai, India. His passion for programming started while creating a website for his school, and that's where the never-ending journey started. He became the secretary of a technology group in college, creating websites yet again, automating symposiums, and much more.

He started his career at a prestigious product-based company; his knowledge was respected and recognized by his seniors, who let him develop tools and automation to sharpen his talents. Lucky guy! People hardly ever get to nurture their talent, but he got a handful of opportunities to sharpen his skills and become a Solution Architect, becoming a jack of all trades but still an expert in .NET.

Prabhakaran has more than 12 years of IT experience in architecting, designing, and developing mission-critical desktop, web, and mobile applications. He has experience in full-stack development spanning ASP.NET MVC, Web API, C#, Mobility expert in Swift, Objective-C, Blackberry Cascades, hybrid apps, SharePoint, JavaScript, jQuery, and MEAN.JS.

I would like to thank my lovely wife, Girija, for standing beside me when I took the decision to write this book. She compromised a lot of quality time and was there beside me throughout this journey, and I dedicate this book to her. I also want to thank my wonderful children, Venba and Inba. They were my stress busters in hectic weekends, and I hope one day they will understand why I was busy with my laptop instead of playing with them. I'd like to thank my parents for taking care of the kids along with my wife while I was hooked on my laptop. My family, including my in-laws, have always supported me in authoring this book, and I really appreciate it.

About the Reviewers

Jason De Oliveira works as a CTO for MEGA International (http://www.mega.com), a software company in Paris (France), providing modeling tools for business transformation, enterprise architecture, and enterprise governance, risk, and compliance management. He is an experienced manager and senior solutions architect, with high skills in software architecture and enterprise architecture.

He loves sharing his knowledge and experience via his blog, speaking at conferences, writing technical books, writing articles in the technical press, giving software courses as MCT, and coaching co-workers in his company. He frequently collaborates with Microsoft and can often be found at the Microsoft Technology Center (MTC) in Paris.

Microsoft has awarded him for more than 6 years with the Microsoft® Most Valuable Professional (MVP C#/.NET) award for his numerous contributions to the Microsoft community. Microsoft seeks to recognize the best and brightest from technology communities around the world with the MVP Award. These exceptional and highly respected individuals come from more than 90 countries, serving their local online and offline communities and having an impact worldwide.

Feel free to contact him via his blog if you need any technical assistance or want to talk about technical subjects (http://www.jasondeoliveira.com).

Jason has worked on the following books:

- *.NET 4.5 Expert Programming Cookbook* (English)
- *WCF 4.5 Multi-tier Services Development with LINQ to Entities* (English)
- *.NET 4.5 Parallel Extensions Cookbook* (English)
- *WCF Multi-layer Services Development with Entity Framework* (English)
- *Visual Studio 2013: Concevoir, développer et gérer des projets Web, les gérer avec TFS 2013* (French)

I would like to thank my lovely wife, Orianne, and my beautiful daughters, Julia and Léonie, for supporting me in my work and for accepting long days and short nights during the week, and, sometimes, even during the weekend. My life would not be the same without them!

Alvin Ashcraft is a software developer living near Philadelphia, PA. He has dedicated his 22-year career to building software with C#, Visual Studio, WPF, ASP.NET, HTML/JavaScript, UWP, and Xamarin apps and SQL Server. He has been awarded as a Microsoft MVP nine times; once for Software Architecture, seven times for C# and Visual Studio & Tools, and for Windows Dev in 2018-2019. You can read his daily links for .NET developers on his blog at `alvinashcraft.com` and UWP App Tips blog at `www.uwpapp.tips`.

He currently works as a Principal Software Engineer for Allscripts, developing clinical healthcare software. He has previously been employed with several large software companies, including Oracle, Genzeon, and Corporation Service Company. There, he helped create software solutions for financial, business, and healthcare organizations using Microsoft platforms and solutions.

He was a technical reviewer for *NuGet 2 Essentials* and *Mastering ASP.NET Core 2.0* by Packt.

I would like to thank my wonderful wife, Stelene, and our three amazing daughters for their support. They were very understanding while I read and reviewed these chapters on evenings and weekends to help deliver a useful, high-quality book for the ASP.NET Core developers.

www.PacktPub.com

For support files and downloads related to your book, please visit www.PacktPub.com.

Did you know that Packt offers eBook versions of every book published, with PDF and ePub files available? You can upgrade to the eBook version at www.PacktPub.com and as a print book customer, you are entitled to a discount on the eBook copy. Get in touch with us at service@packtpub.com for more details.

At www.PacktPub.com, you can also read a collection of free technical articles, sign up for a range of free newsletters and receive exclusive discounts and offers on Packt books and eBooks.

www.packtpub.com/mapt

Get the most in-demand software skills with Mapt. Mapt gives you full access to all Packt books and video courses, as well as industry-leading tools to help you plan your personal development and advance your career.

Why subscribe?

- Fully searchable across every book published by Packt
- Copy and paste, print, and bookmark content
- On demand and accessible via a web browser

Customer Feedback

Thanks for purchasing this Packt book. At Packt, quality is at the heart of our editorial process. To help us improve, please leave us an honest review on this book's Amazon page at https://www.amazon.com/dp/1788294130.

If you'd like to join our team of regular reviewers, you can e-mail us at customerreviews@packtpub.com. We award our regular reviewers with free eBooks and videos in exchange for their valuable feedback. Help us be relentless in improving our products!

To my lovely wife Girija, wonderful kids Venba and Inba

Table of Contents

Preface

Being able to create and maintain data-oriented applications has become crucial in modern programming. This is why Microsoft came up with Entity Framework (EF), so architects can optimize storage requirements while also writing efficient and maintainable application code. This book is a comprehensive guide that will show you how to utilize the power of the EF to build efficient .NET Core applications. It not only teaches all the fundamentals of EF Core, but also demonstrates how to use it practically so you can implement it in your software development.

This book is divided into three modules. The first module focuses on building entities and relationships. Here, you will also learn about different mapping techniques, which will help you choose the one best suited to your application design. Once you have understood the fundamentals of EF, you will move on to learn about validation and querying in the second module. It will also teach you how to execute raw SQL queries and extend the EF to leverage Query Objects using the Query Object Pattern. The final module of the book focuses on performance optimization and managing the security of your application. You will learn to implement fail-safe mechanisms using concurrency tokens. The book also explores row-level security and multitenant databases in detail.

By the end of the book, you will be proficient in implementing EF on your .NET Core applications.

What this book covers

Chapter 1, *Kickstart – Introduction to Entity Framework Core*, teaches you about installing/configuring Entity Framework Core in .NET Core applications. It guides us through performing CRUD (Create/Read/Update/Delete) operations.

Chapter 2, *The Other Way Around – Database First Approach*, explains about reverse engineering and existing database using EF Core. It guides us through performing migrations and also helps us in retaining model changes that won't be lost during migrations.

Chapter 3, *Relationships – Terminology and Conventions*, provides knowledge about relationship terms related to entities, keys, and properties. We will also see different conventions available with respect to relationships.

Chapter 4, *Building Relationships – Understanding Mapping*, helps you explore multiple relationship techniques and explains how to leverage them in your application design. We will also explore how to create relationships using Fluent API.

Chapter 5, *Know the Validation – Explore Inbuilt Validations*, teaches you about how validation works in the framework, explores built-in validations, shows how they should be configured, covers the patterns each validation expects from the user, and shows how the validation error is rendered by the MVC engine.

Chapter 6, *Save Yourself – Hack Proof Your Entities*, helps us with adding validations, explains why we need validations on both the client side and server side, and shows how to achieve it. It also introduces custom validation, and how to create client-side logic for validation and remote validation.

Chapter 7, *Going Raw – Leveraging SQL Queries in LINQ*, teaches you about executing Raw SQL Queries while also teaching you how to execute parameterized queries, compose with LINQ, and, finally, execute without a DbSet or POCO object.

Chapter 8, *Query Is All We Need – Query Object Pattern*, helps you understand the Query Object pattern, and extend EF to leverage query objects.

Chapter 9, *Fail Safe Mechanism – Transactions*, helps you understand the existing behavior of transactions, how to create regular/cross-context transactions, and how to use external DBTransactions.

Chapter 10, *Make It Real – Handling Concurrencies*, elaborates on how concurrency is wired in EF and how to handle it. It explains concurrency tokens in detail and shows how to create a fail-safe mechanism using it.

Chapter 11, *Performance – It's All About Execution Time*, teaches you how to improve EF's performance by properly utilizing the framework, reducing abuses, and much more.

Chapter 12, *Isolation – Building a Multi-Tenant Database*, explores row-level security and multi-tenant databases in detail.

What you need for this book

To work with this text, we assume you are familiar with .NET Core and C#.

You require the following tools to successfully execute the code in this book:

- Visual Studio 2017 Express
- SQL Server 2017 Express
- SQL Server 2017 Developer

Who this book is for

This book is for .NET Core developers who would like to integrate EF Core in their application. Prior knowledge of .NET Core and C# is assumed.

Conventions

In this book, you will find a number of text styles that distinguish between different kinds of information. Here are some examples of these styles and an explanation of their meaning.

Code words in a text, database table names, folder names, filenames, file extensions, pathnames, dummy URLs, and user input are shown as follows: "The new column should be included in the Edit method of PostController."

A block of code is set as follows:

```
public interface IPostDetailQueryHandler
{
    Task<Post> Handle(PostDetailQuery query);
}
```

When we wish to draw your attention to a particular part of a code block, the relevant lines or items are set in bold:

```
public async Task<IActionResult> Index()
{
    return View(await _context.Blogs.FromSql("Select *
        from dbo.Blog").ToListAsync());
}
```

New terms and **important words** are shown in bold. Words that you see on the screen, for example, in menus or dialog boxes, appear in the text like this: "We can see from the following screenshot that the **Url** value is unchanged."

Warnings or important notes appear like this.

Tips and tricks appear like this.

Reader feedback

Feedback from our readers is always welcome. Let us know what you think about this book—what you liked or disliked. Reader feedback is important for us as it helps us develop titles that you will really get the most out of.

To send us general feedback, simply email feedback@packtpub.com, and mention the book's title in the subject of your message.

If there is a topic that you have expertise in and you are interested in either writing or contributing to a book, see our author guide at www.packtpub.com/authors.

Customer support

Now that you are the proud owner of a Packt book, we have a number of things to help you to get the most from your purchase.

Downloading the example code

You can download the example code files for this book from your account at http://www.packtpub.com. If you purchased this book elsewhere, you can visit http://www.packtpub.com/support and register to have the files e-mailed directly to you.

You can download the code files by following these steps:

1. Log in or register to our website using your e-mail address and password.
2. Hover the mouse pointer on the **SUPPORT** tab at the top.
3. Click on **Code Downloads & Errata**.
4. Enter the name of the book in the **Search** box.
5. Select the book for which you're looking to download the code files.
6. Choose from the drop-down menu where you purchased this book from.
7. Click on **Code Download**.

Once the file is downloaded, please make sure that you unzip or extract the folder using the latest version of:

- WinRAR / 7-Zip for Windows
- Zipeg / iZip / UnRarX for Mac
- 7-Zip / PeaZip for Linux

The code bundle for the book is also hosted on GitHub at `https://github.com/PacktPublishing/Mastering-Entity-Framework-Core`. We also have other code bundles from our rich catalog of books and videos available at `https://github.com/PacktPublishing/`. Check them out!

Downloading the color images of this book

We also provide you with a PDF file that has color images of the screenshots/diagrams used in this book. The color images will help you better understand the changes in the output. You can download this file from `https://www.packtpub.com/sites/default/files/downloads/MasteringEntityFrameworkCore20_ColorImages.pdf`.

Errata

Although we have taken every care to ensure the accuracy of our content, mistakes do happen. If you find a mistake in one of our books—maybe a mistake in the text or the code—we would be grateful if you could report this to us. By doing so, you can save other readers from frustration and help us improve subsequent versions of this book. If you find any errata, please report them by visiting http://www.packtpub.com/submit-errata, selecting your book, clicking on the **Errata Submission Form** link, and entering the details of your errata. Once your errata are verified, your submission will be accepted and the errata will be uploaded to our website or added to any list of existing errata under the Errata section of that title.

To view the previously submitted errata, go to https://www.packtpub.com/books/content/support and enter the name of the book in the search field. The required information will appear under the **Errata** section.

Piracy

Piracy of copyrighted material on the Internet is an ongoing problem across all media. At Packt, we take the protection of our copyright and licenses very seriously. If you come across any illegal copies of our works in any form on the Internet, please provide us with the location address or website name immediately so that we can pursue a remedy.

Please contact us at copyright@packtpub.com with a link to the suspected pirated material.

We appreciate your help in protecting our authors and our ability to bring you valuable content.

Questions

If you have a problem with any aspect of this book, you can contact us at questions@packtpub.com, and we will do our best to address the problem.

1

Kickstart - Introduction to Entity Framework Core

I still remember the days when we were spending quite a lot of time on working with relational databases rather than just focusing on solving business problems; those days are definitely gone. To elaborate, let's jot down the issues we had before ORM:

- Data access layers were not portable, which made it hard to change from one platform to another.
- There were no abstractions, which forced us to write manual mapping between objected-oriented objects and data entities.
- Vendor-specific SQL statements, which requires knowledge to port between different RDBMS systems.
- Relied heavily on triggers and stored procedures.

The entire product development process shifted towards tools and open source platforms, and even Microsoft took that path from .NET Core onward. If we keep spending time on writing code which could be achieved through tools, we might end up looking like cavemen.

The Entity Framework was created to address this concern; it was not introduced with the initial .NET framework but rather was introduced in .NET Framework 3.5 SP1.

If we look closely, it was obvious that the .NET team built it for the following reasons:

- To minimize the time spent by the developers/architects on stuff like abstractions and the portable data access layer
- So that the developers do not require vendor specific SQL knowledge
- So that we can build object-oriented business logic by eradicating triggers and SPs

 This book uses Visual Studio 2017 (the latest at the time of writing) and ASP.NET Core 2.0 MVC with Entity Framework 2.0. Even though Entity Framework 2.0 is the latest version, it is still an evolving one, so it would take time for the .NET team to develop all the existing features of Entity Framework 6.2 based on the full .NET Framework.

We will cover the following topics here:

- Prerequisites
- Creating a new project
- Installing Entity Framework 2.0
- Data models
- Database context
- Registering the context in services (.Net Core DI)
- Creating and seeding databases
- Performing CRUD operations

Prerequisites

.NET Core, the open source platform, paved the way for multi-platform support in Visual Studio 2017. The editors came in different flavors, supporting both platform-specific and cross-platform IDEs:

- **Visual Studio**: An exclusive edition for Windows with Community, Professional and Enterprise editions:

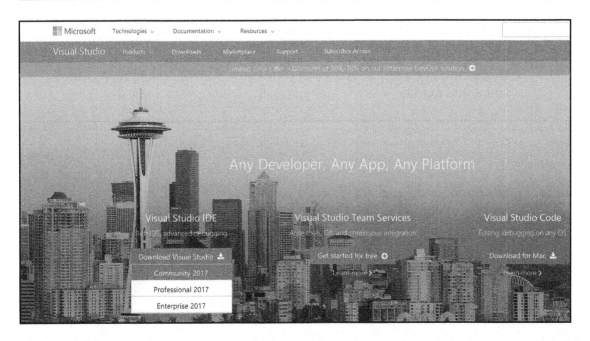

Visual Studio 2017 IDE can be downloaded directly from `https://www.visualstudio.com`.

- **Visual Studio for Mac**: An exclusive edition for macOS, which was actually inherited from Xamarin Studio (Xamarin was acquired by Microsoft):

Visual Studio for Mac can be downloaded from `https://www.visualstudio.com/vs/visual-studio-mac/`.

- **Visual Studio Code**: The cross-platform editor from Microsoft for Windows, Linux, and macOS:

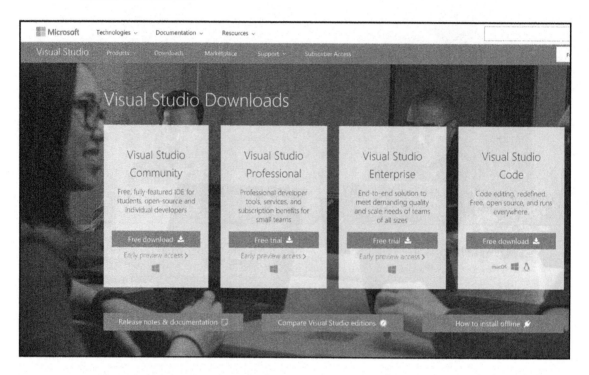

Download the desired version/edition of Visual Studio Code from `https://www.visualstudio.com/downloads/`.

The Visual Studio 2017 installer is segregated into workloads, individual components, and language packs. We will be installing and using **Visual Studio Community 2017** with the workloads **ASP.NET and web development** and **.NET Core cross-platform development**. The workload is a combination of one or more individual components which can also be installed from the **Individual components** tab of the installer, as follows:

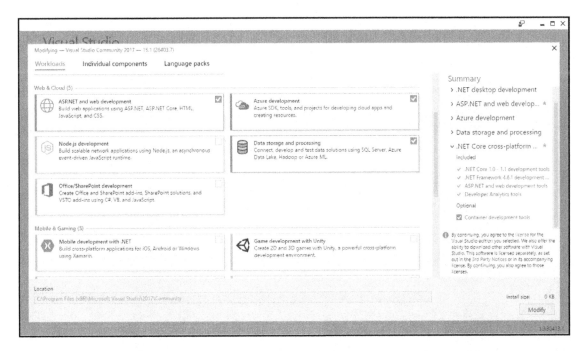

New Visual Studio installer with workloads

We have looked at the different flavors/editions of Visual Studio available to us, and we will be using Visual Studio Community on our journey, which is free of charge for private and test purposes. It is up to the reader to pick an edition which suits their needs (the tools and scaffolding available in the IDE might differ).

Creating a new project

Open Visual Studio and create a new project either from the **File** menu or from the **Start** page.

The Start page

From the **New Project** section, create a new project using any one of the following approaches:

1. Select **Create new project....** On the left pane, select **Templates | Visual C# | .NET Core**. Select the **ASP.NET Core Web Application** template from the list.

2. Search the project templates for the **ASP.NET Core Web Application** and select it. As displayed in the following screenshot, enter `MasteringEFCore.Web` as the **Name** and `MasteringEFCore` as the **Solution name** and click **OK**:

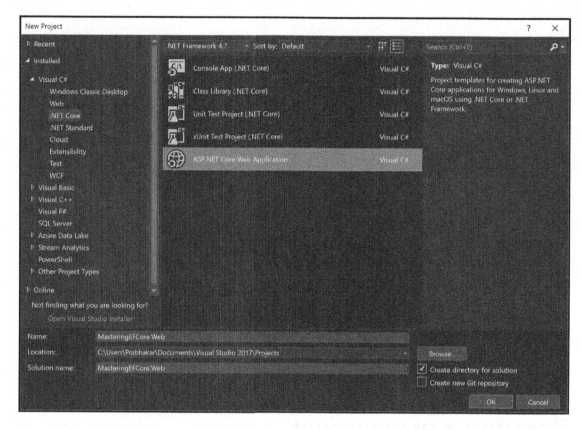

New project

The File menu

From the **File** menu, perform the following steps:

1. Select **New** | **Project**.
2. On the left pane, select **Templates** | **Visual C#** | **.NET Core**.
3. Select the **ASP.NET Core Web Application** template from the list.

4. As displayed in the previous screenshot, enter
   `MasteringEFCore.CodeFirst.Starter` as the **Name** and
   `MasteringEFCore` as the **Solution name** and click **OK**.

Irrespective of the previous two approaches, the selected template will
provide **New ASP.NET Web Application (.NET Core)** dialog, to let us choose
from the following:

- **Empty**
- **Web API**: Creates a Web API project
- **Web Application (Model-View-Controller)**: Creates an MVC Web
  application which also allows us to create APIs

We will be selecting **Web Application (Model-View-Controller)** from the dialog
as shown here:

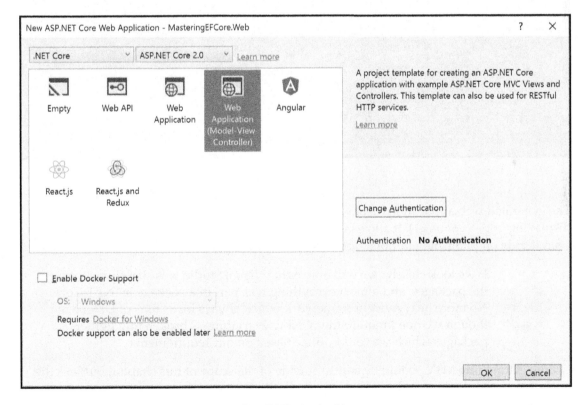

New ASP.NET web project dialog

5. In our case, select **.NET Core**, **ASP.NET Core 2.0**, and the **Web Application (Model-View-Controller)** template, and also keep the Authentication set to **No Authentication**. Click **OK**:

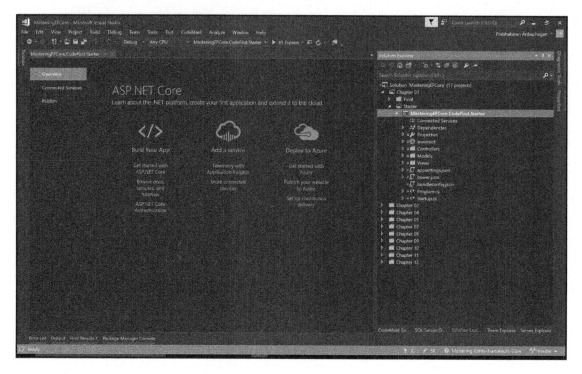

ASP.NET Core web application

The generated web application displays a tabbed interface which is new to us (instead of displaying `index.cshtml`). It allows us to access documentation, connect to any service or even decide on publishing options right from the start page.

If we look closely, we will notice that Visual Studio was silently restoring the packages, and almost everything was part of a package in .NET Core. No more heavyweight framework which always loads tons of DLLs even though we don't require them! Now everything is broken into lighter packages which we could utilize based on our requirements.

I know getting into MVC would be a little outside of the scope of this chapter, but let's dig into a few details before we deep dive into the Entity Framework.

Structuring the web app

A .NET Core web application is composed of the following folders:

- `Dependencies`: SDK, server, and client-side dependencies
- `wwwroot`: All static resources should reside here
- `Connected Services`: To connect external services available in Marketplace
- `launchSettings.json`: Settings required to launch a web application
- `appSettings.json`: Configurations such as logging and connection strings
- `bower.json`: Client-side dependencies should be configured here
- `bundleConfig.json`: Bundling is moved to the JSON configuration now
- `Program.cs`: Everything starts from `Main()` and any program can be made into a web application using the `WebHostBuilder` API
- `Startup.cs`: For adding and configuring startup services like MVC support, logging, static files support and so on
- `Controllers`, `Views`: Part of MVC and contains actions and corresponding views

The structure we had discussed so far is illustrated in the following screenshot:

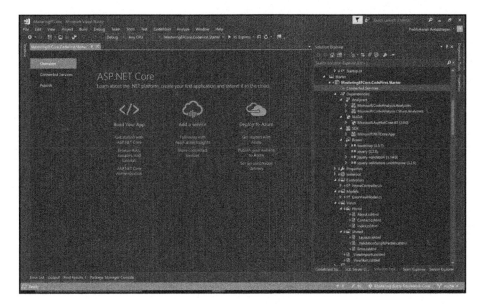

ASP.NET Core Web Application structure

The following highlighted sections in `Views\Shared\_Layout.cshtml` should be modified with the desired application name:

```html
<!DOCTYPE html>
<html>
<head>
  <meta charset="utf-8" />
  <meta name="viewport" content="width=device-width,
      initial-scale=1.0" />
  <title>@ViewData["Title"] - MasteringEFCore.Web</title>
  ...
</head>
<body>
 <nav class="navbar navbar-inverse navbar-fixed-top">
  <div class="container">
    <div class="navbar-header">
      ...
      <a asp-area="" asp-controller="Home" asp-action="Index"
        class="navbar-brand">MasteringEFCore.Web</a>
    ...
    <div class="container body-content">
    ...
    <footer>
       <p>&copy; 2017 - MasteringEFCore.Web</p>
    </footer>
    ...
</body>
```

We have created a .NET Core web application with no authentication and explored the structure of the project, which might help us understand MVC in .NET Core. If we expand the dependencies, it is evident that we don't have built-in support for **Entity Framework (EF) Core**. We will look at the different ways of identifying and installing the packages.

Installing Entity Framework

The Entity Framework package should be installed as part of the NuGet package, and can be done in the following ways:

1. Go to the **Package Manager Console** (**Tools** | **NuGet Package Manager** | **Package Manager Console**), select the project where the package should be installed:

Add the following command in the PM Console to install the package on the selected project:

```
Install-Package Microsoft.EntityFrameworkCore.SqlServer
```

The Package Manager Console will be opened as shown in the following screenshot, Kindly use this space to install the package using the preceding command:

PM console

2. Go to the **Package Management** tab (either from **Tools** or from `Dependencies/Project`).
   - For a solution-wide installation, and availability for all projects that are part of the solution, go to **Tools** | **NuGet Package Manager** | **Manage NuGet Packages for Solution...** or right-click on the solution from **Solution Explorer** and select **Manage NuGet Packages for Solution...**
   - For project wise installation, right-click on **dependencies** from the desired project or right-click on the desired project and select **Manage NuGet Packages...**

3. Search for `Microsoft.EntityFrameworkCore.SqlServer`, select the stable version **2.0.0** and install the package. It contains all the dependent packages as well (key dependencies such as `System.Data.SqlClient` and `Microsoft.EntityFrameworkCore.Relational`):

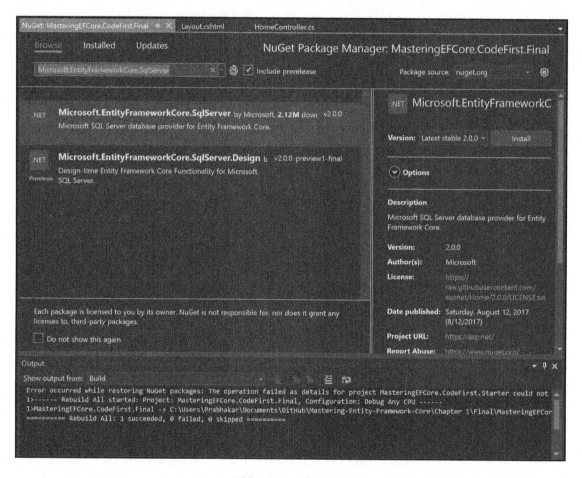

NuGet package manager window

We have looked at different ways of using the **Package Manager** console so far, and installed packages related to EF Core. In the next section, we will start building the schema and later consume the created entities using EF.

Data models

When we think about creating data models in the .NET world way before creating the database, we are a little bit off the legacy track, and yes, it's been widely called the **Code-First approach**. Let's create entity classes using code-first for the `Blogging` application, and put them into the `Models` folder under the project.

Blog entity

Create a `Blog.cs` class file and include the following properties:

```
public class Blog
{
    public int Id { get; set; }
    public string Url { get; set; }
    public ICollection<Post> Posts { get; set; }
}
```

The Entity Framework will look for any property with the name `Id` or `TypeNameId` and marks them as the primary key of the table. The `Posts` property is a navigation property which contains `Post` items related to this `Blog` entity. It doesn't matter whether we use `ICollection<T>` or `IEnumerable<T>` for the navigation property, EF will create a collection for us, `HashSet<T>` by default. We could also create a concrete collection using `List<T>`.

Post entity

Create a `Post.cs` class file and include the following properties:

```
public class Post
{
    public int Id { get; set; }
    public string Title { get; set; }
    public string Content { get; set; }
    public DateTime PublishedDateTime { get; set; }
    public int BlogId { get; set; }
    public Blog Blog { get; set; }
}
```

The `BlogId` property is a foreign key created for the corresponding `Blog` navigation property. As you may notice in this case, we have an individual item as the navigation property, as opposed to a list in the `Blog` entity. This is where relationship type comes into the picture, which we will be exploring more in `Chapter 3`, *Relationships – Terminology and Conventions*.

 EF will allow us to create an individual navigation property without any foreign key in the entity. In those cases, EF will create a foreign key for us in the database table using the `BlogId` pattern (the `Blog` navigation property along with its `Id` primary key). EF will generate them automatically for all navigational properties against the `Id` primary key, but it also allows us to name it differently and decorate it via a custom attribute.

We have built the schema required for the application so far, but it was not configured in EF, so let's see how the data models get connected/configured with EF using database context.

Database context

The main entry point for EF would be any class that inherits the `Microsoft.EntityFrameworkCore.DbContext` class. Let's create a class called `BlogContext` and inherit the same. We will keep the context and other EF related configurations inside the `Data` folder. Create a `Data` folder in the project, and also create `BlogContext.cs` inside this folder:

```
public class BlogContext: DbContext
{
  public BlogContext(DbContextOptions<BlogContext> options)
    : base(options)
  {
  }

  public DbSet<Blog> Blogs { get; set; }
  public DbSet<Post> Posts { get; set; }
}
```

EF interprets `DbSet<T>` as a database table; we have created a `DbSet<T>` property for all the entities for our blogging system. We usually name the properties in plural form as the property will hold list of entities, and EF will be using those property names while creating tables in the database.

Creating a `DbSet` for a parent entity is enough for EF to identify the dependent entities and create corresponding tables for us. EF will be using plural form while deciding table names.

.NET developers and SQL developers debate plural table names and often end up creating entities with two different conventions. As a framework, EF supports those scenarios as well. We could override the default plural naming behavior using Fluent API. Refer to the following Fluent API code:

```
public class BlogContext: DbContext
{
  ...
  protected override void OnModelCreating(ModelBuilder modelBuilder)
  {
    modelBuilder.Entity<Blog>().ToTable("Blog");
    modelBuilder.Entity<Post>().ToTable("Post");
  }
}
```

We have created a database context and configured the data models in it. You may notice we cannot see any connection string pointing to the database. It could have been done using the `OnConfiguring()` method with a hard-coded connection string, but it would not be an ideal implementation. Rather, we will use built-in dependency injection support from .NET Core to configure the same in the next section.

Registering the context in services (.NET Core DI)

The dependency injection support in the ASP.NET framework came too late for the .NET developers/architects who were seeking shelter from third-party tools such as Ninject, StructureMap, Castle Windsor, and so on. Finally, we gained support from ASP.NET Core. It has most of the features from the third-party DI providers, but the only difference is the configuration should happen inside the `Startup.cs` middleware.

First thing's first, let's configure the connection string in our new `appSettings.json`:

```
"ConnectionStrings": {
  "DefaultConnection": "Server
    (localdb)\\mssqllocaldb;Database=MasteringEFCoreBlog;
    Trusted_Connection=True;MultipleActiveResultSets=true"
},
```

Then configure the context as a service (all service configuration goes into `Startup.cs`). To support that, import `MasteringEFCore.Web.Data` and `Microsoft.EntityFrameworkCore` in the `Startup` class. Finally, add the `DbContext` to the services collection by creating and including `DbContextOptionsBuilder` using `UseSqlServer()`:

```
public void ConfigureServices(IServiceCollection services)
{
  // Add framework services.
  services.AddDbContext<BlogContext>(options =>
    options.UseSqlServer(Configuration.GetConnectionString("
      DefaultConnection")));
  services.AddMvc();
}
```

We will be using a lightweight version of SQL Server called **LocalDB** for development. This edition was created with the intention of development, so we shouldn't be using it in any other environments. It runs with very minimal configuration, so it's invoked while running the application. The `.mdf` database file is stored locally.

We have configured the database context using dependency injection, and at this stage, we are good to go. We are almost there. As of now, we have the schema required for the database and the context for EF and services being configured. All of these will end up providing an empty database with literally no values in it. Run the application and see that an empty database is created. It will be of no use. In the next section, let's see how we can seed the database with master data/create tables with sample data, which can be consumed by the application.

Creating and seeding databases

We have created an empty database, and we should have a mechanism by which we can seed the initial/master data that might be required by the web application. In our case, we don't have any master data, so all we can do is create a couple of blogs and corresponding posts. We need to ensure whether the database was created or not before we start adding data to it. The `EnsureCreated` method helps us in verifying this. Create a new `DbInitializer.cs` class file inside the `Data` folder and include the following code:

```
public static void Initialize(BlogContext context)
{
  context.Database.EnsureCreated();
  // Look for any blogs.
```

```
if (context.Blogs.Any())
{
  return;    // DB has been seeded
}
var dotnetBlog = new Blog {
    Url = "http://blogs.packtpub.com/dotnet" };
var dotnetCoreBlog = new Blog { Url =
   "http://blogs.packtpub.com/dotnetcore" };
var blogs = new Blog[]
{
  dotnetBlog,
  dotnetCoreBlog
};
foreach (var blog in blogs)
{
  context.Blogs.Add(blog);
}
context.SaveChanges();
var posts = new Post[]
{
  new Post{Id= 1,Title="Dotnet 4.7 Released",Blog = dotnetBlog,
  Content = "Dotnet 4.7 Released Contents", PublishedDateTime =
   DateTime.Now},
  new Post{Id= 1,Title=".NET Core 1.1 Released",Blog=
  dotnetCoreBlog,
  Content = ".NET Core 1.1 Released Contents", PublishedDateTime
  =
   DateTime.Now},
  new Post{Id= 1,Title="EF Core 1.1 Released",Blog=
  dotnetCoreBlog,
  Content = "EF Core 1.1 Released Contents", PublishedDateTime =
   DateTime.Now}
};
foreach (var post in posts)
{
  context.Posts.Add(post);
}
context.SaveChanges();
}
```

In `Program.cs`, initialize `DbInitializer` in `Main()` by creating the `BlogContext` using dependency injection and pass the same to the `DbInitializer.Initialize()`:

```
public static void Main(string[] args)
{
  var host = BuildWebHost(args);
  using (var scope = host.Services.CreateScope())
```

```
    {
      var services = scope.ServiceProvider;
      try
      {
          var context = services.GetRequiredService<BlogContext>();
          DbInitializer.Initialize(context);
      }
      catch (Exception ex)
      {
        var logger = services.GetRequiredService<ILogger<Program>>();
        logger.LogError(ex, "An error occurred initializing
            the database.");
      }
    }
  }
  host.Run();
}
```

One last piece of the puzzle is missing; we need to add migration whenever we add/manipulate data models, without which EF doesn't know how the database needs to be created/updated. The migration can be performed with the NuGet **Package Manager** console:

Add-Migration InitialMigration

The preceding statement allows EF to create a migration file with tables created from the models configured in the DbContext. This can be done as follows:

Update-Database

The preceding statement applies the migration created to the database. At this moment we are almost done with the EF configuration. We should run the application and verify the database regarding whether or not the proper schema and seed data were updated.

We could verify the table whether it contains seeded data using the following **SQL Server Object Explorer**:

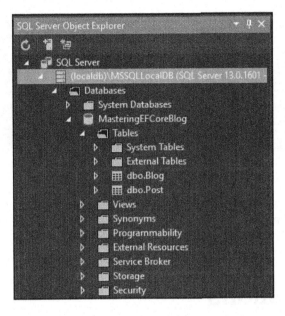

Database created successfully

We can see that the schema was created properly inside the MSSQLLocalDB instance, and we should expand the tables and verify whether the seed data was updated or not. The seed data of the Blog entity was updated properly, which was verified with the following screenshot:

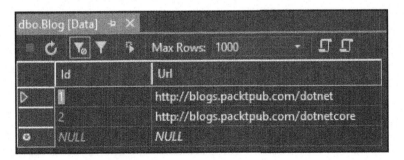

Blog table created with configured schema and seed data

The seed data of the `Post` entity was updated properly, which was verified with the following screenshot.

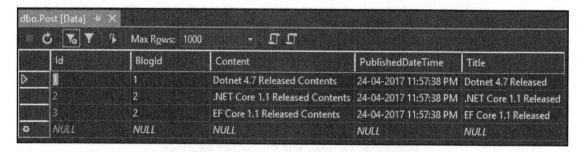

Post table created with configured schema and seed data

We have ensured that the database was created with the proper schema and seed data, and now we should start consuming the entities. In the next section, let's see how we can consume the entities in MVC using scaffolding rather than building everything on our own.

CRUD operations

Creating **CRUD (Create/Read/Update/Delete)** operations manually would take quite a long time. It's a repetitive operation that could be automated. The process of automating this CRUD operation is referred to as **scaffolding**:

1. Right-click on the `Controllers` folder and select **Add | New Scaffolded Item**.
2. A dialog box will be shown to **Add MVC Dependencies**.
3. Select **Minimal Dependencies** from the dialog box.
   Visual Studio adds the NuGet packages required to scaffold the MVC Controller and includes the `Microsoft.EntityFrameworkCore.Design` and the `Microsoft.EntityFrameworkCore.SqlServer.Design` packages. It also includes `ScaffoldingReadme.txt`, which is not required. We could just delete it.

Once the minimal setup is completed, we need to build/rebuild the application otherwise the same **Add MVC Dependencies** dialog will be displayed instead of the **Add Scaffold** dialog.

At this point, the tools required to scaffold **Controller** and **View** are included by Visual Studio, and we are ready to start the process of scaffolding again:

1. Right-click on the `Controllers` folder and select **Add** | **New Scaffolded Item**
2. In the **Add Scaffold** dialog, select **MVC Controller with views, using Entity Framework** as follows:

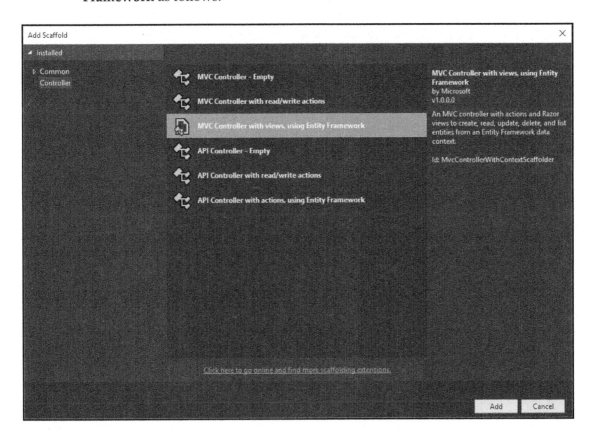

3. In the **Add Controller** dialog, select the appropriate **Model** and **Data context class** (Blog and BlogContext in our case), along with the BlogsController auto-generated controller name:

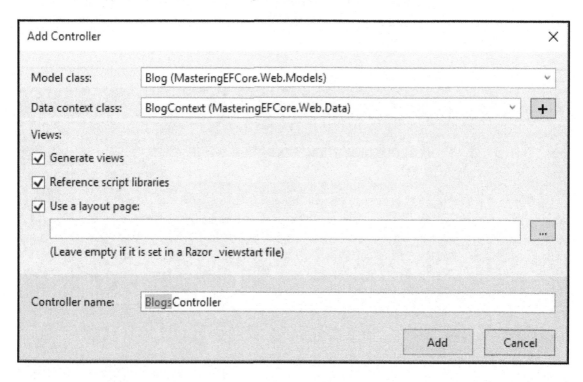

4. Click **Add,** shown as follows:

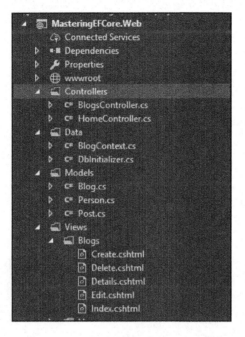

Scaffolded items

5. The scaffolded code includes the CRUD operation in the MVC **Controllers** and **Views**. Examining the scaffolded MVC code would be out of the scope of this chapter, so we will focus on the EF scaffolded part alone:

```
public class BlogsController : Controller
{
  private readonly BlogContext _context;
  public BlogsController(BlogContext context)
  {
    _context = context;
  }
  // GET: Blogs
  public async Task<IActionResult> Index()
  {
    return View(await _context.Blogs.ToListAsync());
  }
  ...
}
```

6. In the preceding code block, you may notice that the dependency injection was used when passing the `BlogContext` (`MasteringEFCoreBlog` database context) to the controller, which was also used in the `Index()` action:

```
<div class="navbar-collapse collapse">
<ul class="nav navbar-nav">
  <li><a asp-area="" asp-controller="Home"
    asp-action="Index">Home</a></li>
  <li><a asp-area="" asp-controller="Blogs"
    asp-action="Index">Blogs</a></li>
  ...
```

7. We need to update the navigation, as displayed in the preceding code, in `Views\Shared\_Layout.cshtml`, without which we won't be able to view the CRUD operations in the `Blogs` module. All set. Let's run and see the CRUD operations in action:

Updated navigation menu with Blogs

The preceding screenshot is the home page of the ASP.NET Core web application. We have highlighted the **Blogs** hyperlink in the navigation menu. The **Blogs** hyperlink would take the user to the **Index** page, which would list all the blog items:

Blogs list

Let's try to create a blog entry in the system, as follows:

Creating a Blog

The **Create** page provides input elements required to populate the entity which needs to be created, so let's provide the required data and verify it:

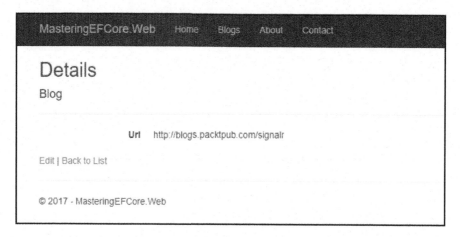

Blog detail page

The **Details** page displays the entity, and the preceding screenshot displays the entity that was just created. The **Edit** page provides input elements required and also pre-populates with existing data, which could be edited by using and updating the data:

Editing a Blog

The **Delete** page provides a confirmation view that lets the users confirm whether or not they would like to delete the item:

Deleting a Blog

 This **Delete** page will be displayed when the user selects the **Delete** hyperlink in the item row on the list page. Instead of deleting the blog directly from the action, we will be routing the user to the **Delete** page to get confirmation before performing the action.

We have identified how to perform CRUD operations using EF Core; since exploring MVC was out of the scope of this book. We stuck to analyzing scaffolding related to EF only.

Summary

We started our journey with Entity Framework by knowing what difference it made when compared with the legacy approach at a high level. We also looked at building the .NET environment and creating and configuring the .NET Core web application with Entity Framework. We explored NuGet packages and package manager, which will be extensively used in the entire book. We also identified and installed the packages required for the Entity Framework in this chapter. Using the Code-First approach, we built the schema, configured them with EF and created and seeded the database with schema and seed data. Finally, we consumed the built schema in our MVC application using the scaffolding tool (which was installed along the way), and also looked at the usage of the database context in the controllers. The Code-First approach can be used for building new systems, but we need a different approach for existing systems. That's where the **Database-First** approach comes into the picture. Let's explore this in Chapter 2, The Other Way Around – Database First Approach.

2

The Other Way Around – Database First Approach

In Chapter 1, *Kickstart - Introduction to Entity Framework Core*, we were exposed to the **Entity Framework** (**EF**) Code-First approach, which might not be useful in all scenarios. We need a provision to reverse engineer existing databases using EF Core, which guides us in performing migrations and helps us in retaining model changes that won't be lost during migrations.

When EF was first released, it supported only the database-first approach, which means we could use the framework only on the existing database. As opposed to the Code-First approach discussed in the previous chapter, the database-first approach will be widely used while we decide to use EF in the existing system.

The topics we will cover here are:

- Preparing the database
- Creating a new project
- Installing Entity Framework
- Reverse engineering the database
- Registering context in services (.Net Core DI)
- Performing CRUD operations

Preparing the database

We will use the same blogging system used in Chapter 1, *Kickstart - Introduction to Entity Framework Core*. In this case, we will create SQL queries required for the existing database and then we will build our blogging system using the database-first approach. Let's write the SQL query of Blog and Post, which were required for the blogging system.

Blog entity script

We will create a Blog table, then alter it to add a primary key constraint, and finally, insert some dummy data into the table. The complete script is available in the GitHub repository at https://github.com/PacktPublishing/Mastering-Entity-Framework-Core/blob/master/Chapter%202/Final/MasteringEFCore.DatabaseFirst.Final/dbo.Blog.sql.

The script required for creating the Blog table and inserting the data is displayed as follows:

```
// Code removed for brevity
CREATE TABLE [dbo].[Blog] (
    [Id]  INT           IDENTITY (1, 1) NOT NULL,
    [Url] NVARCHAR (MAX) NULL
);
GO
// Code removed for brevity
INSERT INTO [Blog] (Url) VALUES
('http://blogs.packtpub.com/dotnet'),
('http://blogs.packtpub.com/dotnetcore'),
('http://blogs.packtpub.com/signalr')
GO
```

We have looked at the Blog table SQL script, now let's look at the Post table script that will introduce a non-clustered index and foreign key.

Post entity script

We will create a Post table and a non-clustered index for better performance, later alter them to add a primary key and foreign key constraints, and finally, insert some dummy data into the table. The complete script is available in the GitHub repository at https://github.com/PacktPublishing/Mastering-Entity-Framework-Core/blob/master/Chapter%202/Final/MasteringEFCore.DatabaseFirst.Final/dbo.Post.sql.

The script required for creating the `Post` table and inserting the data is displayed below:

```
// Code removed for brevity
CREATE TABLE [dbo].[Post] (
  [Id]                 INT           IDENTITY (1, 1) NOT NULL,
  [BlogId]             INT           NOT NULL,
  [Content]            NVARCHAR (MAX) NULL,
  [PublishedDateTime]  DATETIME2 (7)  NOT NULL,
  [Title]              NVARCHAR (MAX) NOT NULL
);
GO
// Code removed for brevity
INSERT INTO [Post] ([BlogId], [Title], [Content],
    [PublishedDateTime]) VALUES
(1, 'Dotnet 4.7 Released', 'Dotnet 4.7 Released Contents',
    '20170424'),
(2, '.NET Core 1.1 Released', '.NET Core 1.1 Released Contents',
    '20170424'),
(2, 'EF Core 1.1 Released', 'EF Core 1.1 Released Contents',
    '20170424')
GO
```

While inserting data time values, we should use the `YYYYMMDD` format, such as *20170424*, and if we are tuned with the `DD-MM-YYYY hh:mm:ss xm` format, then we need to perform an explicit conversion, such as `convert(datetime,'24-04-2017 01:34:09 PM',5)`, otherwise we would get the message, **the conversion of a varchar data type to a datetime data type resulted in an out-of-range value.**

We need to figure out how to execute the previous script using LocalDB:

1. Open the **SQL Server Object Explorer** from the **View** menu.
2. Expand **SQL Server** and **(localdb)\MSSQLLocalDB**.
3. Right-click on **Databases** and select **Add New Database**.
4. In the **Create Database** dialog box, provide the **Database Name** as `MasteringEFCoreDbFirst` and **Database Location** as your project path, and click **OK**.
5. Expand **Databases**, right-click on the **MasteringEFCoreDbFirst** database, and select **New Query**.

6. Copy the `Blog.sql` content and paste it into the **New Query** window, and click the execute icon or *Ctrl+Shift+E*:

The script execution of the Blog script is shown as follows:

Execute Blog.sql on the New Query window

7. Copy the `Post.sql` content and paste it in the **New Query** window, and click the execute icon or *Ctrl+Shift+E*:

The script execution of the Post script is shown here:

```sql
      /****** Object: Table [dbo].[Post] Script Date: 26-04-2017 08:28:49 PM ******/
      SET ANSI_NULLS ON
      GO

      SET QUOTED_IDENTIFIER ON
      GO

      CREATE TABLE [dbo].[Post] (
          [Id]                INT             IDENTITY (1, 1) NOT NULL,
          [BlogId]            INT             NOT NULL,
          [Content]           NVARCHAR (MAX)  NULL,
          [PublishedDateTime] DATETIME        NOT NULL,
          [Title]             NVARCHAR (MAX)  NOT NULL
      );
      GO

      CREATE NONCLUSTERED INDEX [IX_Post_BlogId]
          ON [dbo].[Post]([BlogId] ASC);
      GO

      ALTER TABLE [dbo].[Post]
          ADD CONSTRAINT [PK_Post] PRIMARY KEY CLUSTERED ([Id] ASC);
      GO

      ALTER TABLE [dbo].[Post]
          ADD CONSTRAINT [FK_Post_Blog_BlogId] FOREIGN KEY ([BlogId]) REFERENCES [dbo].[Blog] ([Id]) ON DELETE CASCADE;
      GO

      INSERT INTO [Post] ([BlogId], [Title], [Content], [PublishedDateTime]) VALUES
      (1, 'Dotnet 4.7 Released', 'Dotnet 4.7 Released Contents', '20170424'),
      (2, '.NET Core 1.1 Released', '.NET Core 1.1 Released Contents', '20170424'),
      (2, 'EF Core 1.1 Released', 'EF Core 1.1 Released Contents', '20170424')
      GO
```

(3 row(s) affected)

Query executed successfully at 01:46:33 PM | (localdb)\MSSQLLocalDB (13.... | D

Execute Post.sql on New Query window

We have prepared the database for the Database-First approach; now let's see how we could leverage Entity Framework on the existing database.

Creating new project

We have exhaustively seen how to create a new project in `Chapter 1`, *Kickstart - Introduction to Entity Framework Core*. Kindly refer to the steps involved in creating the project and use the following project information:

Project name: `MasteringEFCore.DatabaseFirst`

Solution name: `MasteringEFCore`

Installing Entity Framework

The Entity Framework package inclusion and the steps involved were also discussed extensively in `Chapter 1`, *Kickstart - Introduction to Entity Framework Core*. So let's focus on the packages that are required for the reverse engineering (database-first approach). The basic package required for the Entity Framework to integrate with SQL Server is as follows:

Add the following command in the PM Console to install the following package:

```
Install-Package Microsoft.EntityFrameworkCore.SqlServer
```

We could also search and install the `Microsoft.EntityFrameworkCore.SqlServer` package using **NuGet Package Manager** window:

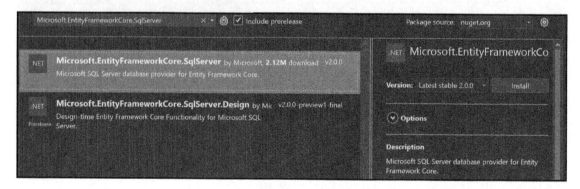

Microsoft.EntityFrameworkCore.SqlServer NuGet package

The packages required for the reverse engineering (auto-generating the models from the database) are listed below, we could add the following command in the PM Console to install these packages:

```
Install-Package Microsoft.EntityFrameworkCore.Tools
Install-Package Microsoft.EntityFrameworkCore.SqlServer.Design
```

We could also search and install the preceding listed packages using **NuGet Package Manager** window as shown here:

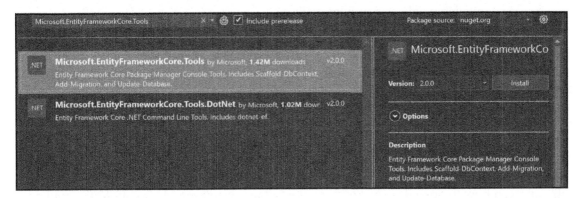

Microsoft.EntityFrameworkCore.Tools NuGet package

Install the `Microsoft.EntityFrameworkCore.Tools` package. This package exposes the Entity Framework commands to the **NuGet Package Manager** console, with which we could perform certain operations such as scaffolding database context:

Microsoft.EntityFrameworkCore.SqlServer.Design NuGet package

Install the `Microsoft.EntityFrameworkCore.SqlServer.Design` package. This package lets us scaffold the models from the SQL Server database.

At the time of writing, `Microsoft.EntityFrameworkCore.SqlServer.Design 2.0.0` was available only as a preview release.

We have installed the packages required to reverse engineer the existing database entities in EF Core. In the next section, we will start reverse engineering to configure EF Core against the database.

Reverse engineering the database

Reverse engineering can be performed on the **NuGet Package Manager** console. We have already seen how to open it, so just execute the following command to scaffold the context and models files:

```
Scaffold-DbContext "Server
(localdb)\mssqllocaldb;Database=MasteringEFCoreDbFirst;
Trusted_Connection=True;"
  Microsoft.EntityFrameworkCore.SqlServer -OutputDir Models
```

Sometimes we might get errors stating that **The package could not be located**. The workaround would be opening the project in a separate solution. If we get an **Unable to open the database** error, then providing access in the SQL Management Studio (connecting the locals from the studio) would resolve the issue. **SQL Server Management Studio (SSMS)** is a free version and can be downloaded from `https://docs.microsoft.com/en-us/sql/ssms/download-sql-server-management-studio-ssms`.

Please refer to the following screenshot:

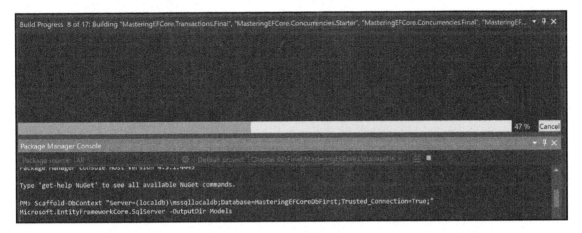

The scaffolding process generates database context files and corresponding data models (in our case, three files in total).

Configuring data context

The auto-generated database context (which is presented in the following code) will include:

- Virtual properties of the tables/entities to hold corresponding data.
- The `OnConfiguring` method, which will configure EF with the database.
- The `OnModelCreating` method, which will ensure certain constraints and relationships are built while creating the database. It would not be used in our database-first approach as we already have them in place.

The database context should contain the following configuration:

```
public partial class MasteringEFCoreDbFirstContext : DbContext
{
  public virtual DbSet<Blog> Blog { get; set; }
  public virtual DbSet<Post> Post { get; set; }
  protected override void OnConfiguring(DbContextOptionsBuilder
    optionsBuilder)
  {
    if (!optionsBuilder.IsConfigured)
    {
      // Move this connection string to config file later
```

```
ptionsBuilder.UseSqlServer(@"Server=
    (localdb)\mssqllocaldb;Database=MasteringEFCoreDbFirst;
    Trusted_Connection=True;");
    }
}
protected override void OnModelCreating(ModelBuilder
modelBuilder)
{
    modelBuilder.Entity<Post>(entity =>
    {
        entity.HasIndex(e => e.BlogId).HasName("IX_Post_BlogId");
        entity.Property(e => e.Title).IsRequired();
        entity.HasOne(d => d.Blog).WithMany(p => p.Post)
            .HasForeignKey(d => d.BlogId);
    });
    }
}
```

In case you have noticed the warning, we need to remove the section using dependency injection, which will be performed in the *Registering Context in Services (.NET Core DI)* section.

Working with the Blog entity

We have discussed in detail the `Blog` model in Chapter 1, *Kickstart - Introduction to Entity Framework Core*, but still, the following highlighted part looks pretty new to us:

- The `Blog()` constructor initializes the `Post` property, which ensures that the collection has a concrete HashSet list created and ready to accept any new items
- The `Post` property has a `virtual` keyword, which instructs EF to lazy load the navigational property `Post`:

```
public partial class Blog
{
    public Blog()
    {
        Post = new HashSet<Post>();
    }
    public int Id { get; set; }
    public string Url { get; set; }
    public virtual ICollection<Post> Post { get; set; }
}
```

There is nothing much to explore in the `Blog` class so, let's move on to the `Post` class.

Working with the Post entity

In `Chapter 1`, *Kickstart - Introduction to Entity Framework Core*, even the `Post` model was discussed in detail, except we have a virtual `Blog` property, which is nothing but a navigational property:

```
public partial class Post
{
  public int Id { get; set; }
  public int BlogId { get; set; }
  public string Content { get; set; }
  public DateTime PublishedDateTime { get; set; }
  public string Title { get; set; }
  public virtual Blog Blog { get; set; }
}
```

We have seen the differences between the model created manually in `Chapter 1`, *Kickstart - Introduction to Entity Framework Core*, and the auto-generated models. Let's see how the database context configuration could be made generic rather than hardcoding the connection string inside the code.

Registering context in services (.NET Core DI)

The warning displayed in the `OnConfiguring(DbContextOptionsBuilder optionsBuilder)` method needs to be addressed. So let's remove that method (highlighted in the following code) and perform configuration inside the `Startup.cs` file using dependency injection.

Refactoring the OnConfiguring() method

If we recap on how we have configured the database context, the auto-generated code had a hardcoded connection string used for configuration. To avoid it, we should have a mechanism to pass on the database context options to the `DbContext` base class; let's see how to do it:

```
public partial class MasteringEFCoreDbFirstContext : DbContext
{
    public virtual DbSet<Blog> Blog { get; set; }
    public virtual DbSet<Post> Post { get; set; }
    protected override void OnConfiguring(DbContextOptionsBuilder
      optionsBuilder)
    {
        // Move this connection string to config file later
        optionsBuilder.UseSqlServer(@"Server=
        (localdb)\mssqllocaldb;Database=MasteringEFCoreDbFirst;
        Trusted_Connection=True;");
    }
}
```

Also include a constructor for the `MasteringEFCoreDbFirstContext` class, which will initialize the `DbContext` through dependency injection from the `Startup` class:

```
public
    MasteringEFCoreDbFirstContext(
      DbContextOptions<MasteringEFCoreDbFirstContext> options)
    : base(options)
    {
    }
```

We have seen how to pass on the options to the database context base class, now we will see how the options were configured with a connection string.

Refactoring the ConfigureServices method

We will use the `ConfigureServices()` method to include the database context framework service to the service collection. Add the following `using` statements to configure the `DbContext` options and to add database context to the services list:

```
using Microsoft.EntityFrameworkCore;
using MasteringEFCore.DatabaseFirst.Final.Models;
```

As we did in Chapter 1, *Kickstart - Introduction to Entity Framework Core*, we will configure context as a service and add DbContext (created using UseSqlServer() through DbContextOptionsBuilder) to the services collection:

```
public void ConfigureServices(IServiceCollection services)
{
  // Add framework services.
  services.AddDbContext<MasteringEFCoreDbFirstContext>(options =>
  options.UseSqlServer(Configuration.GetConnectionString(
    "DefaultConnection")));
  services.AddMvc();
}
```

We have configured the database context in the framework, but if we watch closely, we see that the connection string is coming from a configuration. Next, we will see how the configuration is included in appsettings.json.

The appsettings.json setting

The application settings, as we explored earlier, are based on JSON, and in order to include a setting, we need to add a JSON key-value pair. In our case, ConnectionStrings is the key and the value is again a JSON object that defines DefaultConnection:

```
{
  "ConnectionStrings": {
  "DefaultConnection": "Server=
    (localdb)\\mssqllocaldb;Database=MasteringEFCoreDbFirst;
    Trusted_Connection=True;MultipleActiveResultSets=true"
  },
  "Logging": {
    "IncludeScopes": false,
    "LogLevel": {
      "Default": "Warning"
    }
  }
}
```

In this section, we have configured the database context in the `ConfigureServices()` method and also leveraged `appsettings.json` to make the connection configurable. At this point, all the configuration necessary is completed and EF is ready to consume the database for further implementation. Let's see how the CRUD operations could be performed using EF (we have already seen them in `Chapter 1`, *Kickstart - Introduction to Entity Framework Core*, but still, we will explore a few parts with respect to rendering that which were not covered earlier).

Performing CRUD operations

We have already seen how to create CRUD operations right from scaffolding controllers to their corresponding views for the `Blog` model, so we will create them for the `Post` model in this section:

1. Right-click on the `Controllers` folder and select **Add | New Scaffolded Item.**

2. **Add Scaffold** dialog box, select **MVC Controller with views, using Entity Framework**:

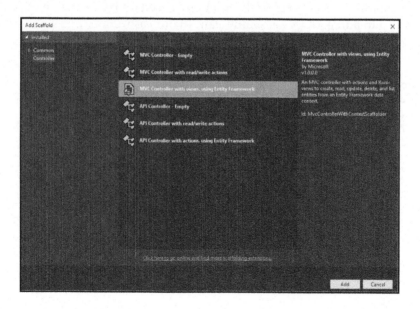

3. In the **Add Controller** dialog box, select the appropriate **Model class** and **Data Context** class (Post and MasteringEFCoreDbFirstContext in our case) along with the auto-generated controller name, PostsController:

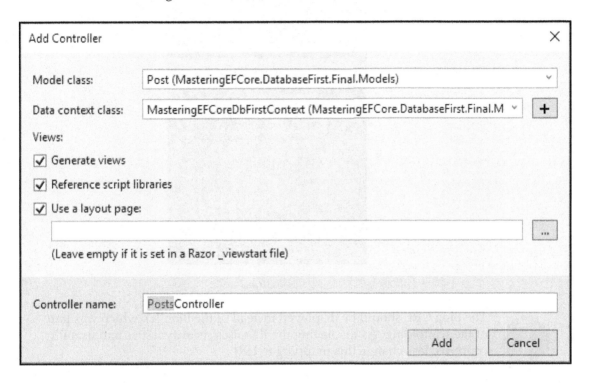

4. Next click **Add** as shown in the following screenshot:

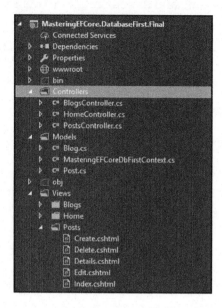

Scaffolded items

 The Blog URL should be displayed instead of the Blog ID, which was part of the scaffolding. As displaying the ID raises security issues and usability concerns, let's change this mapping to URL.

Let's start our changes from the `Index.cshml` file, where we have listed `Blog.Id` instead of `Blog.Url`:

```
@foreach (var item in Model) {
  <tr>
    ...
    <td>
        //@Html.DisplayFor(modelItem => item.Blog.Id)
        @Html.DisplayFor(modelItem => item.Blog.Url)
    </td>
  </tr>
}
```

The changes are reflected on the screen, where we can see Blog URLs rendered instead of the IDs that were listed before:

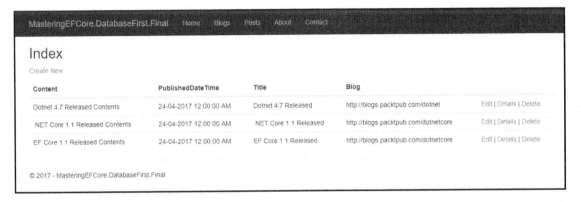

MasteringEFCore.DatabaseFirst.Final   Home   Blogs   Posts   About   Contact

Index

Create New

Content	PublishedDateTime	Title	Blog	
Dotnet 4.7 Released Contents	24-04-2017 12:00:00 AM	Dotnet 4.7 Released	http://blogs.packtpub.com/dotnet	Edit	Details	Delete
.NET Core 1.1 Released Contents	24-04-2017 12:00:00 AM	.NET Core 1.1 Released	http://blogs.packtpub.com/dotnetcore	Edit	Details	Delete
EF Core 1.1 Released Contents	24-04-2017 12:00:00 AM	EF Core 1.1 Released	http://blogs.packtpub.com/dotnetcore	Edit	Details	Delete

© 2017 - MasteringEFCore.DatabaseFirst.Final

Posts list view

We have scaffolded CRUD operations and modified Blog ID usage to URLs in the `Post` index action. Let's update the same on the other actions as well.

Creating controller action

The changes we made in the previous section need to be updated in the `SelectList` collection, which will be used by MVC to render the drop-down list. By default, MVC scaffolding provides a `SelectList` (we have commented on that line) that has `Id` in the `Value` field and needs to be modified to `Url`, otherwise it will display only numeric values on the screen (a serious security issue and not so user-friendly):

```
public IActionResult Create()
{
  //ViewData["BlogId"] = new SelectList(_context.Blog, "Id", "Id");
  ViewData["BlogId"] = new SelectList(_context.Blog, "Id", "Url");
  return View();
}
```

The following screenshot shows the `Url` mapped to the **BlogId** control, but there is something additional that needs to be fixed. The **BlogId** should be either just `Blog` or `Blog` URL.

I will leave this part as an exercise, kindly make changes to all the labels associated with the **BlogId** column:

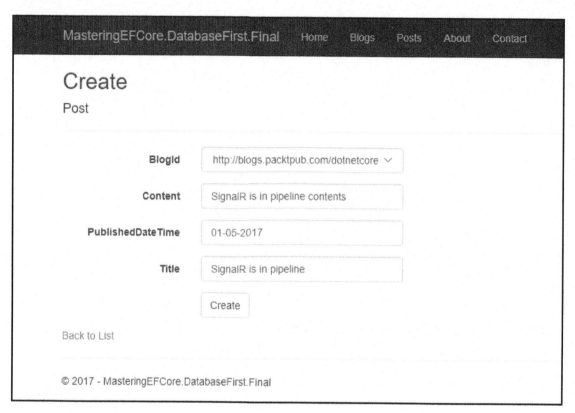

Posts create view

The same change needs to be applied to the `Post` action of `Create` as well:

```
[HttpPost]
[ValidateAntiForgeryToken]
public async Task<IActionResult>
Create([Bind("Id,BlogId,Content,PublishedDateTime,Title")]
    Post post)
{
  ...
  ViewData["BlogId"] = new SelectList(_context.Blog, "Id", "Url",
    post.BlogId);
  return View(post);
}
```

The changes are reflected in the newly included/added items displayed on the screen (the **Index** action was already modified to list the Blog URLs):

List view with new post

We have updated the references to the Blog ID with Blog URLs in the Post **Create** (HTTP, GET, and POST) action. Let's update the same on the other actions as well.

Edit controller action

The same changes that we discussed with respect to the `SelectList` collection must be made to the **Edit** action as well:

```
public async Task<IActionResult> Edit(int? id)
{
  ...
  ViewData["BlogId"] = new SelectList(_context.Blog, "Id", "Url",
    post.BlogId);
  return View(post);
}
```

The following screenshot shows the URL mapped to the **BlogId** control, and as part of the exercise, kindly make changes to the **BlogId** label with the literal changes you made in the *Creating controller action* section:

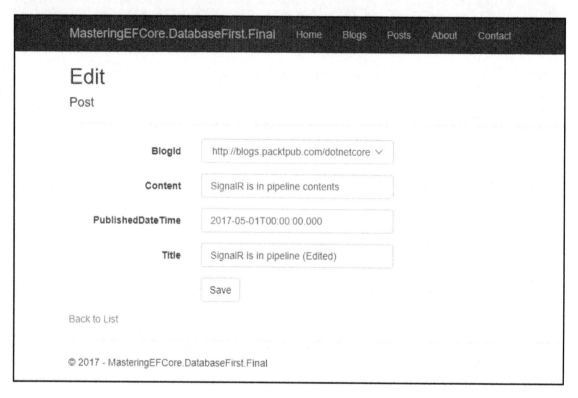

Edit a post

The same change needs to be applied to the Post action of Edit as well:

```
[HttpPost]
[ValidateAntiForgeryToken]
public async Task<IActionResult> Edit(int id,
  [Bind("Id,BlogId,Content,PublishedDateTime,Title")] Post post)
{
  ...
  ViewData["BlogId"] = new SelectList(_context.Blog, "Id", "Url",
    post.BlogId);
  return View(post);
}
```

The changes were reflected in the updated item that was displayed on the screen:

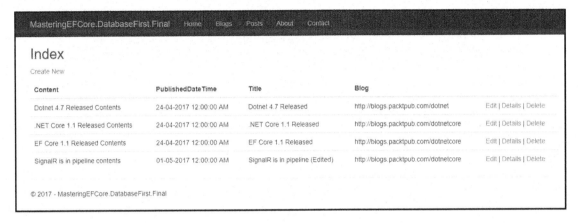

List view with edited post

We have updated the references to the Blog ID with Blog URLs in the `Post` **Edit** (`HTTP`, `Get`, and `Post`) action. Let's update this on the remaining `DELETE` action.

The Delete view

`Blog.Url` should be displayed instead of Blog ID in the `Delete` view as well:

```
<dl class="dl-horizontal">
    ...
    <dd>
        @Html.DisplayFor(model => model.Blog.Url)
    </dd>
</dl>
```

The changes were reflected on the **Delete** confirmation screen that now displays the Blog URL instead of the Blog ID:

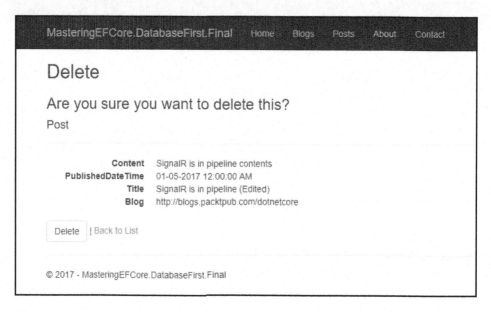

Delete a post

The **Post** list page doesn't display the deleted item, which ensures that the data has been deleted from the table:

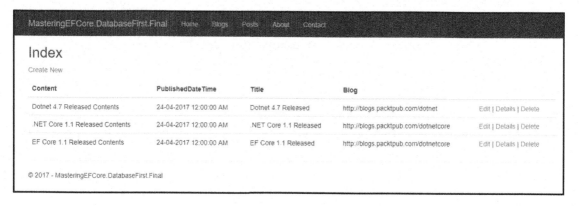

List view after deleting a post

We have identified certain missing pieces of the puzzle in the CRUD operations that were covered in Chapter 1, *Kickstart - Introduction to Entity Framework Core* because there is no specific change that needs to be addressed in the database-first approach.

Summary

We have learned how to leverage Entity Framework on an existing system that has a live database (for illustrative purposes, we have created SQL scripts to create and simulate an existing database). We have explored NuGet packages that expose the APIs required to reverse engineer the database (including database context and corresponding data models). Finally, we have consumed the existing database in our MVC application using the scaffolding tool (which was installed on the way), and have also seen the changes required to the auto-generated code (which were not covered in Chapter 1, *Kickstart - Introduction to Entity Framework Core*). The database-first approach was just a mechanism used for building existing systems (leveraging EF in the existing system). So far, we have used relationships (new or existing ones), but haven't figured out the relationships supported by Entity Framework. Let's explore them in Chapter 3, *Relationships – Terminology and Conventions*.

3
Relationships – Terminology and Conventions

In Chapter 2, *The Other Way Around – Database First Approach*, we re-engineered the existing database using Entity Framework's Database-First approach. Let's now start to understand the terminologies and conventions used in relationships.

Entities are of no use if we don't give them an identity. The relationship terms we will be exploring in this chapter will provide an identity for the entities, which not only describes them, but also helps us in creating relationships between different entities.

The topics we will cover in this chapter are:

- Understanding relationship terms:
    - Data models
    - Principal entity
    - Principal key
    - Dependent entity
    - Foreign key
    - Navigation property
- Conventions in a relationship:
    - Fully-defined relationships
    - No foreign key property
    - Single navigation property
    - Foreign key
    - Inverse property

Understanding relationship terms

We have created and used data models or entities so far, but we haven't figured out how they are related. Let's understand how they are related and the terminologies used for those relationships.

Data models

We will revisit the data models we created and consumed in Chapter 1, *Kickstart - Introduction to Entity Framework Core* (using the Code-First approach), which could be used to understand the relationship terminologies. For illustration purposes, we will tweak those objects to understand different terminologies that were not used in the system.

Blog entity

The Blog entity/data model we created using the Code First approach is displayed as follows:

```
public class Blog
{
    public int Id { get; set; }
    public string Url { get; set; }
    public ICollection<Post> Posts { get; set; }
}
```

We will be using the Blog model to understand the following:

- Principal entity
- Principal key
- Navigational property

The Post entity

The Post entity/data model we created using the Code-First approach is displayed as follows:

```
public class Post
{
    public int Id { get; set; }
    public string Title { get; set; }
    public string Content { get; set; }
```

```
public DateTime PublishedDateTime { get; set; }
public int BlogId { get; set; }
public Blog Blog { get; set; }
}
```

We will be using the `Post` model to understand the following:

- Dependent entity
- Foreign key
- Navigational property
- Reference navigation property
- Inverse navigation property

As part of the *Data model* section, we captured key relationship terms in their appropriate models, now we will focus on each one of them in detail.

Principal entity

The entity that will serve as a parent in a relationship is termed a **principal entity**. In the database world, this entity holds the primary key that will be used by the dependent entities in building relationships. Consider the following diagram:

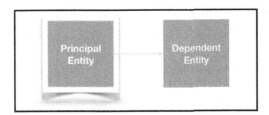

In our blogging system, the `Blog` entity serves as a parent to the `Post` entity, hence we could conclude `Blog` is the principal entity. The relationship we have between the two entities could be termed as an **Association**. Consider the following diagram:

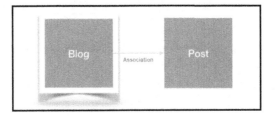

In our blogging system, the `Person` entity serves as a parent to the `User` entity, hence we could conclude `Person` is the Principal entity. The relationship we have between the two entities could be termed a **Containment**. Consider the following diagram:

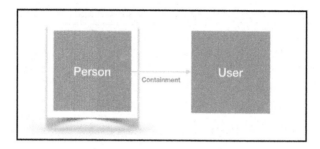

We have seen the principal entity; let's explore the key of the relationships built using a principal entity in the next section.

Principal key

The parent entity needs a unique key to associate itself with the child, and the key used for this purpose is termed as the **principal key**. In our blogging system, the `Id` property of the `Blog` entity would be the unique key/principal key of the blog entry/item that will be used by the dependent `Post` entity to build a relationship with the `Blog` entity:

```
public class Blog
{
    public int Id { get; set; }
    public string Title { get; set; }
    public string Subtitle { get; set; }
    public string Url { get; set; }
    public string Description { get; set; }
    public DateTime CreatedAt { get; set; }
    public DateTime ModifiedAt { get; set; }
    public int CreatedBy { get; set; }
    public int ModifiedBy { get; set; }
    public ICollection<Post> Posts { get; set; }
}
```

The **Blog** table design is shown as follows. In the table design, the highlighted **Id** field would be the unique primary key of the table:

Apart from the primary key, there is a possibility that a non-primary key could be used in building relationships, which could be termed an **alternate key**. In our blogging system, the **Url** property of the **Blog** entity could be an alternate key for building relationships:

We have seen the principal key, which defines the relationships built using the principal entity; let's explore the dependent entity in the next section.

Dependent entity

The entity that cannot survive on its own (always dependent on its parent) ends up being a child. In a relationship, this would be termed a **Dependent entity**. Consider the following diagram:

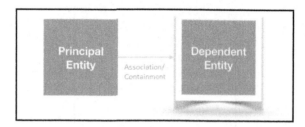

In our blogging system, the Post entity depends on the Blog entity (posts are made for the corresponding blog, so without a blog entry the post wouldn't exist), hence we could conclude Post is the dependent entity. In the database world, this entity holds a foreign key that will hold the reference to the primary entity in the relationships. This is depicted in the following diagram:

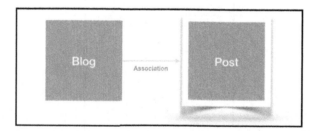

In our blogging system, the User entity depends on the Person entity, hence we could conclude User is the dependent entity. This is depicted in the following diagram:

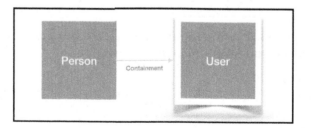

We have seen the dependent entity; let's explore the key of the relationships built using the dependent entity in the next section.

Foreign key

The child entity needs a unique key to associate itself with the parent. The key usually holds the value of the principal key to mark its relationship with the parent and is termed a **foreign key**. In our blogging system, the `BlogId` property of the `Post` entity holds the reference to the parent unique key/principal key to denote the relationship with the `Blog` entity:

```
public class Post
{
    public int Id { get; set; }
    public string Title { get; set; }
    public string Content { get; set; }
    public string Summary { get; set; }
    public DateTime PublishedDateTime { get; set; }
    public string Url { get; set; }
    public long VisitorCount { get; set; }
    public DateTime CreatedAt { get; set; }
    public DateTime ModifiedAt { get; set; }
    public int CreatedBy { get; set; }
    public int ModifiedBy { get; set; }
    public int BlogId { get; set; }
    public Blog Blog { get; set; }
    public int AuthorId { get; set; }
    public User Author { get; set; }
    public int CategoryId { get; set; }
    public Category Category { get; set; }
    public ICollection<TagPost> TagPosts { get; set; }
    public ICollection<Comment> Comments { get; set; }
}
```

In database terminology, we would still call the property a foreign key. The `Post` table design is shown as follows. In the design, the highlighted `BlogId` field would be the foreign key of the table:

We have seen the foreign key, which defines the relationships built using the dependent entity. Let's explore navigation properties, which define the direction or nature of relationships, in the next section.

Navigation property

A property that can be defined as either a principal entity or dependent entity, whether it's referring to its parent or holding one or many dependent entities to it, is called the **navigation property**. We can see that it just holds the references to both parent and child but in a different way, so we could categorize them as the following:

- Collection navigation property
- Reference navigation property
- Inverse navigation property

Let's explore the types of navigation property in detail.

Collection navigation property

We can work out what it actually does from its name, it holds a collection of dependent entities (or references to a list of dependent items) and it always holds references to multiple items. In our blogging system, the `Posts` property of the `Blog` entity could be treated as a collection navigation property:

```
public class Blog
{
    ... // code removed for brevity
    public ICollection<Post> Posts { get; set; }
}
```

The `Blog` and `Post` class diagrams are displayed as follows. In the design, the highlighted `Posts` field in the `Blog` entity would be the collection navigation property:

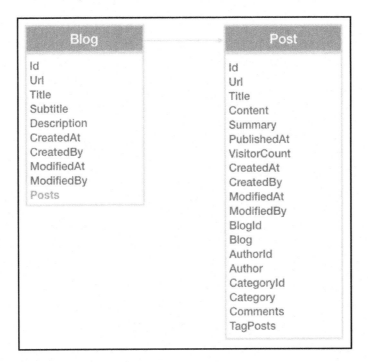

We have seen the property that holds the child collection; let's explore how the dependent entity holds a reference to its parent in the next section.

Reference navigation property

We can work out what it actually does from its name. Yes, it holds a reference to its parent entity and it always holds a reference to a single item. In our blogging system, the `Blog` property of the `Post` entity could be treated as a reference navigation property:

```
public class Post
{
  ... // code removed for brevity
  public int BlogId { get; set; }
  public Blog Blog { get; set; }
}
```

The `Blog` and `Post` class diagrams are shown as follows. In the design, the highlighted `Blog` field in the `Post` entity would be the reference navigation property:

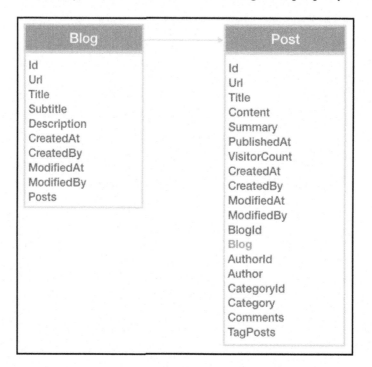

We have seen the property that holds the reference to its parent, and it causes some confusion as to what the inverse navigation property will be.

Inverse navigation property

You guessed it, this is a little bit tricky as it always refers to the other end of the relationship. In our blogging system, the Blog property of the Post entity could be treated as an inverse navigation property of the Posts property of the Blog entity:

```
public class Post
{
    ... // code removed for brevity
    public Blog Blog { get; set; }
}
```

This is also true vice versa, which means the Posts property of the Blog entity could be treated as an inverse navigation property of the Blog property of the Post entity:

```
public class Blog
{
    ... // code removed for brevity
    public ICollection<Post> Posts { get; set; }
}
```

The Blog and Post class diagrams are shown as follows. In the design, the highlighted Blog field in the Post entity and the Posts field in the Blog entity would be the inverse navigation properties:

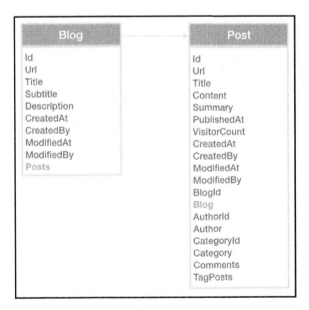

We have explored different relationship terms so far; let's explore the conventions available in a relationship in the next section.

Conventions in a relationship

By now, we should be able to say that relationships are identified by Entity Framework while it is analyzing our data model. So, from the preceding section, it is evident that we should have a navigation property in both the entities for a relationship.

While analyzing the relationship, Entity Framework can only identify a primary key on its own. But, if we use an alternate key for a relationship, then explicitly we should mark it as the principal key using the Fluent API. In our blogging system, the implementation in `OnModelCreating` would be as follows:

```
modelBuilder.Entity<Post>()
.HasOne(p => p.Blog)
.WithMany(b => b.Posts)
.HasForeignKey(p => p.BlogUrl)
.HasPrincipalKey(b => b.Url);
```

It's also evident that, for any relationship, we need a property that should be against a data model and not a scalar datatype (it would be ignored by EF for relationships).

Fully-defined relationships

A relationship that contains all properties/terminologies seen in the previous section could be termed a **fully-defined relationship**. To be precise, it should have navigational properties on both entities involved in a relationship, and the dependent entity should have a foreign key property as well:

```
public class Blog
{
   ... // code removed for brevity
   public ICollection<Post> Posts { get; set; }
}
public class Post
{
   ... // code removed for brevity
   public int BlogId { get; set; }
   public Blog Blog { get; set; }
}
```

The `Blog` and `Post` class diagrams are shown as follows. In the design, the highlighted properties would be the navigational properties:

- The `Blog` field in the `Post` entity and the `Posts` field in the `Blog` entity would be the inverse navigation properties
- The `Blog` field in the `Post` entity would be the reference navigation property
- The preceding two navigation properties complete the relationship, so it's called a fully-defined relationship

The following diagram illustrates fully-defined relationship between `Blog` and `Post` entities:

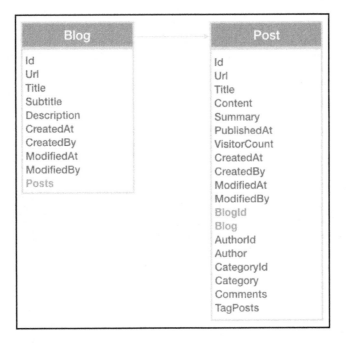

The data models we have used so far have a fully-defined relationship. We will tweak these data models to illustrate the other conventions in future sections.

Fully-defined relationships - under the hood

The EF Core uses the mechanism internally for creating relationship between entities based on the following scenarios:

- If the two entities have navigation properties pointing to each other; EF will configure them as inverse navigation properties

In the following code, the `Posts` property of the `Blog` entity and the `Blog` property of the `Post` entity would be configured as inverse navigation properties:

```
public class Blog
{
    // Code removed for brevity
    public ICollection<Post> Posts { get; set; }
}
public class Post
{
    // Code removed for brevity
    public Blog Blog { get; set; }
}
```

The following image illustrates the relationship created based on the navigational properties:

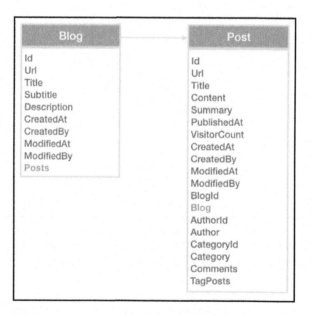

- EF will consider the property a foreign key if the naming convention uses principal entity name with primary key property name:

In the following code, the principal entity `Blog`, with its primary key `Id`, will have the foreign key `BlogId` in the `Post` entity:

```
public class Blog
{
    public int Id { get; set; }
    // Code removed for brevity
}
public class Post
{
    // Code removed for brevity
    public int BlogId { get; set; }
}
```

The following image illustrates the how a foreign key is created in `Post` entity:

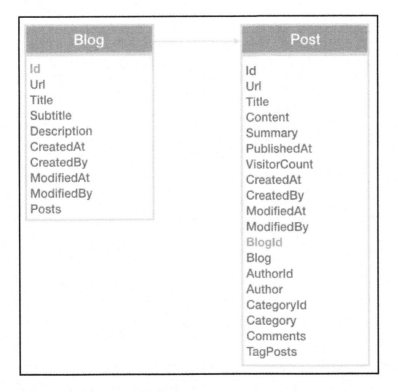

- EF will create a foreign key relationship if the principal entity primary key matches the dependent entity reference key.

In the following code, the primary key `BlogId` of the `Blog` entity will have the foreign key `BlogId` in the `Post` entity:

```
public class Blog
{
  public int BlogId { get; set; }
  // code removed for brevity
}
public class Post
{
  // code removed for brevity
  public int BlogId { get; set; }
}
```

The following image illustrates foreign key is related with its matching principal entity's identifier:

- EF will create a foreign key

In the following code, the `SomeBlog` navigation property of the `Post` entity with the primary key `Id` of the `Blog` entity will have the foreign key `SomeBlogId` in the `Post` entity:

```
public class Blog
{
    public int Id { get; set; }
     // code removed for brevity
}
public class Post
{
    // code removed for brevity
    public Blog SomeBlog { get; set; }
    public int SomeBlogId { get; set; }
}
```

The following image illustrates foreign key is based on dependent entity's navigation property name:

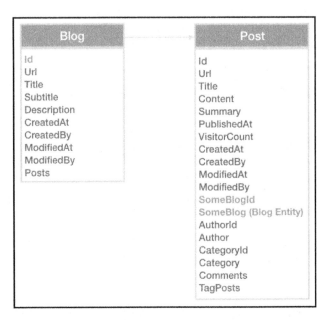

We have explored a fully-defined relationship with the different naming conventions expected by EF on identifying the relationship; let us see about other conventions in the coming sections.

No foreign key property

We usually create entities using fully-defined relationships, but this is not expected by Entity Framework. In a relationship, the foreign key is not required, but it is recommended to have one:

The following code does not contain foreign key in the `Post` entity and still the relationship is formed:

```
public class Blog
{
    // code removed for brevity
    public ICollection<Post> Posts { get; set; }
}
public class Post
{
    // code removed for brevity
    // Foreign key BlogId was removed from here
    public Blog Blog { get; set; }
}
```

The following image illustrates that without foreign key, the relationship is built:

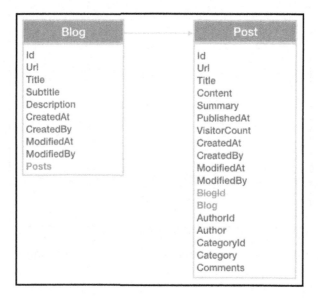

We have removed the `BlogId` foreign key from the `Post` entity, and it still works as expected.

No foreign key property - under the hood

The relationship works even if the foreign key is not available because Entity Framework creates a shadow property for us. It follows the naming convention of **navigational property with primary key name:**

In the following code the foreign key in the `Post` entity is injected by the framework:

```
public class Blog
{
    ... // code removed for brevity
    public ICollection<Post> Posts { get; set; }
}
public class Post
{
    ... // code removed for brevity
    public int BlogId { get; set; } // shadow property created by EF
    public Blog Blog { get; set; }
}
```

The following image illustrates that foreign key is injected by the framework:

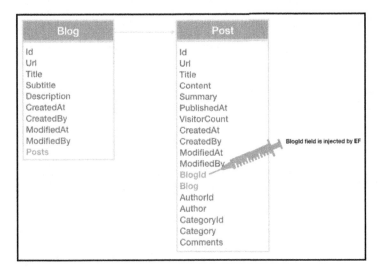

We did something different from the conventional entities removed the foreign key from the navigational properties, but still, the relationship worked as expected. Let us see what other parts can be removed in the coming sections.

Single navigation property

In the same way we removed the foreign key from the entity, we could remove a navigation property completely from an entity and the relationship would still work. In a relationship, the navigation property is not required in the dependent entity, meaning that having a single navigation property on a principal entity is more than sufficient:

In the following code, both the foreign key and navigation property were removed and still relationship works as expected:

```
public class Blog
{
    ... // code removed for brevity
    public ICollection<Post> Posts { get; set; }
}
public class Post
{
    ... // code removed for brevity
    // Foreign key "BlogId" and navigation property "Blog" was
        removed here
}
```

The following image illustrates that both foreign key and navigation key were removed from the entity:

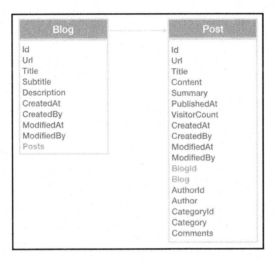

We have removed the `Blog` navigation property from the `Post` entity, and it still works as expected.

Foreign key

We could use a different naming convention for a foreign key and still map that foreign key against the navigation property (using the `ForeignKey` data annotation does the trick). In a relationship, a navigation property is not required in the dependent entity, meaning that having a single navigation property on a principal entity is more than sufficient:

In the following code, the custom foreign key is mapped against the navigation property:

```
public class Blog
{
  ... // code removed for brevity
  public ICollection<Post> Posts { get; set; }
}
public class Post
{
  ... // code removed for brevity
  public int BlogSomeId { get; set; }
  [ForeignKey("BlogSomeId")]
  public Blog Blog { get; set; }
}
```

The following image illustrates that the custom foreign key is mapped against the navigation property:

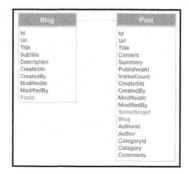

We have modified the foreign key to `BlogSomeId` and configured it against the navigation property which is the `Blog` of the `Post` entity, and it still works as expected.

Inverse property

If we have more than one navigation property in an entity, it makes sense to use an inverse property to pair the navigational properties for a relationship. There will be occurrences where even though we have a fully-defined relationship, we still need an inverse property in order to pair up the navigational properties due to custom naming conventions that don't fall into any of EF's discovery mechanisms:

In the following code, the custom foreign key and navigation property were configured in the inverse navigation property:

```
public class Blog
{
    ... // code removed for brevity
    [InverseProperty("SomeBlog")]
    public ICollection&lt;Post> SomePosts { get; set; }
}
public class Post
{
    ... // code removed for brevity
    public int SomeBlogId { get; set; }
    public Blog SomeBlog { get; set; }
}
```

The following image illustrates that the custom foreign key and navigation property were configured in the inverse navigation property:

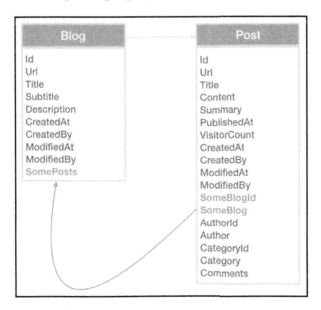

We have introduced the `SomeBlog` inverse property in the `Blog` entity, which pairs with the `SomeBlog` navigation property of the `Post` entity.

Summary

In this chapter, we were introduced to the terminologies and conventions used for relationships in Entity Framework. We started right from a fully-defined relationship, and from there we started trimming the relationship, but still made the relationship work. Finally, we customized and paired up navigational properties with customized properties, and still made the relationship work. This chapter has introduced us to relationships (we also had a peek at the Fluent API), but we didn't get the chance to understand different relationships. Let's explore them in `Chapter 4`, *Building Relationships – Understanding Mapping*.

4
Building Relationships – Understanding Mapping

In Chapter 3, *Relationships – Terminology and Conventions*, we studied terminologies and conventions used in a relationship; let's start using them in building relationships. We have been using only Blog and Post entities so far, which doesn't do any good to the blogging system. Let's expand them to other entities such as Comment, Tag, and so on, and we will leverage them to understand the relationships as well.

The relationship was introduced right from the initial **Entity Framework (EF)** version, but there was a limitation on the bi-directional relationship. In the matured framework, we have support for multiplicity, enabling that multiple entities can be related together.

The topics we will cover in this chapter are:

- Relationships:
  - One-to-one
  - One-to-many
  - Many-to-many
- Fluent API:
  - Identifying navigation property and inverse navigation
  - Identifying single navigation property
  - Relationship-building techniques
  - Cascade delete

Relationships

We could have conventional relationships such as one-to-one, one-to-many, and many-to-many in our entity relationships with ease in EF. Let's explore them in detail in this section. To make it interesting, let's design the database of the blogging system during the course of understanding relationships:

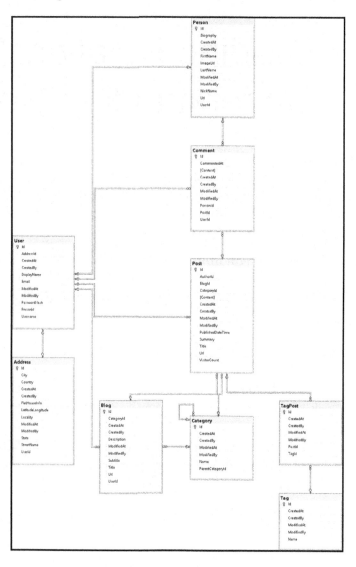

We have seen the proposed design of the blogging system; now let's learn about the relationships and how they could be built using the same design.

The one-to-one relationship

We need a new entity to explain the one-to-one relationship, as the existing entities don't have the provision to explain the same. So let's pick the Address entity from the proposed design and see how the one-to-one relationship is built:

The code illustrating one-to-one relationship between User and Address entities was listed as follows:

```
public class User
{
    public int Id { get; set; }
    public string DisplayName { get; set; }
    public string Username { get; set; }
    public string PasswordHash { get; set; }
    public string Email { get; set; }
    public DateTime CreatedAt { get; set; }
    public DateTime ModifiedAt { get; set; }
    public int CreatedBy { get; set; }
    public int ModifiedBy { get; set; }
    public ICollection<Blog> Blogs { get; set; }
    public ICollection<Post> Posts { get; set; }
    public ICollection<Comment> Comments { get; set; }
    public int? AddressId { get; set; }
    public Address Address { get; set; }
    public int PersonId { get; set; }
    public Person Person { get; set; }
}

public class Address
{
    public int Id { get; set; }
    public string FlatHouseInfo { get; set; }
    public string StreetName { get; set; }
    public string Locality { get; set; }
    public string City { get; set; }
    public string State { get; set; }
    public string Country { get; set; }
    public string LatitudeLongitude { get; set; }
    public DateTime CreatedAt { get; set; }
    public DateTime ModifiedAt { get; set; }
    public int CreatedBy { get; set; }
```

```
public int ModifiedBy { get; set; }
public int UserId { get; set; }
public User User { get; set; }
}
```

As you will notice, we have only a reference navigation property on both the User and Address entities, and additionally, a foreign key is introduced to allow EF to differentiate between the principal and dependent entities.

In the following diagram, the foreign key UserId is mapped against the Id primary key which has one-to-one relationship:

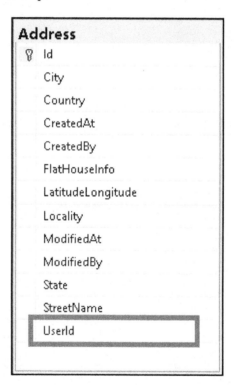

The User entity's Id primary key highlighted below is used as a foreign key in Address entity to form one-to-one relationship:

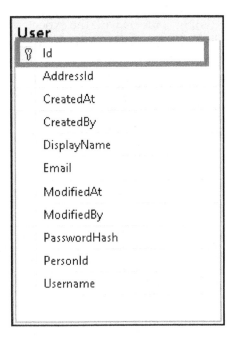

We have identified the provision, the `UserId` field that will allow the entity to configure the relationship. Let us build the relationship using the Fluent API in the next section.

Building one-to-one relationships using the Fluent API

We could configure the relationship using the Fluent API with the `HasOne`, `WithOne`, and `HasForeignKey` methods. The `HasForeignKey` method needs to be generic in a one-to-one relationship (a one-to-many relationship doesn't require this) since we need to explicitly mark the dependent type. In our case, we have specified the `Address` entity for the foreign key:

```
protected override void OnModelCreating(ModelBuilder modelBuilder)
{
  modelBuilder.Entity<Blog>().ToTable("Blog");
  modelBuilder.Entity<Post>().ToTable("Post");
  modelBuilder.Entity<User>()
    .ToTable("User")
    .HasOne(x=>x.Address)
    .WithOne(x=>x.User)
    .HasForeignKey<Address>(x=>x.UserId);
  modelBuilder.Entity<Address>().ToTable("Address");
}
```

The Fluent API configuration will provide us with the expected relationship, which is reflected in the following database diagram. The one-to-one relationship is now built between the User and Address entities, except the AddressId field would be optional as it's not mandatory while creating a user, but a user is required to create an address:

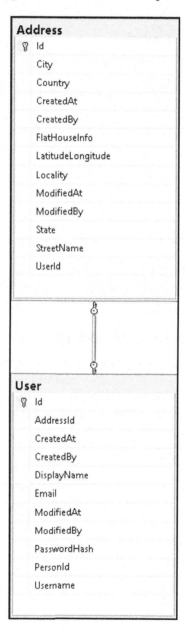

We could capture a lot more relationships in the blogging system that come under one-to-many relationships. The following diagram shows one-to-many relationships between the Person and User entities:

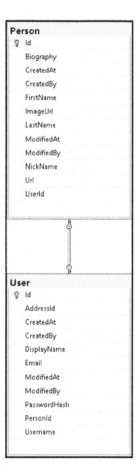

We have already seen the User table design; let's look at the Person table design content:

```
public class Person
{
    public int Id { get; set; }
    public string FirstName { get; set; }
    public string LastName { get; set; }
    public string NickName { get; set; }
    public string Url { get; set; }
    public string Biography { get; set; }
    public string ImageUrl { get; set; }
```

```
        public DateTime CreatedAt { get; set; }
        public DateTime ModifiedAt { get; set; }
        public int CreatedBy { get; set; }
        public int ModifiedBy { get; set; }
        public int? UserId { get; set; }
        public User User { get; set; }
        public ICollection<Comment> Comments { get; set; }
    }
```

We have looked at the one-to-one relationship in this section. Let us explore the one-to-many relationship in the next section.

The one-to-many relationship

So far, the illustrations carried out between the `Blog` and `Post` entities have had a one-to-many relationship. If we watch closely, we might be able to figure it out; the `Blog` entity is the principal entity and the `Post` entity is the dependent entity where the `Blog` entity can contain one or more posts (violà! one-to-many was already in place):

```
public class Blog
{
  public int Id { get; set; }
  public string Title { get; set; }
  public string Subtitle { get; set; }
  public string Url { get; set; }
  public string Description { get; set; }
  public DateTime CreatedAt { get; set; }
  public DateTime ModifiedAt { get; set; }
  public int CreatedBy { get; set; }
  public int ModifiedBy { get; set; }
  public ICollection<Post> Posts { get; set; }
}

public class Post
{
  public int Id { get; set; }
  public string Title { get; set; }
  public string Content { get; set; }
  public string Summary { get; set; }
  public DateTime PublishedDateTime { get; set; }
  public string Url { get; set; }
  public long VisitorCount { get; set; }
  public DateTime CreatedAt { get; set; }
  public DateTime ModifiedAt { get; set; }
  public int CreatedBy { get; set; }
```

```
    public int ModifiedBy { get; set; }
    public int BlogId { get; set; }
    public Blog Blog { get; set; }
    public int AuthorId { get; set; }
    public User Author { get; set; }
    public int CategoryId { get; set; }
    public Category Category { get; set; }
    public ICollection<TagPost> TagPosts { get; set; }
    public ICollection<Comment> Comments { get; set; }
}
```

The preceding fully-defined relationship in the model would provide the following relationship. It doesn't require Fluent API configuration unless we have a lot of navigation properties:

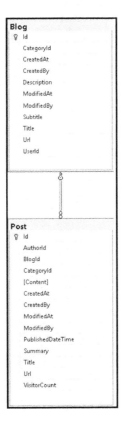

Since we have a one-to-many relationship, and it is clearly evident that Blog is a principal entity and Post is a dependent entity, EF doesn't need any explicit configuration to define the nature of the relationship, and hence it is done implicitly.

We could capture a lot more relationships in the blogging system that comes under one-to-many relationships. The following diagram shows other one-to-many relationships in the blogging system:

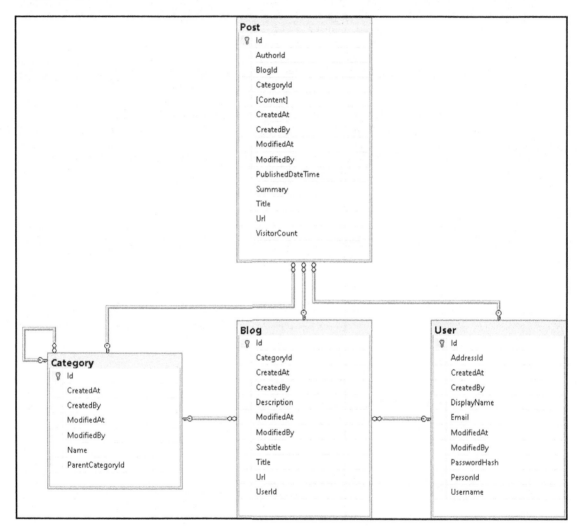

The other one-to-many relationships were between the following entities:

- Blog and Post
- Blog and User
- Blog and Category

From the preceding entities, we have already seen all the table designs except the Category class. Let's look at its design content:

```
public class Category
{
    public int Id { get; set; }
    public string Name { get; set; }
    public DateTime CreatedAt { get; set; }
    public DateTime ModifiedAt { get; set; }
    public int CreatedBy { get; set; }
    public int ModifiedBy { get; set; }
    public int? ParentCategoryId { get; set; }
    public Category ParentCategory { get; set; }
    public ICollection<Category> Subcategories { get; set; }
    public ICollection<Blog> Blogs { get; set; }
    public ICollection<Post> Posts { get; set; }
}
```

We have seen three relationships so far in the blogging system design; the following diagram shows couple of other one-to-many relationships in the blogging system:

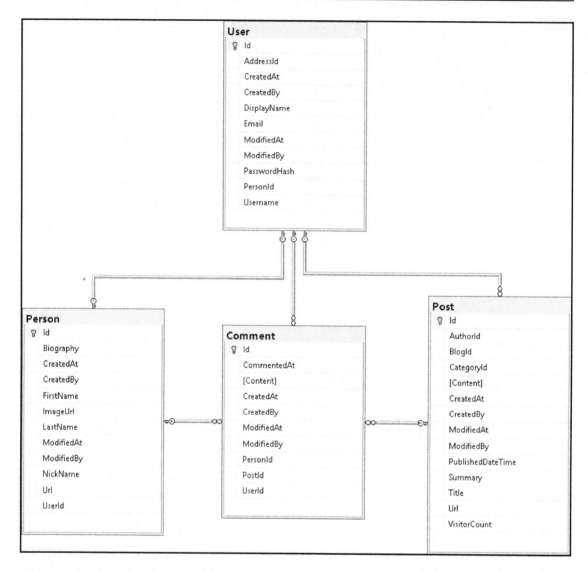

The couple of other one-to-many relationships were between the following entities:

- Post **and** Comment
- User **and** Comment
- Person **and** Comment

From the preceding entities, we have already seen all the table designs except `Comment`. Let's look at its design content:

```
public class Comment
{
    public int Id { get; set; }
    public string Content { get; set; }
    public DateTime CommentedAt { get; set; }
    public DateTime CreatedAt { get; set; }
    public DateTime ModifiedAt { get; set; }
    public int CreatedBy { get; set; }
    public int ModifiedBy { get; set; }
    public int PostId { get; set; }
    public Post Post { get; set; }
    public int? PersonId { get; set; }
    public Person Person { get; set; }
    public int? UserId { get; set; }
    public User User { get; set; }
}
```

We have come across the `Comment` entity that has some different relationships. It has a self-referencing relationship (to be blunt, it points to itself), it also falls under the one-to-many relationship, and the only difference is that the parent and the dependent entities were the same in this case:

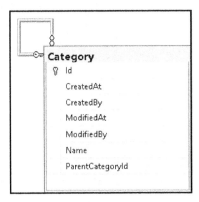

We have covered the one-to-many relationship along with the blogging system design. Let us explore the many-to-many relationship in the next section.

The many-to-many relationship

The many-to-many relationship is a tricky one; we need to understand how these kinds of relationships are built. Usually, we will build two different entities that require a many-to-many relationship, create an entity that will be purely used to join the first two entities, and then map one-to-many between this entity (created to join two separate one-to-many relationships) and the two entities (created first) separately:

```csharp
public class Post
{
    public int Id { get; set; }
    public string Title { get; set; }
    public string Content { get; set; }
    public string Summary { get; set; }
    public DateTime PublishedDateTime { get; set; }
    public string Url { get; set; }
    public long VisitorCount { get; set; }
    public DateTime CreatedAt { get; set; }
    public DateTime ModifiedAt { get; set; }
    public int CreatedBy { get; set; }
    public int ModifiedBy { get; set; }
    public int BlogId { get; set; }
    public Blog Blog { get; set; }
    public int AuthorId { get; set; }
    public User Author { get; set; }
    public int CategoryId { get; set; }
    public Category Category { get; set; }
    public ICollection<TagPost> TagPosts { get; set; }
    public ICollection<Comment> Comments { get; set; }
}

public class Tag
{
    public int Id { get; set; }
    public string Name { get; set; }
    public DateTime CreatedAt { get; set; }
    public DateTime ModifiedAt { get; set; }
    public int CreatedBy { get; set; }
    public int ModifiedBy { get; set; }
    public ICollection<TagPost> TagPosts { get; set; }
}

public class TagPost
{
    public int Id { get; set; }
    public DateTime CreatedAt { get; set; }
    public DateTime ModifiedAt { get; set; }
```

```
    public int CreatedBy { get; set; }
    public int ModifiedBy { get; set; }
    public int TagId { get; set; }
    public Tag Tag { get; set; }
    public int PostId { get; set; }
    public Post Post { get; set; }
}
```

The Post and Tag entities require many-to-many relationships for which the TagPost entity is created, and its only job is to join the Post and Tag entities.

The following diagram, illustrates many-to-many between Post and Tag entities through TagPost entity:

The Tag entity table diagram is displayed as follows

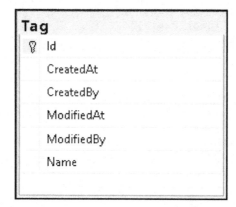

The TagPost entity which will contain PostId and TagId to form many-to-many relationship is displayed as follows

In order to have a many-to-many relationship between the Post and Tag entities, we created a TagPost (a kind of walk down table) entity purely to allow EF to join the Post and Tag entities. It is achieved by having a one-to-many relationship between the Tag and TagPost and Post and TagPost entities.

Building many-to-many relationship using the Fluent API

We should configure the relationship in the Fluent API in two different one-to-many relationships between the `Tag` and `TagPost` and `Post` and `TagPost` entities. The `HasForeignKey` method doesn't need to be generic, since one-to-many relationships don't need to mark the dependent type explicitly:

The many-to-many relationship between Tag and Post entities require the following configuration:

```
protected override void OnModelCreating(ModelBuilder modelBuilder)
{
  modelBuilder.Entity<Blog>().ToTable("Blog");
  modelBuilder.Entity<Post>().ToTable("Post");
  modelBuilder.Entity<User>()
    .ToTable("User")
    .HasOne(x=>x.Address)
    .WithOne(x=>x.User)
    .HasForeignKey<Address>(x=>x.UserId);
  modelBuilder.Entity<Address>().ToTable("Address");
  modelBuilder.Entity<Tag>().ToTable("Tag");
  modelBuilder.Entity<TagPost>()
    .ToTable("TagPost")
    .HasOne(x => x.Tag)
    .WithMany(x => x.TagPosts)
    .HasForeignKey(x => x.TagId);
  modelBuilder.Entity<TagPost>()
    .ToTable("TagPost")
    .HasOne(x => x.Post)
    .WithMany(x => x.TagPosts)
    .HasForeignKey(x => x.PostId);

}
```

The Fluent API configuration would provide us with the expected relationship, which is reflected in the following database diagram. The many-to-many relationship is now built between the `Post` and `Tag` entities through the `TagPost` entity:

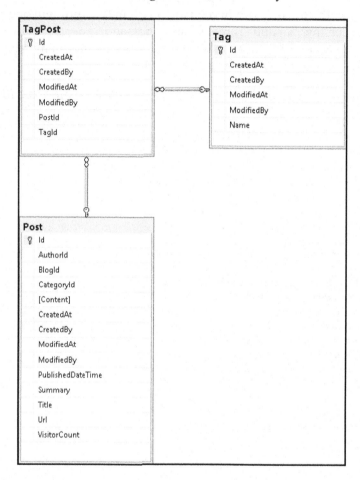

We have learned about the many-to-many relationship in this section. Let us explore more about the Fluent API in the next section.

Fluent API

We already had a sneak peek into the Fluent API, without which the relationship can never be complete (in a few cases, it is mandatory).

Identifying navigation property and inverse navigation

We used the Fluent API in one-to-one and many-to-many relationships. We will use the same method to leverage the terminologies we have seen so far. The HasOne and HasMany methods allow us to identify the navigation property in the dependent entity or simply a reference navigation property.

The following code configures the foreign key explicitly in the one-to-many relationship:

```
modelBuilder.Entity<TagPost>()
  .ToTable("TagPost")
  .HasOne(x => x.Tag)
  .WithMany(x => x.TagPosts)
  .HasForeignKey(x => x.TagId);
```

The following diagram, the TagId highlighted is required for the foreign key of the relationship:

The `HasOne` method identifies the `Tag` navigation in the `TagPost` entity. The `WithOne` and `WithMany` methods allow us to identify the inverse navigation in the principal entity or simply a collection navigation property.

The code required for inverse navigation property configuration is shown below:

```
modelBuilder.Entity<TagPost>()
    .ToTable("TagPost")
    .HasOne(x => x.Tag)
    .WithMany(x => x.TagPosts)
    .HasForeignKey(x => x.TagId);
```

The following diagram illustrates that we require an inverse navigation property for the relationship:

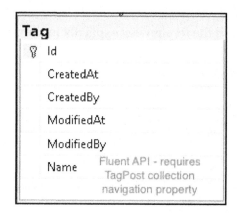

The `HasOne` method identifies the `TagPosts` inverse navigation in the `Tag` entity.

We have seen Fluent API identification and usages from a many-to-many relationship; let's use the same approach to identify the usage in terminologies.

Identifying the single navigation property

In the single navigation property, we will never have a navigation property in a dependent entity, which makes it hard for us in identifying the reference navigation property. This is where `HasMany` comes into the picture, helping us to identify the relationship:

The following code contains entity and its configuration of single navigation property, where `Blog` entity contains the navigation property and configuration uses `HasOne()` to complete the relationship:

```
public class Blog
{
  public int Id { get; set; }
  public string Url { get; set; }
  public ICollection<Post> Posts { get; set; }
}
public class Post
{
  public int Id { get; set; }
  public string Title { get; set; }
  public string Content { get; set; }
  public DateTime PublishedDateTime { get; set; }
  // Foreign key "BlogId" and navigation property "Blog" was
      removed here
}

// onModelCreating method implementation inside context class
    modelBuilder.Entity<Blog>()
    .HasMany(x => x.Posts)
    .WithOne()
```

The following diagram, illustrates the relationship built between entities with single navigation property:

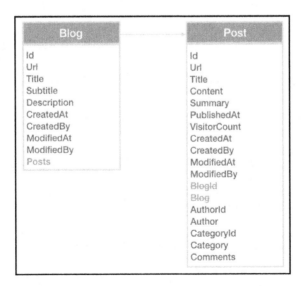

As you may have guessed, we started with `HasMany` and ended up with `WithOne` and, of course, we don't have any overload for `WithOne` as we don't have any reference property, and EF will configure against the dependent entity internally.

Relationship-building techniques

Let's build a relationship using the same approach and see the usages for the following terminologies as well.

Building relationship using a foreign key

We have seen that the foreign key property was applied using a data annotation approach, but what if we had to apply the same thing from the Fluent API? It is still possible. With the `HasForeignKey` Fluent API method exposed to us, we could use it in configuration to achieve the same:

The code required for custom foreign key mapping in entity and configuration were displayed here:

```
public class Blog
{
  public int Id { get; set; }
  public string Url { get; set; }
  public ICollection<Post> Posts { get; set; }
}
public class Post
{
  public int Id { get; set; }
  public string Title { get; set; }
  public string Content { get; set; }
  public DateTime PublishedDateTime { get; set; }
  public int SomeBlogId { get; set; }
  [ForeignKey("SomeBlogId")]
  public Blog Blog { get; set; }
}

// onModelCreating method implementation inside context class
   modelBuilder.Entity<Post>()
     .HasOne(x => x.Blog)
     .WithMany(x => x.Posts)
     .HasForeignKey(x => x.SomeBlogId);
```

We have modified the foreign key as `SomeBlogId` and configured against the `Blog` navigation property of the `Post` entity, and it is configured using the Fluent API.

Building relationships using a principal key

The principal key doesn't require a Fluent API configuration if it's a primary key, but what if we had to apply a relationship against an alternate key? Then, we need the Fluent API to complete the configuration. We could achieve the same using the `HasPrincipalKey` Fluent API method exposed to us:

The code required for custom foreign key mapping in entity and configuration using principal key instead of primary key were displayed as follows:

```
public class Blog
{
  public int Id { get; set; }
  public string Url { get; set; }
  public ICollection<Post> Posts { get; set; }
}
public class Post
{
  public int Id { get; set; }
  public string Title { get; set; }
  public string Content { get; set; }
  public DateTime PublishedDateTime { get; set; }
  public int SomeBlogId { get; set; }
  [ForeignKey("SomeBlogId")]
  public Blog Blog { get; set; }
}

// onModelCreating method implementation inside context class
   modelBuilder.Entity<Post>()
     .HasOne(x => x.Blog)
     .WithMany(x => x.Posts)
     .HasForeignKey(x => x.SomeBlogId)
     .HasPrincipalKey(x => x.Url); // not a valid
         relationship in real time
```

We have created a relationship using the modified foreign key `BlogSomeId` against the alternate key `Url` from `Blog`. This was achieved using the `HasPrincipalKey` Fluent API method.

Building relationships using the IsRequired method

We can configure the relationship as required or optional using the same Fluent API with the IsRequired method. We can use the same approach to define whether a relationship is mandatory or optional:

```
public class Blog
{
   public int Id { get; set; }
   public string Url { get; set; }
   public ICollection<Post> Posts { get; set; }
}
public class Post
{
   public int Id { get; set; }
   public string Title { get; set; }
   public string Content { get; set; }
   public DateTime PublishedDateTime { get; set; }
   public int BlogSomeId { get; set; }
   [ForeignKey("BlogSomeId")]
   public Blog Blog { get; set; }
}

// onModelCreating method implementation inside context class
   modelBuilder.Entity<Blog>()
      .Property(x => x.Url)
      .IsRequired()
   modelBuilder.Entity<Post>()
      .HasOne(x => x.Blog)
      .WithMany(x => x.Posts)
      .IsRequired();
```

The first configuration applies the Url property on the Blog entity to be a mandatory/required field, and the second configuration enforces the relationship as mandatory.

Cascade delete

The relationship we have created so far allows us to build the data with relationship, and the deletion mechanism need to be configured as well. What would happen if we try to delete a principal entity row? Would that do nothing on dependent elements or remove them as well? Let's see the different ways available to perform those operations:

- **Cascade**: If we delete the principal entity row, the dependent entity rows get deleted as well
  The following code would configure that the dependent rows would be deleted as well if the primary row is deleted:

  ```
  public class Blog
  {
    public int Id { get; set; }
    public string Url { get; set; }
    public ICollection<Post> Posts { get; set; }
  }
  public class Post
  {
    public int Id { get; set; }
    public string Title { get; set; }
    public string Content { get; set; }
    public DateTime PublishedDateTime { get; set; }
    public int BlogSomeId { get; set; }
    [ForeignKey("BlogSomeId")]
     public Blog Blog { get; set; }
  }

  // onModelCreating method implementation inside context class
  modelBuilder.Entity<Post>()
      .HasOne(x => x.Blog)
      .WithMany(x => x.Posts)
      .OnDelete(DeleteBehavior.Cascade);
  ```

  This enforces EF to delete `Post` elements if a `Blog` element is deleted.

- **SetNull**: If we delete the principal entity row, the dependent entity row's foreign key will be set to null values:
  The following code would configure the dependent rows to be set to null if the primary row is deleted:

  ```
  public class Blog
  {
    public int Id { get; set; }
  ```

```
    public string Url { get; set; }
    public ICollection<Post> Posts { get; set; }
}
public class Post
{
    public int Id { get; set; }
    public string Title { get; set; }
    public string Content { get; set; }
    public DateTime PublishedDateTime { get; set; }
    public int BlogSomeId { get; set; }
    [ForeignKey("BlogSomeId")]
    public Blog Blog { get; set; }
}

// onModelCreating method implementation inside context class
    modelBuilder.Entity<Post>()
      .HasOne(x => x.Blog)
      .WithMany(x => x.Posts)
      .OnDelete(DeleteBehavior.SetNull);
```

This enforces EF to set null values on the Blog column of the Post entity elements if a Blog element is deleted:

- **Restrict**: If we delete the principal entity row, the dependent entity's rows remain untouched:
  The following code would configure that the dependent rows would retain their values even though the primary row is deleted:

```
public class Blog
{
    public int Id { get; set; }
    public string Url { get; set; }
    public ICollection<Post> Posts { get; set; }
}
public class Post
{
    public int Id { get; set; }
    public string Title { get; set; }
    public string Content { get; set; }
    public DateTime PublishedDateTime { get; set; }
    public int BlogSomeId { get; set; }
    [ForeignKey("BlogSomeId")]
    public Blog Blog { get; set; }
}

// onModelCreating method implementation inside context class
    modelBuilder.Entity<Post>()
```

```
.HasOne(x => x.Blog)
.WithMany(x => x.Posts)
.OnDelete(DeleteBehavior.Restrict);
```

This does nothing on the `Post` entity elements if a `Blog` element is deleted.

We have seen different scenarios of delete behavior on dependent entities if a principal entity gets deleted, and this completes the relationship configuration.

Data migration issue with EF Core 2.0

In `Chapter 1`, *Kickstart - Introduction to Entity Framework Core*, we saw that data migration has to be performed whenever we add/update the data model. The data migration using the `Add-Migration` command stopped working in EF Core 2.0. As a workaround, we need to leverage .NET **Command Line Interface (CLI)** commands to achieve the same.

The first problem is that we were unable to add the `Microsoft.EntityFrameworkCore.Tools.DotNet` package; it throws the error **Package 'Microsoft.EntityFrameworkCore.Tools.DotNet.2.0.1' has a package type 'DotnetCliTool' that is not supported by project 'MasteringEFCore.BuildRelationships.Final'** displayed in the following screenshot:

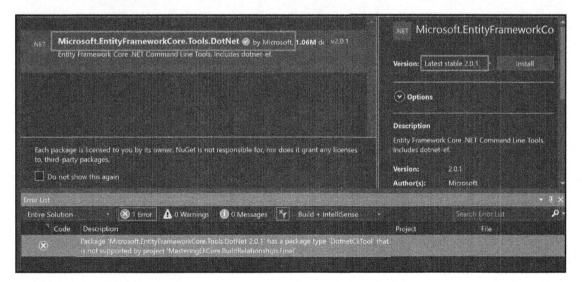

It could be resolved by unloading the project file and including the
`DotNetCliToolReference` code block manually in the `.csproj` file content, then
reloading the project and restoring the NuGet package. This should resolve the package-
related issue:

```
<ItemGroup>
  <DotNetCliToolReference Include=
    "Microsoft.EntityFrameworkCore.Tools.DotNet" Version="2.0.1" />
</ItemGroup>
```

Go to the `Developer Command Prompt` for VS 2017 (search for the command in the Start
menu), and execute the following .NET CLI command to add the migration:

```
dotnet ef migrations add
```

The following screenshot adds the migration `"Models with relationship"` and the
execution log shows `Done. To undo this action, use 'ef migrations remove'`, which means the data migration was successful:

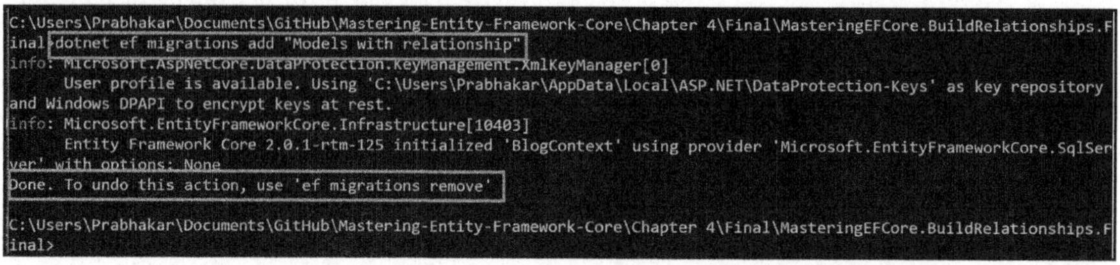

The database update could be performed using the following .NET CLI command:

```
dotnet ef database update
```

The following screenshot confirms that the database was updated successfully with a `Done`
success message, as shown in the following screenshot:

```
       CONSTRAINT [PK_TagPost] PRIMARY KEY ([Id]),
       CONSTRAINT [FK_TagPost_Post_PostId] FOREIGN KEY ([PostId]) REFERENCES [Post] ([Id]) ON DELETE CASCADE,
       CONSTRAINT [FK_TagPost_Tag_TagId] FOREIGN KEY ([TagId]) REFERENCES [Tag] ([Id]) ON DELETE CASCADE
   );
info: Microsoft.EntityFrameworkCore.Database.Command[20101]
       Executed DbCommand (2ms) [Parameters=[], CommandType='Text', CommandTimeout='30']
       CREATE UNIQUE INDEX [IX_Address_UserId] ON [Address] ([UserId]);
info: Microsoft.EntityFrameworkCore.Database.Command[20101]
       Executed DbCommand (1ms) [Parameters=[], CommandType='Text', CommandTimeout='30']
       CREATE INDEX [IX_Blog_AuthorId] ON [Blog] ([AuthorId]);
info: Microsoft.EntityFrameworkCore.Database.Command[20101]
       Executed DbCommand (1ms) [Parameters=[], CommandType='Text', CommandTimeout='30']
       CREATE INDEX [IX_Post_BlogId] ON [Post] ([BlogId]);
info: Microsoft.EntityFrameworkCore.Database.Command[20101]
       Executed DbCommand (24ms) [Parameters=[], CommandType='Text', CommandTimeout='30']
       CREATE INDEX [IX_Post_UserId] ON [Post] ([UserId]);
info: Microsoft.EntityFrameworkCore.Database.Command[20101]
       Executed DbCommand (1ms) [Parameters=[], CommandType='Text', CommandTimeout='30']
       CREATE INDEX [IX_TagPost_PostId] ON [TagPost] ([PostId]);
info: Microsoft.EntityFrameworkCore.Database.Command[20101]
       Executed DbCommand (1ms) [Parameters=[], CommandType='Text', CommandTimeout='30']
       CREATE INDEX [IX_TagPost_TagId] ON [TagPost] ([TagId]);
info: Microsoft.EntityFrameworkCore.Database.Command[20101]
       Executed DbCommand (36ms) [Parameters=[], CommandType='Text', CommandTimeout='30']
       INSERT INTO [__EFMigrationsHistory] ([MigrationId], [ProductVersion])
       VALUES (N'20171123090841_Models with relationship', N'2.0.1-rtm-125');
Done.

C:\Users\Prabhakar\Documents\GitHub\Mastering-Entity-Framework-Core\Chapter 4\Final\MasteringEFCore.BuildRelationships.F
inal>
```

I love to fool people in the beginning and then provide them with a solution, and that makes sure that they never forget it. Let me break the ice, the migration issue could be simply resolved by removing and adding the `Microsoft.EntityFrameworkCore.Tools` NuGet package.

Yes, we have explored .NET CLI commands within the context of a data migration issue, and also learned how to resolve it using both CLI and package update in this section.

Summary

We have learned and built different kinds of relationships supported by EF in this chapter. We started with regular one-to-one, one-to-many, and many-to-many relationships, and from there applied a few Fluent API methods to achieve relationships. Then, we covered different usages of the Fluent API on the terminologies we saw in Chapter 3, *Relationships – Terminology and Conventions*. Finally, we have seen the behavior of `Delete` operations on dependent entities if a principal entity gets deleted. These sections dealt with relationships, but never looked at validations, except where required. Let's explore them in the next chapter.

5
Know the Validation – Explore Inbuilt Validations

We have learned and built different kinds of relationships supported by EF in this chapter. We started with regular one-to-one, one-to-many, and many-to-many relationships, and from there applied a few Fluent API methods to achieve relationships. Then, we covered different usages of the Fluent API on the terminologies we saw in Chapter 3, *Relationships – Terminology and Conventions*. Finally, we have seen the behavior of Delete operations on dependent entities if a principal entity gets deleted. These sections dealt with relationships, but never looked at validations, except where required. Let's explore them in the next chapter.

We have explored about different kind in-built relationships, leveraged Fluent API methods in creating relationships. We have also looked at the use of the Fluent API on navigational properties, mandating certain fields using isRequired(), implementing principal and foreign keys using HasPrincipalKey() and HasForeignKey() methods, and much more.

In this chapter, we will address the following concerns with respect to data security:

- What should be done to the data before we send it over the network?
    - Add certain rules/conditions to the data (defined in the model)
    - Validate the models both on the client-side and server-side (supported out of the box)

- How are the validations handled in ASP.NET?
  - We started with JavaScript-based validation, then control-driven validations were performed and finally from MVC we started using data model-driven validations
  - We will be exploring how MVC handles validation through the data model
- Do we need to explicitly use HTML5 validation?
  - Not required, as rendering the MVC engine internally converts the data-model driven validations into HTML5 data-attribute driven validations

We will be covering all built-in validations in this chapter, listed as follows:

- Built-in validations
- `Required` field validation
- `EmailAddress` field validation
- `Compare` field validation
- `Url` field validation
- `MinLength` field validation
- `MaxLength` field validation
- `RegularExpression` field validation

Diving into built-in validations

Data security plays a vital role in any application's development, as almost everything revolves around data. So it is crucial that we store valid data in the database, ensuring that the data passed on from the user to the application server is safely transmitted; the data reaching the server also should contain valid data (probably having a valid datatype, length, and so on).

We started performing validations using JavaScript in ASP.NET Web Forms initially; sadly, most of the ASP.NET developers in the initial days used JavaScript only for validations. Then we moved onto control-driven validation which wraps up all the scripting inside ASP controls accepting parameters required for validation. Finally, we were exposed to data model-driven validation, which allows developers to configure validation through data annotation, automatically handling both client-side (using jQuery unobtrusive validation) and server-side (using MVC model binder validation).

The **Entity Framework (EF)** allows us to achieve the same, using annotation/attribute validation, which reduces a lot of coding with respect to security (client-side and server-side validations are simplified due to this requirement). EF provides us with certain built-in validations:

- Required
- EmailAddress
- Compare
- Url
- MinLength
- MaxLength
- RegularExpression

The preceding list briefly covers most of the validators. If you would like to take a look at a complete list of validators, please visit https://msdn.microsoft.com/en-us/library/ system.componentmodel.dataannotations(v=vs.110).aspx. Let's take a look at each of the validators listed in detail.

Required field validation

We will start with the Required built-in validation which allows validators to check whether the field has a value or not. The required validation is necessary to ensure that the mandatory fields are filled in or updated by the user before transmitting the data to the server for further processing.

The following steps will help us in understanding how validation works:

1. The Required field validator is added using data annotation in the model.

2. The MVC engine performs validation on both client-side and server-side using this configuration.

3. When MVC engine generates the form view with the input field, it also scaffolds the `<span>` element along with each input field to hold error messages.

4. When we run the application and submit the form without providing any value in the input field, which has `aria-required` field validation, a validation error would be added to the model state errors list.

5. The errors would be displayed in the `<span>` associated with each element of the form.

The validation error would be captured in the `Required` data annotation if the field is `NULL` or `""` (empty) or has white space in it.

Data type of the field value can be anything. So why on earth is the validator checking for an empty string? It's simple. Because most of the datatypes were translated from a string into their appropriate types by the model binder, so it's easy for the framework to check whether the value exists or not using `String` as the default datatype.

The `Required` attribute/data annotation can be added in the `Blog` code shown as follows; the `DataAnnotations` reference should be included to configure validation. The following screenshot displays the intelli-sense that allows us to import required namespace (triggered using `Ctrl + .`):

```
Blog.cs  ×  BlogsController.cs
MasteringEFCore.Validations.Final          $ MasteringEFCore.Validations.Final.Models.Blog         Url
  1        using System.Collections.Generic;
  2
  3      □namespace MasteringEFCore.Validations.Final.Models
  4       {
  5      □   public class Blog
  6          {
  7            public int Id { get; set; }
  8            [Required]
  9            ○ .    string Url { get; set; }
 10
 11            using System.ComponentModel.DataAnnotations;    ►    ⊗ CS0246 The type or namespace name 'RequiredAttribute' could not
 12            System.ComponentModel.DataAnnotations.Required         be found (are you missing a using directive or an assembly reference?)
 13            Generate type 'Required'                         ►  using System.Collections.Generic;
 14       }                                                       using System.ComponentModel.DataAnnotations;
 15   }
                                                                  Preview changes
```

The source code required to add `Required` validation is shown here; it consumes built-in validation and throws a default error message:

```
public class Blog
{
  public int Id { get; set; }
  [Required]
  public string Url { get; set; }
  public ICollection<Post> Posts { get; set; }
  public int AuthorId { get; set; }
  public User Author { get; set; }
}
```

The scaffolded HTML code has data-attribute driven validation which is consumed by jQuery validate unobtrusive library, the highlighted scaffolded HTML content in the following screenshot is consumed by the library:

```
▲ <form action="/Blogs/Create" method="post" novalidate="novalidate">
  ▲ <div class="form-group">
      <label class="control-label" for="Url">Url</label>
      <input name="Url" class="form-control input-validation-error" id="Url"
      aria-required="true" aria-describedby="Url-error" type="text"
      data-val-required="The Url field is required." data-val="true" value
      ="" />
    ▷ <span class="text-danger field-validation-error" data-valmsg-replace
      ="true" data-valmsg-for="Url">...</span>
    </div>
  ▷ <div class="form-group">...</div>
  ▷ <div class="form-group">...</div>
      <input name="__RequestVerificationToken" type="hidden" value="CfDJ8DLg-L
      bAetFJslxRp6SZ1z-oUwc6FnlJWlAD_KayOildb55oDB_ZOx2nE6J2uwQVRiensHgYEhWd8E
      8kSBKDmwNkYtucHwpCLs9THwY7aRaBxBwMJ54goCFkdbo-F7J4wdLxcOb5KpoC0fSNg6EAQO
      s" />
  </form>
```

The preceding method would force EF to emit the standard validation error message, **The Url field is required**, if the field contains invalid data during validation. The scaffolded <span> element is used for populating the validation error as displayed in the following screenshot:

We can also perform validation using a custom error message using the ErrorMessage field; the configuration is highlighted as follows:

```
public class Blog
{
    public int Id { get; set; }
    [Required]
    public string Url { get; set; }
    public ICollection<Post> Posts { get; set; }
    [Required(ErrorMessage = "Author is required, kindly
        pick one!")]
    public int AuthorId { get; set; }
    public User Author { get; set; }
}
```

The preceding configuration would use the custom error message in the data-val-required attribute instead of the standard validation error message:

```
▲ <form action="/Blogs/Create" method="post" novalidate="novalidate">
  ▷ <div class="form-group">…</div>
  ▲ <div class="form-group">
      <label class="control-label" for="AuthorId">AuthorId</label>
      <select name="AuthorId" class="form-control" id="AuthorId"
      data-val-required="Author is required, kindly pick one!"
      data-val="true"></select>
    </div>
  ▷ <div class="form-group">…</div>
    <input name="__RequestVerificationToken" type="hidden" value="CfD
    J8DLg-LbAetFJslxRp6SZ1z-b4jVCS7PjXp-Zauvw1pO_dluOIPRtCOlvEXWfBTcy
    BOfpUrgKnNqg-29zwdcYYBb0aJoYqPzY21zYWSqURiNIFD7A9WNeXwPw0mBvidhcO
    NWnaikpz1PhyIqwkqtTEZo" />
```

The MVC scaffolding engine, for a <select> field, would not include the <span> element required to display the error message, so kindly include the following section:

```
<form asp-action="Create">
  <div asp-validation-summary="ModelOnly" class="text-danger">
  </div>
  // Code removed for brevity
  <div class="form-group">
    <label asp-for="AuthorId" class="control-label"></label>
    <select asp-for="AuthorId" class ="form-control"
      asp-items="ViewBag.AuthorId </select>
    <span asp-validation-for="AuthorId" class="text-danger">
    </span>
  </div>
  // Code removed for brevity
</form>
```

The preceding method would force EF to emit a custom error message, **Author is required, kindly pick one!**, if the field contains invalid data during validation, which is shown in the following screenshot:

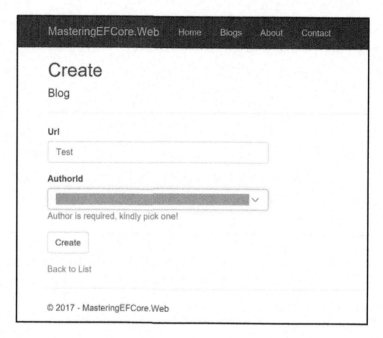

The displayed error message will be cleared once the user starts typing any value into the field.

 The client-side validation logic works based on the jQuery validate library and is performed on the fly when the user types the value by using the jQuery validate unobtrusive library.

We have explored `Required` field validation by configuring it in the `Blog` entity; let's configure the validation for the remaining entities of the blogging system in the next section.

Incorporating the Required validation in blogging system models

We will update our blogging system models to accommodate the `Required` field validation in the following entities:

- **Data model entities**: `Address`, `Blog`, `Category`, `Comment`, `Person`, `Post`, `Tag`, `TagPost`, and `User`
- **View model entities**: `RegistrationViewModel` and `LoginViewModel`

The preceding listed implementation is performed and available at the following Git repository commit—`https://goo.gl/4jyHa2`.

We have introduced a couple of view models in this commit which will be used in the authentication mechanism. We have looked, exhaustively, at `Required` field validations; let's explore the `EmailAddress` validation in the next section.

EmailAddress field validation

The `Required` validation was straightforward, but email validation is a little bit different; each developer would adopt different approaches for the validation. The emergence of jQuery validation provided consistent behavior for most of the validations. Later, the standard set by the HTML5 team is not adopted widely by all browsers and development teams.

Let's explore the `EmailAddress` built-in validation which would allow us to validate whether the value is a valid email or not. The following steps will help us in understanding how validation works:

1. The data annotation was already discussed; we will be using the `EmailAddress` attribute in this section.

2. The MVC engine scaffolding part, the validations, populating model state errors, and displaying errors on the screen, almost the entire process, would be the same for the remaining of the chapters. We can additionally cover how the validation is performed in each section as each of the in-built validation follow different patterns.

The validation error can be captured in the `EmailAddress` data annotation in the following scenarios:

- If the field does not have the @ symbol followed by one or more character(s) (for instance, `a` or `a@`), then the validation error will be reported to the user

- After providing the @ symbol following one or more character, if we introduce a . (period) then the validation engine will expect the field value to be followed by one or more characters, and if not satisfied it will throw a validation error (for instance, `a@a.`)

The `EmailAddress` attribute/data annotation can be configured as follows:

```
public class User
{
    // Code removed for brevity
    [EmailAddress]
    public string Email { get; set; }
}
```

As seen in the previous section, the scaffolded HTML code follows the same data attribute-driven approach for validation. The highlighted section in the following screenshot illustrates that the validation is performed using data-attribute driven validation:

```
⊿ <form action="/Users/Create" method="post" novalidate="novalidate">
  ⊿ <div class="form-horizontal">
      <h4>User</h4>
      <hr />
    ▷ <div class="form-group">...</div>
    ▷ <div class="form-group">...</div>
    ▷ <div class="form-group">...</div>
    ⊿ <div class="form-group">
        <label class="col-md-2 control-label" for="Email">Email</label>
      ⊿ <div class="col-md-10">
          <input name="Email" class="form-control valid" id="Email" aria-invalid="false"
          aria-describedby="Email-error" type="email" data-val="true" data-val-email="Provi
          de a valid email address" value="" />
          <span class="text-danger field-validation-valid" data-valmsg-replace="true"
          data-valmsg-for="Email"></span>
        </div>
      </div>
```

The preceding method will force EF to emit a standard validation error message, **The Email field is not a valid e-mail address.**, if the field contains invalid data during validation, as shown in the following screenshot:

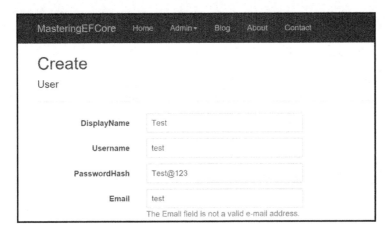

We can see that just after providing a value after the @ symbol, the error is removed, even though the email is not yet complete, as shown in the following screenshot:

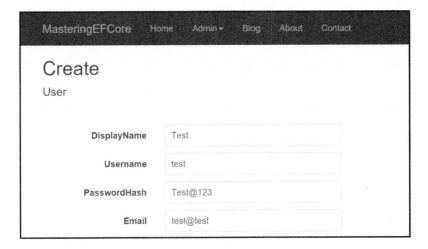

Introducing a . (period) symbol would again throw an error as the email is not complete without the complete domain name in the email, as shown in the following screenshot:

We can also see that after providing one or more characters, the error is removed, and now we have a valid email value, shown as follows:

We can configure the custom error message for each model field, shown as follows:

```
public class User
{
  // Code removed for brevity
  [Required(ErrorMessage = "Email is required"]
  [EmailAddress(ErrorMessage = "Provide a valid email address")]
  public string Email { get; set; }
  // Code removed for brevity
}
```

The preceding method will force EF to emit the custom error message, **Provide a valid email address**, if the field contains invalid data during validation, shown as follows:

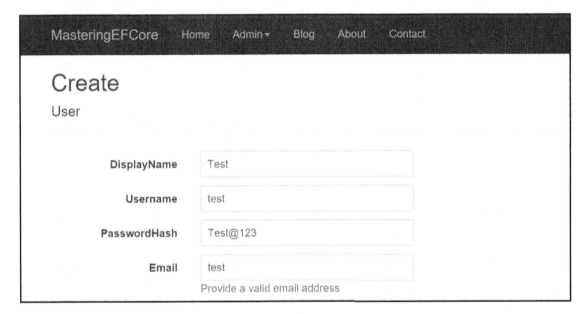

The custom error would still work or be consumed for throwing invalid domain validation errors as well:

The displayed error message will be cleared once the user starts typing a valid email value into the field.

The valid email value was decided by checking the @ symbol of the value; mysteriously, it clears the validation (test@somedomain) before the user completes the email with a valid domain name (gmail.com or yahoo.com). Once the . value is provided again, it displays the error message, expecting the user to provide any domain extension value such as .com or .net (it works perfectly, even if we provide .abc).

Incorporating EmailAddress validation in blogging system models

We will update our blogging system model to accommodate the `EmailAddress` field validation in the **View** model:

```
public class RegistrationViewModel
{
  // Code removed for brevity
  [Required(ErrorMessage = "Email is required")]
  [EmailAddress(ErrorMessage = "Provide a valid email address")]
  public string Email { get; set; }
  [Required(ErrorMessage = "Email is required")]
  [EmailAddress(ErrorMessage = "Provide a valid email address")]
  public string ConfirmEmail { get; set; }
}
```

We have looked, exhaustively, at `EmailAddress` field validations; let's explore the `Compare` validation in the next section.

Compare field validation

We will be exploring `Compare` validation in this section, and since the steps are common for all the built-in validations except the pattern, we will be covering only the validation pattern in the other validation sections. The compare validation will avoid the round-trip between the UI and the service, providing client-side validation for comparing passwords, emails, or even sensitive information such as bank account numbers, which require this compare validation to be in place.

The validation error can be captured in the `Compare` data annotation in the following scenarios:

- If the field is NULL or empty or a whitespace

- If the field has a value which doesn't match the configured field value

The `Compare` attribute/data annotation can be configured as follows:

```
public class RegistrationViewModel
{
  // Code removed for brevity
```

```
        [Required(ErrorMessage = "ConfirmPassword is required")]
        [Compare("Password")]
        public string ConfirmPassword { get; set; }
    }
```

We can verify that if the **Password** and **ConfirmPassword** fields don't match then the standard validation error message '**ConfirmPassword' and 'Password' do not match.** appears:

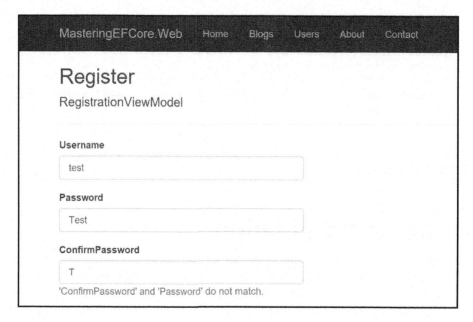

We can configure the custom error message for each model field, shown as follows:

```
    public class RegistrationViewModel
    {
        // Code removed for brevity
        [Required(ErrorMessage = "ConfirmPassword is required")]
        [Compare("Password", ErrorMessage = "Password does not match")]
        public string ConfirmPassword { get; set; }
    }
```

We can also conclude that compare validation consumes the custom validation error message as well. Our test scenario would emit the **Password does not match** validation error message, shown as follows:

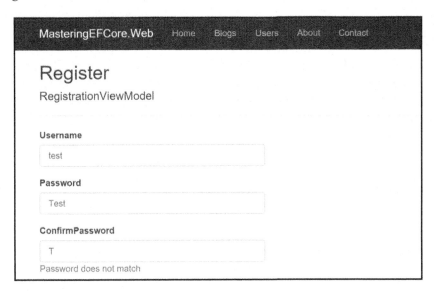

The displayed error message will be cleared once the user starts typing a valid password value in the field.

Incorporating the Compare validation in blogging system models

We will update our blogging system model to accommodate the Compare field validation in the **View** model:

```
public class LoginViewModel
{
    [Required(ErrorMessage = "Username is required")]
    public string Username { get; set; }
    [Required(ErrorMessage = "Password is required")]
    public string Password { get; set; }
    [Required(ErrorMessage = "ConfirmPassword is required")]
    [Compare("Password", ErrorMessage = "Password does not match")]
    public string ConfirmPassword { get; set; }
}
```

We have looked, exhaustively, at the `Compare` field validations. Let's explore the `Url` validation in the next section.

Url field validation

We will look into `Url` validation, how it should be configured, and how it works with the MVC engine. It does the basic syntax check on the URL value rather than verifying the URL itself, so it would be ideal to have a consistent mechanism to perform, such as verification, to have uniform behavior between systems. The `Url` validation is performed based on the pattern -

`<protocol>://<domain-name>.<extension>` . Let's explore the pattern in detail:

- **Protocol**: It should be HTTP, https, or FTP
- **Domain name**: It should be one or more characters
- **Extension**: It should be two or more characters (for instance, `http://a.bc` is valid since it follows the preceding pattern)

The `Url` attribute/data annotation can be used in the following ways:

```
public class Blog
{
  // Code removed for brevity
  [Required(ErrorMessage = "Url is required")]
  [Url]
  public string Url { get; set; }
}
```

The **Url** validation reports the following value as the error **The Url field is not a valid fully-qualified http, https, or ftp URL.** since the value contains only the protocol and does not satisfy the URL pattern:

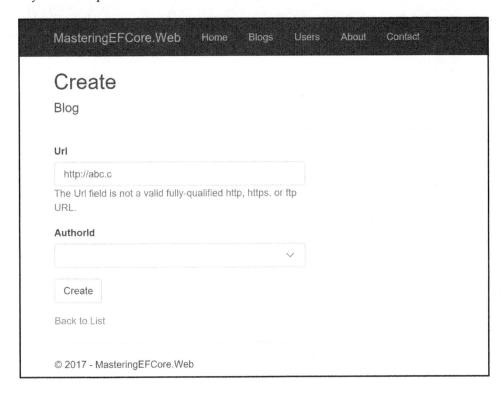

If the field value follows the URL pattern properly, the error will be removed, and we can see that the field value seems to be valid (following the pattern) in the following screenshot:

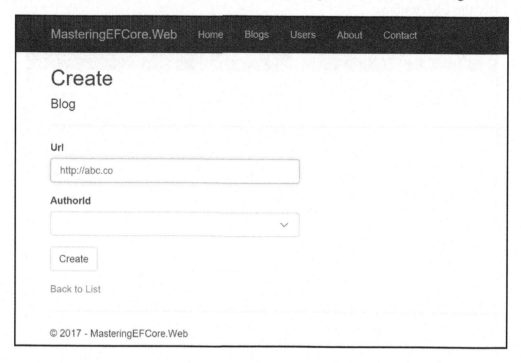

We can configure the custom error message for each model field as follows:

```
public class Blog
{
    // Code removed for brevity
    [Required(ErrorMessage = "Url is required")]
    [Url(ErrorMessage = "Provide a valid url")]
    public string Url { get; set; }
}
```

The preceding method will force EF to emit a custom error message, **Provide a valid url**, if the field contains invalid data during validation, shown as follows:

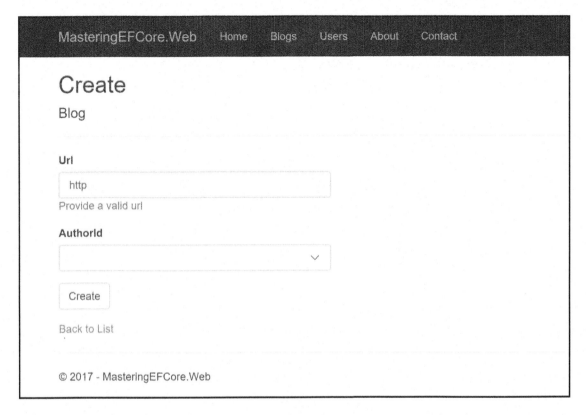

The displayed error message will be cleared once the user starts typing a valid URL value into the field.

Incorporating Url validation in blogging system models

We will update our blogging system model to accommodate `Url` field validation, the data model driven `Url` validation is performed in the below entities:

```
public class Blog
{
  // Code removed for brevity
  [Required(ErrorMessage = "Url is required")]
  [Url(ErrorMessage = "Provide a valid url")]
  public string Url { get; set; }
}
```

```
public class Post
{
  // Code removed for brevity
  [Url(ErrorMessage = "Provide a valid url")]
  public string Url { get; set; }
}

public class Person
{
  // Code removed for brevity
  [Url(ErrorMessage = "Provide a valid url")]
  public string Url { get; set; }
  [Url(ErrorMessage = "Provide a valid image url")]
  public string ImageUrl { get; set; }
}
```

We have exhaustively seen the Url field validations; let's explore about the MinLength validation in the next section.

MinLength field validation

The MinLength validation is helpful for creating constraints on certain fields such as Username, Zip Code, and so on. We will start investigating MinLength validation in this section.

The validation error can be captured in MinLength data annotation in the following scenarios:

- If the field is NULL or empty or whitespace.
- If the field value length is less than configured. For instance, if the MinLength is configured as 6, then if the number of characters provided in the field is less than 6 the min length validation error would be thrown.

The MinLength attribute/data annotation can be configured as follows:

```
public class RegistrationViewModel
{
  [Required(ErrorMessage = "Username is required")]
  [MinLength(6)]
  public string Username { get; set; }
  // Code removed for brevity
}
```

If field value does not meet the minimum length requirement, then the validation error **The field Username must be a string or array type with a minimum length of '6'** would be thrown, whereas the field name and length of the error message is based on the field name and configuration, shown as follows:

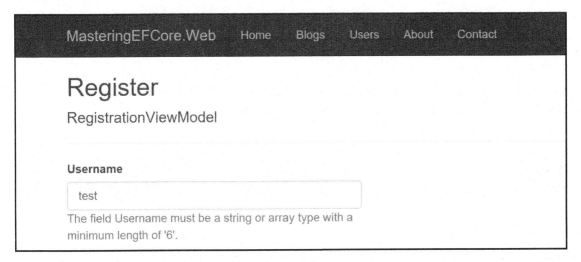

Once satisfied with the length constraint, the error message will be removed from the user interface, shown as follows:

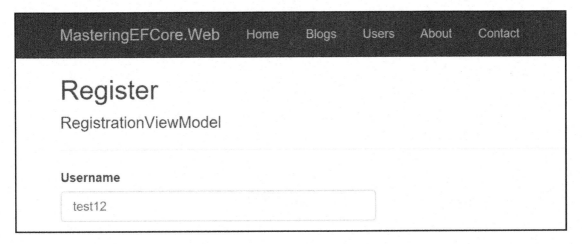

We can configure the custom error message for each model field as follows:

```
public class RegistrationViewModel
{
    [Required(ErrorMessage = "Username is required")]
    [MinLength(6, ErrorMessage = "Username needs minimum
        6 characters")]
    public string Username { get; set; }
    // Code removed for brevity
}
```

The preceding method will force EF to emit a custom error message, **Username needs minimum 6 characters**, if the field contains invalid data during validation, shown as follows:

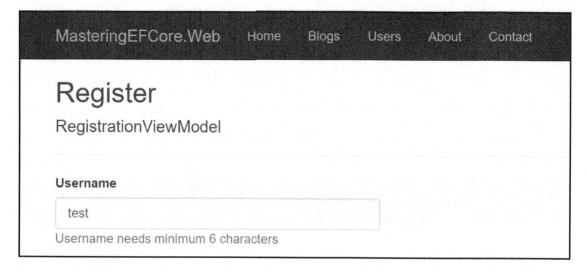

We have looked, exhaustively, at `MinLength` field validation; let's explore `MaxLength` validation in the next section.

MaxLength field validation

The `MaxLength` validation is helpful for creating constraints on certain fields such as Username, Zip code, and so on. We will investigate `MaxLength` validation in this section.

The validation error can be captured in the `MaxLength` data annotation if the field value length is greater than the configured length. For instance, if the maximum length is configured as 30, then if the length of total characters provided in the field is greater than 30, the max length validation error would be thrown.

The `MaxLength` attribute/data annotation can be configured as follows:

```
public class RegistrationViewModel
{
    [Required(ErrorMessage = "Username is required")]
    [MinLength(6, ErrorMessage = "Username needs minimum 6
     characters")]
    [MaxLength(30)]
    public string Username { get; set; }
    // Code removed for brevity
}
```

If the field value does not meet the maximum length requirement, then the validation error, **The field Username must be a string or array type with a maximum length of '30'.** would be thrown, whereas the field name and length of the error message is based on the field name and configuration, as follows:

We can configure the custom error message for each model field, shown as follows:

```
public class RegistrationViewModel
{
    [Required(ErrorMessage = "Username is required")]
```

```
    [MinLength(6, ErrorMessage = "Username needs minimum
        6 characters")]
    [MaxLength(6, ErrorMessage = "Username cannot exceed
        30 characters")]
    public string Username { get; set; }
    // Code removed for brevity
}
```

The preceding method will force EF to emit a custom error message, **Username cannot exceed 30 characters**, if the field contains invalid data during validation, shown as follows:

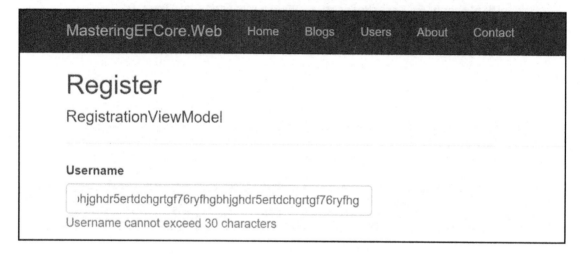

We have looked, exhaustively, at `MaxLength` field validation; let's explore `RegularExpression` validation in the next section.

RegularExpression field validation

Regular expression validation is the only solution used for most validations such as email, phone number, zip code, username, password, and so on. Most of the patterns used with regular expressions are wrapped into separate validations. Still, the usage is vast and requires a method to define custom validation. That's where `RegularExpression` validation comes in handy. Lets investigate regular expressions in this section.

If the field value doesn't follow the defined regular expression pattern, then a validation error would be returned by the engine. For instance, if the regular expression is configured to contain only letters of the alphabet, then any other character inclusion would throw a validation error.

The `RegularExpression` attribute/data annotation can be configured as follows:

```
public class Person
{
    public int Id { get; set; }
    [Required(ErrorMessage = "First Name is required")]
    [RegularExpression("^[a-zA-Z]+$")]
    public string FirstName { get; set; }
    // Code removed for brevity
}
```

If the field value does not match the regular expression, then the validation error, **The field Username must match the regular expression '^[a-zA-Z]+$'.**", would be thrown, which is shown as follows:

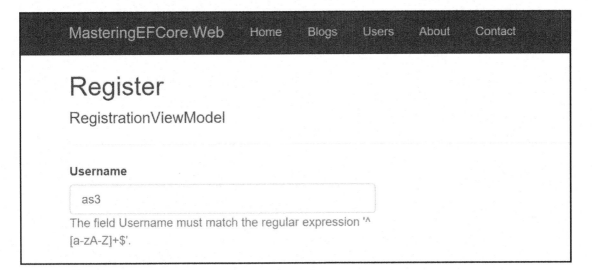

We can configure the custom error message on each model field, as follows:

```
public class Person
{
    public int Id { get; set; }
    [Required(ErrorMessage = "First Name is required")]
    [RegularExpression("^[a-zA-Z]+$", ErrorMessage = "Only
        alphabets were allowed")]
```

```
    public string FirstName { get; set; }
    // Code removed for brevity
}
```

The preceding method will force EF to emit a custom error message, **Only alphabets were allowed**, if the field contains invalid data during validation, which is shown as follows:

We have looked, exhaustively, at RegularExpression field validation and other built -in validations in this chapter. We also built validations for the blogging system we are building along the way.

Summary

We have explored various built-in validations provided by EF in this chapter. We started with the Required field validator which was widely used, then looked into the email address validator, and then we covered other validators such as compare, MinLength, MaxLength and RegularExpression field validators. Finally, we configured these field validators for the blogging system we are building in this book. This chapter dealt only with built-in validations but never discussed how client-side validations are performed or custom validations handled. Let's explore this and a few other things in Chapter 6, *Save Yourself – Hack Proof Your Entities*.

6

Save Yourself – Hack Proof
Your Entities

In Chapter 5, *Know the Validation – Explore Inbuilt Validations*, we understood about in-built validations available in the Entity Framework Core. We explored each one of the validation in detail by starting with how the validation were handled earlier, the way how framework handles it, the configurations required and the rendering performed by the framework.

In this chapter, we will address the following concerns with respect to data security:

- What should be done to the data before we send it over the network?
    - Could you make a wild guess on what should be performed before we send the data over the network?

- What if someone hacks the client-side validation? Or the scripting stops working?
    - We could shield ourselves by introducing server-side validation.

- Beyond client-side and server-side validations, do we need anything in addition?
    - Yes, usual server-side validations would look for any errors and validators of all properties of the model would be taken into account by manual validations.

- Hoping we have custom implementations of validations as well?
    - Yeah, we do have provision to create custom validators and .NET Core's data-attribute approach for custom validators as well.

- Damn, we should have covered almost everything. Guess we didn't leave behind anything else?
    - Except for one thing—remote validation. For instance, checking username availability could be done using remote validation from the client-side without adding any client-side code.

After addressing the concerns, we have a fair idea of what we will be covering in this chapter:

- Client-side validation
- Consequences if the client-side scripting stops working
- Server-side validation
- Manual validation
- Custom validation
- Create client-side logic for custom validation
- Remote validation

Client-side validation

The client-side validation is really a boon to modern web applications. There were many instances that proved jQuery is helpful on both the development and the user experience front. The client-side validations were the biggest advantage we had in saving multiple round trips between client/browser to the server just to perform basic validations.

The jQuery, jQuery Validate, and jQuery Validate Unobtrusive libraries helped us in performing those basic validations on the client (browser) end rather than relying on the server in performing the same. There were multiple discussions or even arguments regarding validating the models at the client-side, which opens security considerations. The following sections will address this issue.

The task to enable client-side validation is just to provide a section for MVC to inject validation errors in the user interface, which has nothing to do with validation-related attributes (as it will be available in the model):

```
<div class="form-group">
  <label asp-for="Title" class="col-md-2 control-label"></label>
  <div class="col-md-10">
    <input asp-for="Title" class="form-control" />
    <span asp-validation-for="Title" class="text-danger"></span>
  </div>
</div>
```

The MVC templating engine will generate the HTML tags with `data-` attributes, which will have the same behavior for both built-in and custom validations. The rendered HTML content for the previously mentioned `Title` field with the `Required` validation is displayed as follows:

```
<div class="form-group">
  <label class="col-md-2 control-label" for="Title">Title</label>
  <div class="col-md-10">
    <input class="form-control" type="text" data-val="true" data-val-
       required="Title is required" id="Title" name="Title"
        value="" />
    <span class="text-danger field-validation-valid"
       data-valmsg-for="Title" data-valmsg-replace="true"></span>
  </div>
</div>
```

The validation is performed when the user tries to submit the form, which will end up in populating the error messages using client-side validation. Further, when we try to edit the messages, the Unobtrusive Validation library kicks in and does the validation way before the user submits the form again.

We have seen what client-side validation does; now, let's see what happens if the JavaScript stops working in the next section.

Validating data without client-side scripting

We live in a world that recognizes the open source, performance-oriented, single page applications (reducing server round trips) as professional applications. Microsoft was too comfortable to move beyond server-side development. Later, they started experimenting client-side validations mainly, thanks to MVC2. Now, with MVC Core, they're back in the game!

This brings us to the million dollar question—is the client-side programming really safe? How long will it take for the hacker to break the client-side validation and get into the server? In today's world, even a dummy who has just started to learn how to hack could do that in minutes. To be blunt, we have no control on the client, and we cannot blindly trust the data we receive from the client (which could be hacked/injected by anybody using tools such as Fiddler, REST Client, and many more).

Knowing that the data we receive may not be authentic, why do we still need client-side validation? Simple. We need better user experience, and we cannot simply ignore a mechanism that will provide us with a mechanism to achieve it. Not only authenticity, but also if somebody disables the JavaScript in their client, then we may be processing unsafe data (not validated) received from the client.

The JavaScript could be disabled using the browser settings. The following screenshot shows how that can be performed using Chrome settings (**Content | JavaScript**):

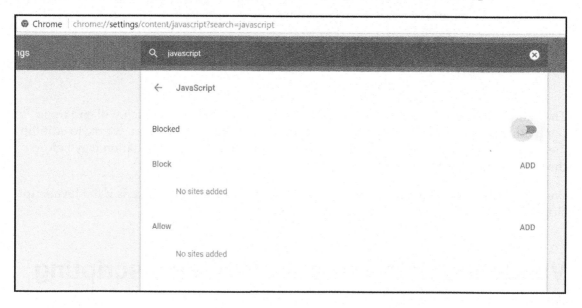

It will enable users to submit any form without client-side validation, so the following form will be submitted without any issues despite not having values in **Title**, **Content**, **Summary**, and so on:

The model that reaches the server without validation is still processed, which opens up security issues. However, we have additional control over the model at the web server. We could see that the values in **Title**, **Content**, and **Summary** were bound as **null** at the server:

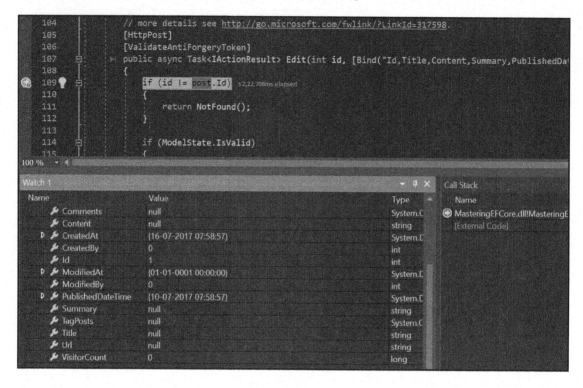

The model needs to be validated before we persist the data back to the data store, and the validation of the posted model is performed by the MVC engine while model binder performs its operation. We should make sure that the model state is `IsValid` and then proceed with the data persistence; it ensures that invalid data doesn't get persisted in the system:

```
113
114    if (ModelState.IsValid)
115    {
116        try
117        {
118            _context.Update(post);
119            await _context.SaveChangesAsync();
120        }
121        catch (DbUpdateConcurrencyException)
122        {
123            if (!PostExists(post.Id))
124            {
125                return NotFound();
126            }
127            else
128            {
129                throw;
130            }
131        }
132        return RedirectToAction("Index");
133    }
134    ViewData["AuthorId"] = new SelectList(_context.Users, "Id", "Id", post.AuthorId);   ≤1ms elapsed
135    ViewData["BlogId"] = new SelectList(_context.Blogs, "Id", "Url", post.BlogId);
```

100 %

Watch 1				Call Stack
Name	Value		Type	Name
VisitorCount	0		long	MasteringEFCore.dll!MasteringEFCore
ModelState.IsValid	false		bool	[External Code]

We have figured out how the data is validated without client-side validation; now let's look at the server-side validation in the next section.

Server-side validation

How can we protect our application, even though we are still leveraging client-side logic while retaining the security of the application? The problem can be resolved in two ways: one is to perform anti-forgery token verification (making sure that the transmitted data has not been tampered with) and the other is to validate the model again in the server side (double-checking ensures that the model is still safe).

A pure MVC Core web application that uses an MVC templating engine can perform the anti-forgery verification in a straightforward manner. MVC generates the anti-forgery token by default for us and all we have to do is verify it at the server side. We could still configure the view to support anti-forgery token generation by enabling `asp-antiforgery` in the `<form>` tag, as follows:

```
<form asp-action="Create" asp-antiforgery="true">
  <div class="form-horizontal">
  ...
```

The old-fashioned way of generating an anti-forgery token is still available and can be done in the following way:

```
<form asp-action="Create">
  @Html.AntiForgeryToken()
  <div class="form-horizontal">
  ...
```

The anti-forgery token can be validated in the server side by configuring it using the custom `ValidateAntiForgeryToken` attribute on the action level:

```
[ValidateAntiForgeryToken]
public async Task<IActionResult> Create(User user)
```

The anti-forgery token can be validated in the server side by configuring it using the custom `AutoValidateAntiForgeryToken` attribute on the controller level:

```
[AutoValidateAntiForgeryToken]
public class UsersController : Controller
```

The same verification can also be done on a global level using `AutoValidateAntiforgeryTokenAttribute` configured in `StartUp.cs` inside the `ConfigureServices()` method, as follows:

```
public void ConfigureServices(IServiceCollection services)
{
  // Add framework services.
  services.AddDbContext<BlogContext>(options =>
    options.UseSqlServer(Configuration.GetConnectionString
      ("DefaultConnection")));
  services.AddMvc(options =>
    options.Filters.Add(new AutoValidateAntiforgeryTokenAttribute()));
  services.AddAuthorization(options =>
  {
    options.AddPolicy("Administrators", policy =>
      policy.RequireRole("Administrators"));
```

```
    });
  }
```

An AngularJS templating engine works a little different in processing the anti-forgery; it uses the XSRF-TOKEN cookie to address the issue. We have a provision in MVC to configure and send the information that would be leveraged by the AngularJS $http service. Exploring those details would be out of context for this book, so just know that we have a provision to use them in a pure JavaScript templating engine as well.

We have figured out how the client-side validation is shielded from attacks; now let's look at the manual validation in the next section.

Manual validation

There may be instances that require manual intervention before we persist something to the database, such as mapping the view model back to the data model. We need a provision in EF to achieve the manual validation to the model in addition to validations performed during model binding of the action invoker (in layman's terms, when the data binding happens in action parameters from request context).

The manual validation can be performed using two ways (ValidateModel and TryValidateModel) in Entity Framework; however, in EF Core, we could use only one and it is TryValidateModel.

We can leverage TryValidateModel() with the user registration module, which contains a view model rather than presenting the actual model itself. We were supposed to validate the data before persisting the view model data into the datastore; in our case, mapping the data between view model to data model and then persisting them into a database:

```
public async Task<IActionResult> Register(RegistrationViewModel
  registrationViewModel)
{
  var user = new User
  {
    Username = registrationViewModel.Username,
    Email = registrationViewModel.Email,
    PasswordHash = Cryptography.Instance.HashPassword(
        registrationViewModel.Password)
  };
  if (TryValidateModel(user))
  {
    await _context.Users.AddAsync(user);
    ViewBag.Message = "User created successfully";
```

```
      return RedirectToAction("Index");
   }
   else
   {
      ViewBag.Message = "Error occurred while validating the user";
   }

   return View(user);
}
```

The preceding implementation illustrates how we perform manual validation, and it does the following:

- Maps the data from **Registration View Model** to **User Data Model**
- We should always suspect that the mapped data may not be valid
- It is always safer to validate the mapped data manually before we persist the data back to the data store
- If we have any validation errors, we would be publishing the information to the user through the `ViewBag` message

The `IsValid` property of the model would be false before we trigger `TryValidateModel`, and later it will be updated based on validation. We have seen how to perform manual validation, and now we will move to custom validation in the next section.

Custom validation

The built-in validations exposed in the framework may be solving most of our technical validation problems, but there may be some business needs/requirements that require additional provision on top of built-in validations.

The custom validation can be performed at two levels:

- Field level
- Class level

The field-level custom validator can be created using the following:

- Inherit the custom validation class from the `ValidationAttribute` base type
- Override the `IsValid` method and handle your business validation
- The `IsValid` method accepts two parameters—`value` and `validationContext`

- The `value` field is the actual field value against which the attribute is configured
- The `validationContext` field would have `ObjectInstance` of the model that contains the configured field

In our blogging system, we can provide a business validation to the publication date; it needs a validation that prohibits the user from publishing the post in a past date. Let's call the custom validation attribute `FutureOnly` and perform the following validation in the overridden `IsValid` method:

```
public class FutureOnlyAttribute : ValidationAttribute
{
  protected override ValidationResult IsValid(object value,
      ValidationContext validationContext)
  {
    var post = (Post) validationContext.ObjectInstance;
    return post.PublishedDateTime.CompareTo(DateTime.Now) < 0
        ? new ValidationResult("Publishing Date cannot be in past,
          kindly provide a future date")
        : ValidationResult.Success;
  }
}

public class Post
{
  public int Id { get; set; }
  [Required(ErrorMessage = "Title is required")]
  public string Title { get; set; }
  [Required(ErrorMessage = "Content is required")]
  public string Content { get; set; }
  public string Summary { get; set; }
  [FutureOnly]
  public DateTime PublishedDateTime { get; set; }
  [Url(ErrorMessage = "Provide a valid url")]
  public string Url { get; set; }
  public long VisitorCount { get; set; }
  public DateTime CreatedAt { get; set; }
  public DateTime ModifiedAt { get; set; }
  public int CreatedBy { get; set; }
  public int ModifiedBy { get; set; }
  [Required(ErrorMessage = "Blog is required")]
  public int BlogId { get; set; }
  public Blog Blog { get; set; }
  [Required(ErrorMessage = "Author is required")]
  public int AuthorId { get; set; }
  public User Author { get; set; }
  [Required(ErrorMessage = "Category is required")]
```

```
public int CategoryId { get; set; }
public Category Category { get; set; }
public ICollection<TagPost> TagPosts { get; set; }
public ICollection<Comment> Comments { get; set; }
}
```

The preceding implementation will verify whether the publication date is future only, and, if it encounters any past date, it will throw a **Publishing Date cannot be in past, kindly provide a future date** validation error.

Let's provide an invalid value in the `FutureOnly` attribute field and see how the validation is performed:

The `IsValid` parameter deals with the actual value passed on both the `value` and `validationContext` parameters; as mentioned earlier, both of them will have the value provided by the user. We are considering `validationContext` in our implementation and it is evident that the provided value is in a past date (when compared to the current date), hence the validation error will be thrown; it is shown as follows:

The class-level custom validator can be created using the following:

- Inheriting the validate object interface, `IValidatableObject`
- Implementing the `Validate` method and handling your business validation
- The `Validate` method must yield the validation errors if it had any

In our blogging system, we can remove the `FutureOnly` attribute included in the model and replace it with class-level validation. The business validation will be triggered automatically (during model binding), and, as it happened in the field-level validation, it updates the model state and error collection. The business validation using `IValidatableObject` is furnished as follows:

```
public class Post : IValidatableObject
{
    public int Id { get; set; }
    [Required(ErrorMessage = "Title is required")]
    public string Title { get; set; }
    [Required(ErrorMessage = "Content is required")]
    public string Content { get; set; }
    public string Summary { get; set; }
    public DateTime PublishedDateTime { get; set; }
    [Url(ErrorMessage = "Provide a valid url")]
    public string Url { get; set; }
    public long VisitorCount { get; set; }
    public DateTime CreatedAt { get; set; }
    public DateTime ModifiedAt { get; set; }
    public int CreatedBy { get; set; }
    public int ModifiedBy { get; set; }
    [Required(ErrorMessage = "Blog is required")]
    public int BlogId { get; set; }
    public Blog Blog { get; set; }
    [Required(ErrorMessage = "Author is required")]
    public int AuthorId { get; set; }
    public User Author { get; set; }
    [Required(ErrorMessage = "Category is required")]
    public int CategoryId { get; set; }
    public Category Category { get; set; }
    public ICollection<TagPost> TagPosts { get; set; }
    public ICollection<Comment> Comments { get; set; }

    public IEnumerable<ValidationResult> Validate(ValidationContext
        validationContext)
    {
        var post = (Post)validationContext.ObjectInstance;
        if (post.PublishedDateTime.CompareTo(DateTime.Now) < 0)
            yield return
                new ValidationResult("Publishing Date cannot be in past,
                kindly provide a future date", new []{ "PublishedDateTime"
                });
    }
}

// One way to consume manual business validation
```

```
var results = new List<ValidationResult>();
var isBusinessValid = Validator.TryValidateObject(post,
    new ValidationContext(post, null, null), results, false);
```

The `IValidatableObject` implementation also does business validation, and updates the error collection with the validation error, **Publishing Date cannot be in past, kindly provide a future date**, if it encounters any business validation issues.

The same scenario was present in the earlier `FutureOnly` attribute validation. Providing a past date would be validated in the `Validate` method. The only difference in both of the approaches was the former does the implementation once and applies to all applicable fields, whereas the latter requires implementation for each field done on the class level. In layman's terms, if we need to include one more field for the validation, we will need to perform the validation for the field again in the `Validate` method:

We explored custom validation that is performed at server side; now, let's explore the custom validation that could be leveraged at a client side as well in the next section.

Creating client-side logic for custom validation

The custom validator we created in this chapter should provide client-side validation support as well. By default, EF will only perform server-side validation (out of the box), but the client-side validation should be performed manually. The framework has provision to inject custom validation and its errors in the context attributes. However, we need to perform/implement client-side validation on our own.

The FutureOnly custom validation attribute can be configured to support client-side validation using IClientModelValidator, which expects us to implement the AddValidation method. We should be injecting the required custom validation values in the context attributes; the required implementation is displayed as follows:

```csharp
public class FutureOnlyAttribute : ValidationAttribute,
  IClientModelValidator
{
  protected override ValidationResult IsValid(object value,
   ValidationContext validationContext)
  {
    var post = (Post) validationContext.ObjectInstance;
    return post.PublishedDateTime.CompareTo(DateTime.Now) < 0
        ? new ValidationResult("Publishing Date cannot be in past,
        kindly provide a future date")
        : ValidationResult.Success;
  }

  public void AddValidation(ClientModelValidationContext context)
  {
    if (context == null)
    {
      throw new ArgumentNullException(nameof(context));
    }
    context.Attributes["data-val"] = "true";
    context.Attributes["data-val-futureonly"] = "Publishing Date
      cannot be in past, kindly provide a future date";
  }
}
```

The context attributes don't have the custom attributes unless we manually configure them inside the element's context; the following screenshot shows that the context doesn't have those custom attributes:

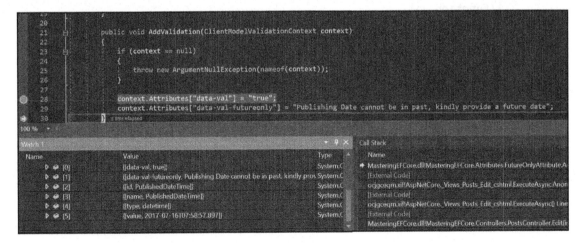

The MVC rendering engine will render HTML content with the data attributes required for client-side validation, and the values that we injected in `AddValidation` were added as attributes to the element context:

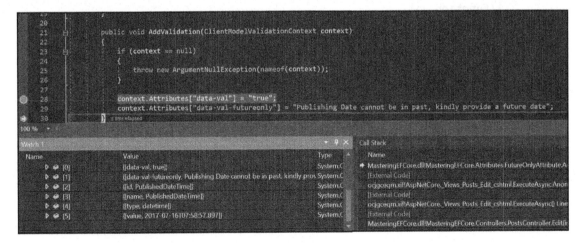

This injected data attribute will be leveraged while implementing the client-side validation, the rendered HTML code required for validation is highlighted as follows:

```
<div class="form-group">
    <label class="col-md-2 control-label"
for="PublishedDateTime">PublishedDateTime</label>
        <div class="col-md-10">
            <input name="PublishedDateTime" class="form-control valid"
id="PublishedDateTime" aria-invalid="false" aria-required="true"
    aria-describedby="PublishedDateTime-error" type="datetime"
    value="" data-val-required="The PublishedDateTime field is
    required." data-val="true" data-val-futureonly="Publishing Date
    cannot be in past, kindly provide a future date">
<span class="text-danger field-validation-valid" data-valmsg-
replace="true"
    data-valmsg-for="PublishedDateTime"></span>
        </div>
</div>
```

The client-side validation should be performed by configuring them in the `jQuery` validator, which also requires an unobtrusive adaptor. The implementation required for the `FutureOnly` custom field validation is furnished below, which will be processed in `PublishedDate`, which consumes the `FutureOnly` custom validation:

```
@section Scripts {
  @{await Html.RenderPartialAsync("_ValidationScriptsPartial");}
  <script>
  $(function () {
    jQuery.validator.addMethod('futureonly',
    function (value, element, params) {
        return (new Date($(params[0]).val())) > (new Date());
  });
    jQuery.validator.unobtrusive.adapters.add('futureonly',
        [ 'element' ],
    function (options) {
      var element = $(options.form).find('input#PublishedDateTime')[0];
      options.rules['futureonly'] = [element];
      options.messages['futureonly'] = options.message;
    });
  }(jQuery));
  </script>
}
```

The preceding implementation will let the JavaScript engine embed unobtrusive validation to the custom attribute element during the page load, which lets the application perform client-side validation. We could verify in the below screenshot that the client-side validation is executed before sending the data over the network:

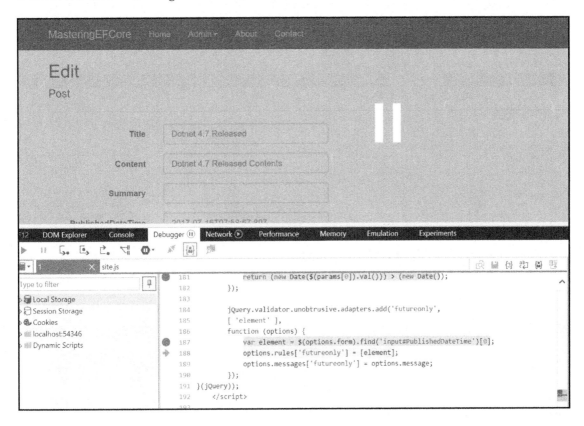

When the user moves over to the other control, unobtrusive validation kicks in, which validates the control using custom JavaScript implementation, shown as follows:

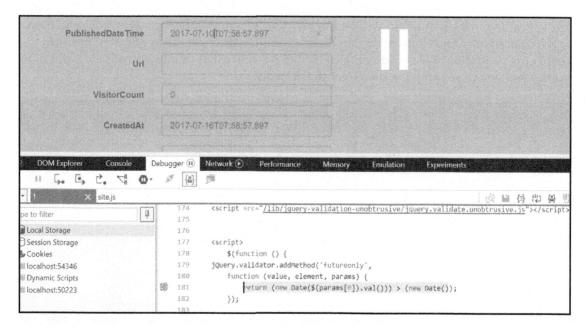

The validation outcome would either let the user continue with his input operation or display an error and stop the user from submitting the form (without reaching the server). In the following example, it was an invalid date and the custom error message is populated in the error collection, which was also displayed in the view as shown in the following screehshot:

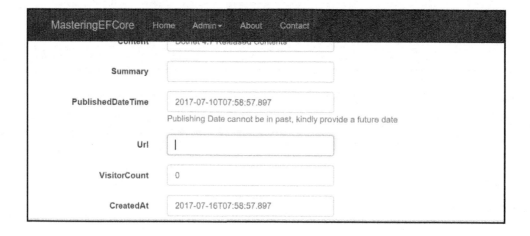

We explored the complete configuration and implementation required for the client-side validation of custom validator; now, let's explore the remote validation feature available with us that will perform something in addition to the custom validation.

Remote validation

The validations we have done so far were configured at model level, and when we say model, it happens within its own domain. We may have a requirement where we need to operate across models. Entity Framework has a provision to achieve the same since it is data driven and the validation required outside the model is not available in Entity Framework. To fill this gap, MVC has a provision to achieve the same using RemoteAttribute, which allows the user to consume the controller action that follows a certain pattern in the implementation.

The remote validation requires the following boundary conditions:

- RemoteAttribute requires two properties—controller and action
- Configured field name should be used as the action parameter name
- The action should return a Json data
- The returned data must have a boolean value

The blogging system has a similar requirement that requires remote validation:

- Validation should be performed without submitting the entire form
- Username can be verified on the fly when the user types in the value
- The remote validation should verify the value against the database and respond whether the username is available or not

RemoteAttribute should be implemented in the user model described as follows:

- Create an action named IsUsernameAvailable in the Users controller.
- The action should have the parameter name as username and type as String.
- Perform the validation on the username value against the users table and capture the result in a boolean variable.

- Return the boolean value in the `Json` method against the `data` parameter. This is shown in the following code snippet:

```
public async Task<IActionResult> IsUsernameAvailable(string
   username)
{
   var usernameAvailable =
      await _context.Users.AnyAsync(x =>
         x.Username.Equals(username,
         StringComparison.OrdinalIgnoreCase));
   return Json(data: !usernameAvailable );
}
```

- Configure `RemoteAttribute` in the `User` model against the `Username` property.
- The validation should pass the parameter's controller as `Users` and action as `IsUsernameAvailable`

The following code would configure the remote validation in the `User` entity:

```
public class User
{
   public int Id { get; set; }
   [Required(ErrorMessage = "Display Name is required")]
   public string DisplayName { get; set; }
   [Required(ErrorMessage = "Username is required")]
   [Remote(action: "IsUsernameAvailable", controller:"Users")]
   public string Username { get; set; }
   [Required(ErrorMessage = "Password is required")]
   public string PasswordHash { get; set; }
   [Required(ErrorMessage = "Email is required")]
   [EmailAddress(ErrorMessage = "Provide a valid email address")]
   public string Email { get; set; }
   public DateTime CreatedAt { get; set; }
   public DateTime ModifiedAt { get; set; }
   public int CreatedBy { get; set; }
   public int ModifiedBy { get; set; }
   public ICollection<Blog> Blogs { get; set; }
   public ICollection<Post> Posts { get; set; }
   public ICollection<Comment> Comments { get; set; }
   public int? AddressId { get; set; }
   public Address Address { get; set; }
   public int PersonId { get; set; }
   public Person Person { get; set; }
}
```

It would be wise to perform unit testing on the remote validation since we are relying on an external functionality to validate a model field. Let's validate the code against a success scenario by providing a username that is available (the highlighted watch console window, as you can see in the following screenshot, shows that the username "prabhakaran" is still available):

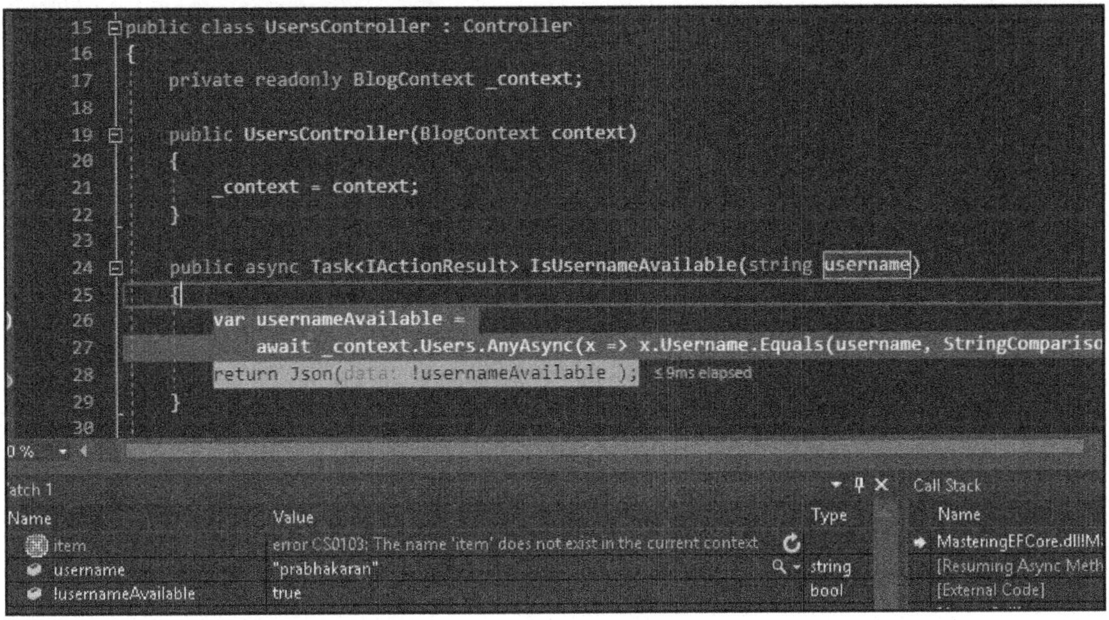

The valid username will not be throwing any validation errors on the **Create User** screen. We can see the username on the screen and then highlight on the very next field and there are still no validation errors; it means that the username is available (displaying the content in the **Username** field is old-fashioned EF!). This is shown in the following screenshot:

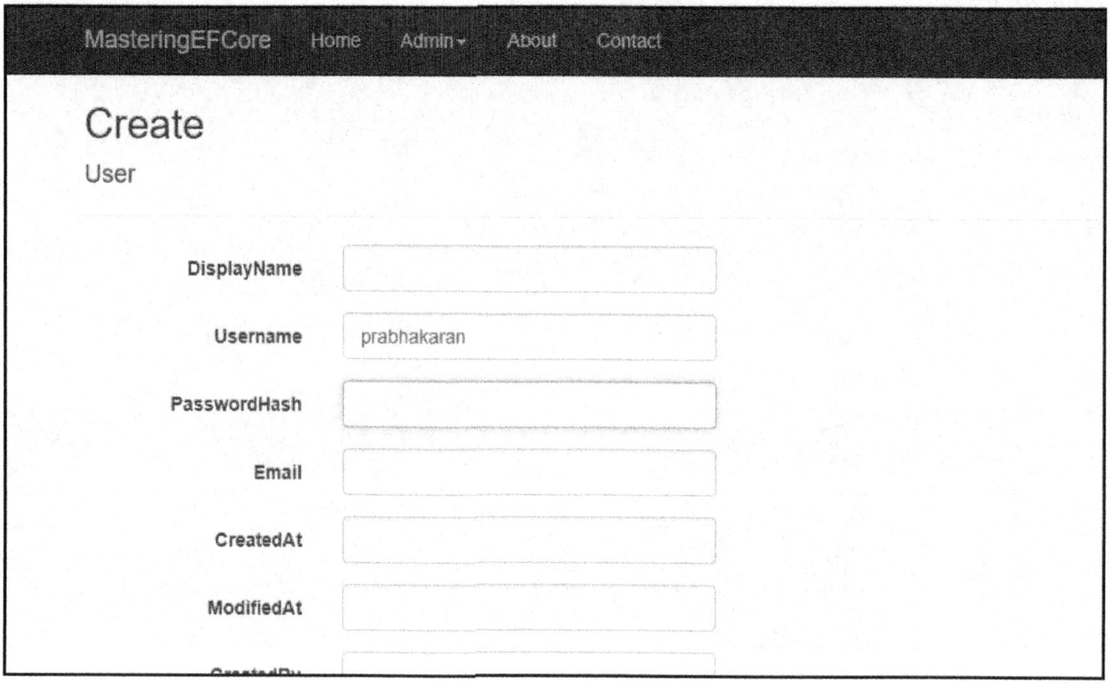

Let's validate the code against a failure scenario by providing a username that is not available (the highlighted watch console window, as you can see in the following screenshot, shows that the **username** "prabhakar" is not available):

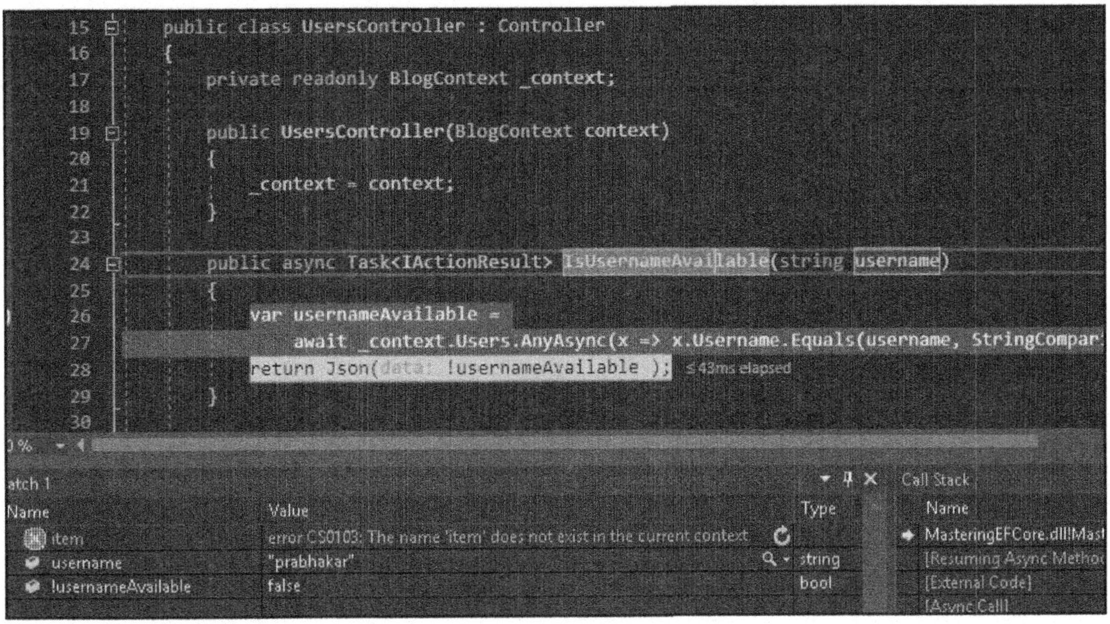

```
15      public class UsersController : Controller
16      {
17          private readonly BlogContext _context;
18
19          public UsersController(BlogContext context)
20          {
21              _context = context;
22          }
23
24          public async Task<IActionResult> IsUsernameAvailable(string username)
25          {
26              var usernameAvailable =
27                  await _context.Users.AnyAsync(x => x.Username.Equals(username, StringCompar
28              return Json(data: !usernameAvailable );    ≤ 43ms elapsed
29          }
30
```

Name	Value	Type
item	error CS0103: The name 'item' does not exist in the current context	
username	"prabhakar"	string
!usernameAvailable	false	bool

Call Stack

Name
MasteringEFCore.dll!Mast
[Resuming Async Method
[External Code]
[Async Call]

This invalid username will be throwing a validation error in the **Create User** screen. We can see that the username furnished in the text field is not available in the database and the corresponding validation error is displayed next to the text field:

One last thing, in the boundary condition, we mentioned that the parameter name should match the field name configured for the remote validation. Do we need to know what would happen if there is a deviation? If the parameter name is different from the name configured? Well, the value binding will not happen, instead the value would be null.

We never discussed assignment as of now, so let's take that as a task and get the proper validation performed as displayed in the following screenshot:

```
15    public class UsersController : Controller
16    {
17        private readonly BlogContext _context;
18
19        public UsersController(BlogContext context)
20        {
21            _context = context;
22        }
23
24        public async Task<IActionResult> IsUsernameAvailable(string item)
25        {
26            var usernameAvailable =
27                await _context.Users.AnyAsync(x => x.Username.Equals(item, StringComparison.OrdinalIg
28            return Json(data: !usernameAvailable );
```

Name	Value	Type	Name
item	null	string	MasteringEFCore.dll!MasteringEFCore.(
			[External Code]

We learned about remote validation in this chapter, and that wraps up the custom validations we can perform beyond the built-in validations available in the framework.

Summary

We learned about custom validations that were provided by Entity Framework and MVC in this chapter. We started with client-side validation, which changed the user experience completely, then looked at what would happen if somebody hacks in and bypasses the client-side validation. We overcame those issues by applying second-level validation at the server side. We saw the urge in performing manual validation rather than the framework doing it for us out of the box; we then performed some custom validation that was required beyond the built-in validations. We also applied the same validation to the client side by leveraging IClientModelValidator. Finally, we performed a remote validation that was not even a part of Entity Framework but was available in the MVC Framework.

So far, we were accessing the data only through data context, and we have never written any plain SQL queries. In a few valid scenarios, we had a need for the provision to bypass the data context for better performance or to avoid heavy lifting tasks done by the framework. We will figure this out in Chapter 7, *Going Raw – Leveraging SQL Queries in LINQ*.

7
Going Raw – Leveraging SQL Queries in LINQ

We have learned about custom validations, leveraging client-side validation, responding if somebody hacks into the system and bypasses the client-side validation, and additional layer security at the server side. Finally, we performed remote validation from the MVC framework.

In this chapter, we will address the following concerns with respect to data security:

- Do we have a provision in **Entity Framework (EF)** to control SQL queries?
    - We can perform or execute inline SQL queries directly from EF.
- What if someone hacks the system and performs SQL injection? Do SQL queries actually open up those security issues?
    - We could use parametrized queries to avoid SQL injection.
- If we go down the plain SQL queries route, can we leverage LINQ queries?
    - Yes, we can still leverage them in LINQ queries.
- Can we execute the queries without the `DBSet` class or **POrtable COmponents (POCO)** object?
    - Yes, we do have a provision to execute queries without `DBSet` or a POCO object.

After addressing these concerns, we have a fair idea of what we will be covering in this chapter:

- Basic raw SQL queries
- Building parameterized queries
- Composing with LINQ
- Executing SQL query without a DBSet class or POCO

Basic raw SQL queries

The main idea of abstracting SQL queries from the framework is to perform implementation irrespective of the data source that we will be using in the application. We might think that creating raw SQL queries must be defeating the very purpose of EF Core's existence. There are a few valid requirements that might need raw SQL instead of leaving Entity to do the work for us.

It could be anything, something that could not be achieved through LINQ queries or performance that was not optimized by Entity-generated queries. The reason could be anything, but, at the end of the day, we all work for an outcome, an optimized outcome with better performance. We might be ready to take extreme measures in not aligning with the framework/APIs, provided the reason is substantiated more than the API usage.

We could perform basic SQL queries or execute stored procedures or functions from EF in raw mode. The framework has a provision in the DBSet through the FromSql method that does the job for us, allowing us to execute raw SQL using EF. It also allows us to create LINQ queries based on SQL queries; because was made possible since it has been exposed from the DBSet type.

Let's extend the blogging system by making the blogs controller execution into raw SQL queries, and we will begin with the Index action using a raw SQL query, displayed as follows:

```
public async Task<IActionResult> Index()
{
  return View(await _context.Blogs.FromSql("Select *
    from dbo.Blog").ToListAsync());
}
```

The preceding listed implementation produces the following output in the view, and it doesn't make much difference to the existing rendered view:

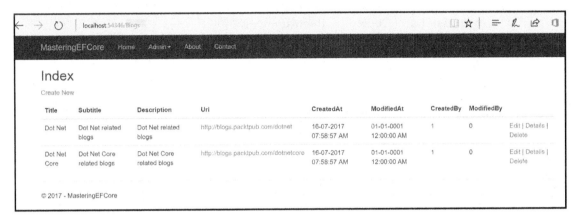

We will create a new action just to illustrate the **stored procedure (SP)** `GetLatestBlogs` execution using raw SQL query EF. The implementation of an SP using `FromSql` is listed as follows:

```
public async Task<IActionResult> LatestBlogs()
{
    return View("Index", await _context.Blogs.FromSql("EXEC
    [dbo].[GetLatestBlogs]").ToListAsync());
}
```

The preceding listed implementation produces the following output in the view. All it does is render the SP's outcome within an existing `Index` view:

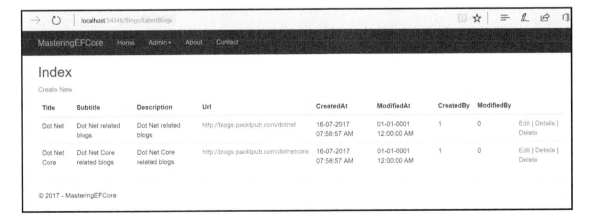

FromSql could perform raw SQL queries only if the returned data is of the DBSet type being accessed. In the preceding example, we used Blogs and DBSet, and it would expect the query to return blogs, and other entities would not be accepted by the framework.

Let's try to return a different type other than the one being configured against the DBSet and see how EF is behaving:

```
public async Task<IActionResult> Index()
{
    return View(await _context.Blogs.FromSql("Select *
    from dbo.Post").ToListAsync());
}
```

The preceding query would trigger an invalid operation since the data returned doesn't match the type it is trying to map:

An unhandled exception occurred while processing the request.

InvalidOperationException: The required column 'Description' was not present in the results of a 'FromSql' operation.

Microsoft.EntityFrameworkCore.Query.Sql.Internal.FromSqlNonComposedQuerySqlGenerator.CreateValueBufferFactory(IRelationalValueBufferFactoryFactory relationalValueBufferFactoryFactory, DbDataReader dataReader)

Stack   Query   Cookies   Headers

InvalidOperationException: The required column 'Description' was not present in the results of a 'FromSql' operation.

Microsoft.EntityFrameworkCore.Query.Sql.Internal.FromSqlNonComposedQuerySqlGenerator.CreateValueBufferFactory(IRelationalValueBufferFactoryFactory relationalValueBufferFactoryFactory, DbDataReader dataReader)

Microsoft.EntityFrameworkCore.Internal.NonCapturingLazyInitializer.EnsureInitialized<TParam, TValue>(ref TValue target, TParam param, Func<TParam, TValue> valueFactory)

Microsoft.EntityFrameworkCore.Query.Internal.ShaperCommandContext.NotifyReaderCreated(DbDataReader dataReader)

Microsoft.EntityFrameworkCore.Query.Internal.AsyncQueryingEnumerable+AsyncEnumerator+<BufferlessMoveNext>d__9.MoveNext()

System.Runtime.ExceptionServices.ExceptionDispatchInfo.Throw()

System.Runtime.CompilerServices.TaskAwaiter.HandleNonSuccessAndDebuggerNotification(Task task)

Microsoft.EntityFrameworkCore.Storage.Internal.SqlServerExecutionStrategy+<ExecuteAsync>d__6.MoveNext()

System.Runtime.ExceptionServices.ExceptionDispatchInfo.Throw()

System.Runtime.CompilerServices.TaskAwaiter.HandleNonSuccessAndDebuggerNotification(Task task)

Microsoft.EntityFrameworkCore.Query.Internal.AsyncQueryingEnumerable+AsyncEnumerator+<MoveNext>d__8.MoveNext()

System.Runtime.ExceptionServices.ExceptionDispatchInfo.Throw()

System.Runtime.CompilerServices.TaskAwaiter.HandleNonSuccessAndDebuggerNotification(Task task)

Microsoft.EntityFrameworkCore.Query.Internal.AsyncLinqOperatorProvider+SelectAsyncEnumerable+SelectAsyncEnumerator+<MoveNext>d__4.MoveNext()

System.Runtime.ExceptionServices.ExceptionDispatchInfo.Throw()

System.Runtime.CompilerServices.TaskAwaiter.HandleNonSuccessAndDebuggerNotification(Task task)

Microsoft.EntityFrameworkCore.Query.Internal.AsyncLinqOperatorProvider+SelectAsyncEnumerable+SelectAsyncEnumerator+<MoveNext>d__4.MoveNext()

With the preceding displayed error, it is evident that something beyond the type mismatch is happening here since the error doesn't specify anything about the type mismatch.

 FromSql expects that the column names returned from the database match with the ones available in the mapping object. If there is a mismatch in the object then an invalid operation exception would be thrown by the framework.

If we have any requirement to consume anonymous types in the raw SQL queries using FromSql, we definitely won't get them until EF Core 2.0, and the same is available on the following shared link at https://github.com/aspnet/EntityFramework/issues/1862, which says:

> *"This is something we are still trying to get in 2.0, but the schedule is tight and there is a high risk that we will need to punt it to the next minor release after 2.0." - Diego Vega.*

> *"Unfortunately, we don't have time to do this for the 2.0 release. We are considering it a high priority for post 2.0." - Arthur Vickers*

The preceding listed responses were from a Entity Framework GitHub repository owner and member, so it's official that we might not get this feature this year.

Let's try to limit the columns returned from the database and see whether we have any impact on the application. The SELECT statement is tweaked with limited columns from the Blog entity:

```
public async Task<IActionResult> Index()
{
    return View(await _context.Blogs.FromSql("Select [Id],[Title],
    [Subtitle],[Description],[Url] from dbo.Blog").ToListAsync());
}
```

The framework doesn't support inline queries that don't provide data to all the properties/fields of the data model. It would start throwing errors, as follows, until all the fields were satisfied in the SQL query:

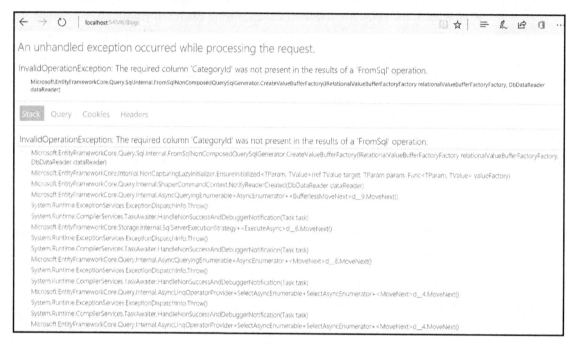

We have seen queries or SPs without any parameters so far, and only a few cases use them in real-time applications. We will explore inline queries that accept parameters and see how we could utilize them safely in the next section.

Building parameterized queries

Building and executing parameterless queries would have fewer usages, whereas most usages in any application would be based on parameters/conditions. Introducing parameters in flat/raw queries would expose us to a threat of SQL injection. How are we going to protect our application from such a threat? We cannot ignore them in a real-world application, as we have applications that are hugely dependent on inline queries.

SQL injection is a technique used by hackers to exploit any system, and it would shake it to its core in terms of security. It could be performed by embedding user inputs blindly with inline SQL queries.

The most commonly injected value would be `OR 1 = 1`, which would pump an entire record set instead of using the input value for filtering. For instance, in our blogging system, if a hacker tries to retrieve user information he could tweak the following query (assuming we have such a query in the system):

`SELECT * FROM USERS WHERE Id =  + userId +.` `userId` could be a field storing the user input value.

Considering the `userId` passed as 5 from the application, it could be constructed as follows:
`SELECT * FROM USERS WHERE Id = 5`
The preceding query displays or returns only one user matching the `Id` as 5.

If the hacker injects the previously mentioned value, it would be as follows:

`SELECT * FROM USERS WHERE Id = 5 OR 1 = 1`

The preceding SQL injection would return all users' information, rather than returning only the user matching `ID` 5. This is a simple SQL injection.

Parameterized queries are the mechanism used to protect us from such threats. They ensure that the SQL injection doesn't happen, and the previously mentioned injection problem would not happen with the parameterized queries:

```
public async Task<IActionResult> Details(int? id)
{
  if (id == null)
  {
    return NotFound();
  }

  var blog = await _context.Blogs.FromSql("Select * from dbo.Blog WHERE
      Id = {0}", id).FirstOrDefaultAsync();
  if (blog == null)
  {
    return NotFound();
  }

  return View(blog);
}
```

Instead of directly passing the input value as a parameter in the FromSql method, we could also use the SqlParameter object to construct the parameter, which also ensures that the query is safe from SQL injection. The following code would illustrate parameterised query execution in EF Core:

```
public async Task<IActionResult> Details(int? id)
{
  if (id == null)
  {
    return NotFound();
  }

  var blog = await _context.Blogs.FromSql("Select * from dbo.Blog
    WHERE Id = @id", new SqlParameter("id", id)).FirstOrDefaultAsync();
  if (blog == null)
  {
    return NotFound();
  }

  return View(blog);
}
```

The following screenshot displays a blog item as usual without any changes to its previous state. The only difference is its rendering through a parameterized query:

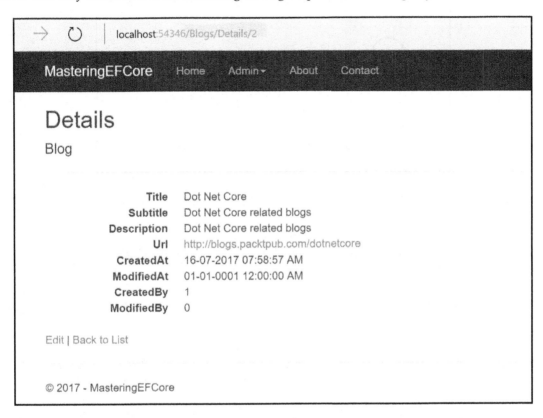

If we try to inject the value through any of the following means, the system would still be handling the injection of the model binder itself since we are dealing with identifiers that were exposed as an integer. Let's visit the following paths:

```
http://localhost:54346/Blogs/Details/1OR1=1
```

```
http://localhost:54346/Blogs/Details?id=1OR1=1
```

Trying to access anyone of the preceding link would throw the following error:

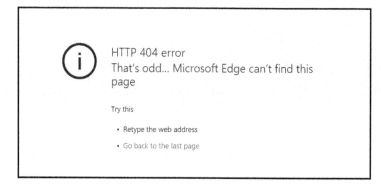

For the sake of argument, let's change the parameter type of the identifier to a string and try injecting the value again to the `Details` action to see how SQL injection is really handled by parameterized queries. It is evident in the following screenshot that the parameterized query is trying to convert the value to an integer that actually fails and the execution is stopped, thereby protecting the application against SQL injection:

Still not convinced? Me neither. Unless we handle injection for a string column, I won't be convinced. Let's tweak the system just for the purpose of illustration by adding the following action, which would filter blogs using a wildcard search in the `Title` column, returning the first item from the result set and finally rendering them in an existing `Details` view:

```
public async Task<IActionResult> GetBlogByTitle(string keyword)
{
  if (keyword == null)
  {
    return NotFound();
  }

  var blog = await _context.Blogs.FromSql("Select * from dbo.Blog WHERE
    Title like '%' + @keyword + '%'",
  new SqlParameter("keyword", keyword)).FirstOrDefaultAsync();
  if (blog == null)
  {
    return NotFound();
  }

  return View("Details", blog);
}
```

Try to inject the values as we did earlier, by visiting the following paths:

```
http://localhost:54346/Blogs/GetBlogByTitle/keyword=core OR 1=1
http://localhost:54346/Blogs/GetBlogByTitle?keyword=core OR 1=1
```

Still, the system would be handling the injection, but now at the database end as it would be treated as a string value. The query fails to return any records, thereby returning `NotFound()` from the action:

We have exhaustively seen the inline parameterized queries. Let us explore them using stored procedures, which are also one of the techniques in handling SQL injections. The SP execution looks similar to the parameterized inline query, still protecting the application from SQL injection. Let's tweak the system just for the purpose of illustration by adding the following action which would filter blogs by category, return the list of blog items, and finally render them in an existing `Index` view:

```
public async Task<IActionResult> BlogsByCategory(int categoryId)
{
    return View("Index", await _context.Blogs.FromSql("EXEC
      [dbo].[GetBlogsByCategory] @categoryId = {0}",
      categoryId).ToListAsync());
}
```

The preceding query could be tweaked to accommodate the `SqlParameter` object, which streamlines the parameterized query in a more readable manner. The following would consume `SqlParameter` in the parameterised SQL execution:

```
public async Task<IActionResult> BlogsByCategory(int categoryId)
{
    return View("Index", await _context.Blogs.FromSql("EXEC
      [dbo].[GetBlogsByCategory] @categoryId = @Id",
      new SqlParameter("id", categoryId)).ToListAsync());
}
```

The following screenshot displays a list of filtered blog items in the `Index` view; only it is processed from a different action and mainly uses parameterized queries:

We have seen parameterized inline queries or SPs so far, which satisfy the use cases in real-time applications. We will further explore leveraging them with the LINQ queries to filter/process data in the *Composing with LINQ* section.

Composing with LINQ

We have performed flat SQL queries so far. This doesn't involve LINQ queries. If we had a mechanism that could leverage flat queries composed of LINQ to SQL queries, then we could get the best of both worlds. Fortunately, we do have built-in support in Entity Framework, and the flat SQL queries could be composed of LINQ queries, and we will cover them in detail in this section.

Let's comment the current implementation in `LatestBlogs()` and perform the SP implementation using flat queries composed with LINQ. Ideally, what we are trying to achieve is to get the table data using a LINQ query and compose the result with a LINQ query to perform filtering and ordering from a LINQ query (this might not be a real-world scenario, but it works well for illustration):

```
public async Task<IActionResult> LatestBlogs()
{
    //return View("Index", await _context.Blogs.FromSql("EXEC [dbo].
        [GetLatestBlogs]").ToListAsync());
    var comparisonDateTime = DateTime.Now.AddMonths(-3);
    return View("Index", await _context.Blogs
        .FromSql("Select * from dbo.Blog")
        .Where(x=>x.CreatedAt >= comparisonDateTime)
        .OrderByDescending(x=>x.Id)
        .ToListAsync());
}
```

We can see the outcome as expected, and it reflects that of the earlier result set for the latest blogs in the following screenshot:

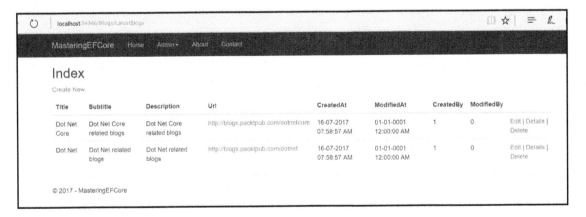

Let's dig in further and see what is happening internally and how Entity Framework is processing these queries. We might be thinking that EF Core would be retrieving blog entries and does a LINQ query with in-memory data. The following **SQL Server Profiler** trace will prove us wrong. If we closely watch the highlighted part of the trace, it is evident that Entity Framework is performing a LINQ to an SQL query by translating the LINQ query into the required SQL query and executing it in one shot in the database. Cool, right? The following screenshot would illustrate that the parameterised execution is translated into SQL statement:

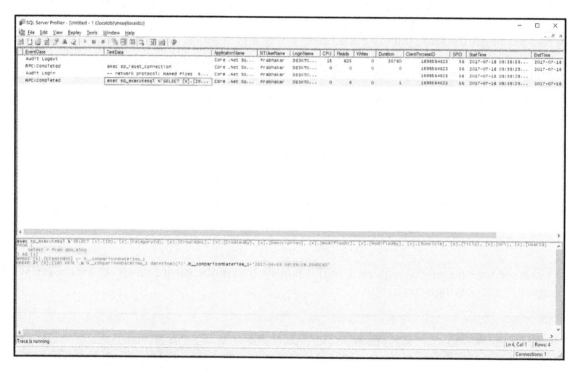

We have looked at the mechanism to compose flat SQL queries with LINQ, but we haven't covered the `Include()` data, which is a powerful feature of Entity Framework. You guessed it right, we could perform the `Include()` operation on flat SQL queries composed of LINQ queries as well. All we need to do is have the `.Include()` method as usual before the `.ToList()` call, which translates the LINQ queries into SQL queries. The following code would consume the `.Include()` functionality:

```
public async Task<IActionResult> LatestBlogs()
{
    //return View("Index", await _context.Blogs.FromSql("EXEC [dbo].
        [GetLatestBlogs]").ToListAsync());
```

```
var comparisonDateTime = DateTime.Now.AddMonths(-3);
return View("Index", await _context.Blogs
  .FromSql("Select * from dbo.Blog")
  .Where(x=>x.CreatedAt >= comparisonDateTime)
  .OrderByDescending(x=>x.Id)
  .Include(x => x.Posts)
  .ToListAsync());
}
```

We can see the outcome of the query in the following screenshots. The first screenshot shows that the total blogs returned has a count of **2**, out of which the first blog has a total of two posts. We can see the blog `Id` used in the post matching with the `Id` field of the first blog:

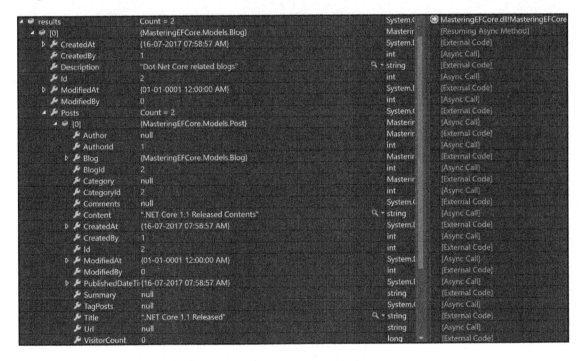

The same is applied to the second post item inside the first blogs **Posts** array, which ensures that the `Include()` method worked as expected, returning corresponding posts to the blog item:

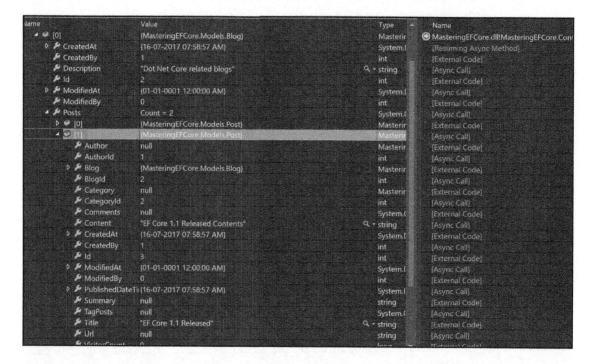

As an additional check, we could verify the second blog item and its corresponding single post, which was included as well:

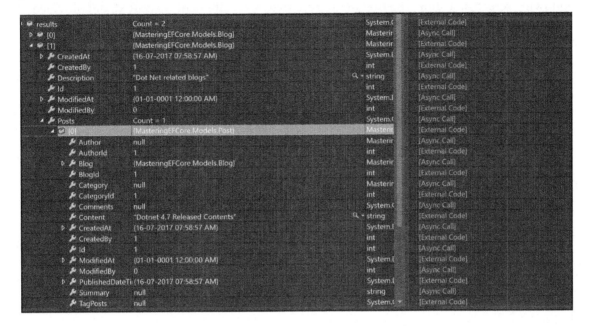

We have seen how the `Include()` functionality worked with the flat SQL query composed with LINQ; let's see how it has been translated into an SQL query (LINQ to SQL). The following screenshot shows us that there were two SQL statements executed, out of which the first statement was similar to the earlier one that retrieves data from the `Blog` table:

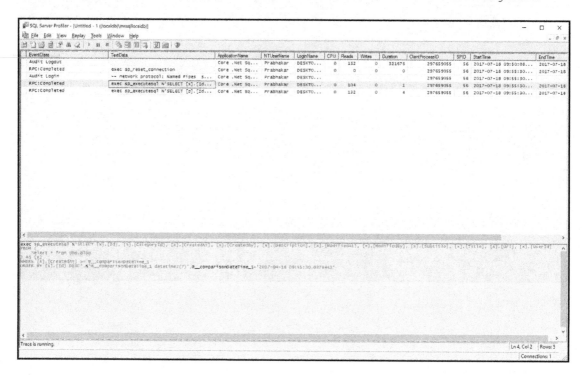

The second statement does the trick for us, executing the code required to include the post table data with the LINQ query. This is depicted in the following screenshot:

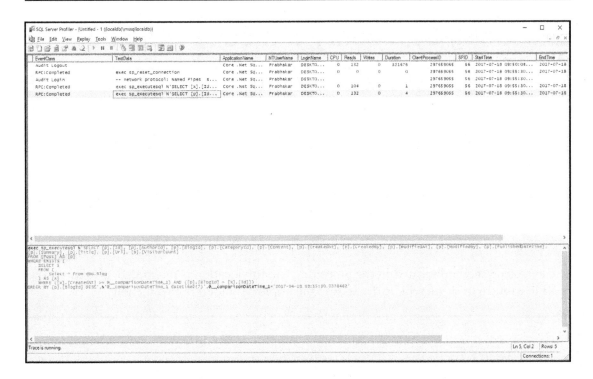

We have seen how to consume flat SQL queries with LINQ to SQL queries in this section, and so far we have seen the execution of flat SQL queries with respect to DBSet or a POCO object. Let's investigate whether the same could be achieved anonymously in the *Executing SQL query without a DBSet or POCO* section.

Executing SQL query without a DBSet or POCO

We need to investigate whether Microsoft supports flat SQL execution anonymously without requiring a `DBSet` or POCO object. Since it's open source, it is easy for us to investigate this. We could directly get into their source code in the GitHub repository (`https://github.com/aspnet/EntityFramework`) and investigate whether they have any implementation of the expected behavior.

Microsoft does have a couple of extension methods for a relational database as a façade, which is available at `https://github.com/aspnet/EntityFramework/blob/0024373adae7e331ed217de2b4bd12be5eedf925/src/EFCore.Relational/RelationalDatabaseFacadeExtensions.cs`.

The extension method located in the preceding GitHub location is illustrated as follows. We need to capture it, as we will be discussing the implementation in this section:

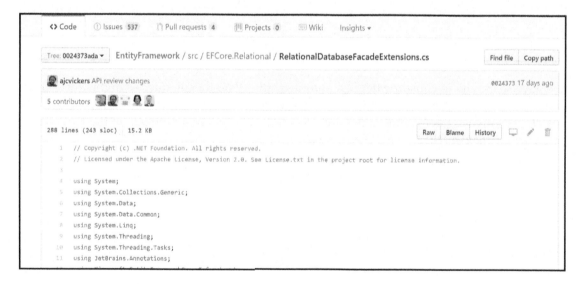

They have an implementation for raw SQL queries, but it is a limited implementation. It has `ExecuteSqlCommand` that supports only `ExecuteNonQuery` functionality, which means we couldn't use this method for processing SQL queries that return result sets:

```
106    public static int ExecuteSqlCommand(
107        [NotNull] this DatabaseFacade databaseFacade,
108        RawSqlString sql,
109        [NotNull] params object[] parameters)
110        => ExecuteSqlCommand(databaseFacade, sql, (IEnumerable<object>)parameters);
111
112    // Note that this method doesn't start a transaction hence it doesn't use ExecutionStrategy
113    public static int ExecuteSqlCommand(
114        [NotNull] this DatabaseFacade databaseFacade,
115        [NotNull] FormattableString sql)
116        => ExecuteSqlCommand(databaseFacade, sql.Format, sql.GetArguments());
117
118    // Note that this method doesn't start a transaction hence it doesn't use ExecutionStrategy
119    public static int ExecuteSqlCommand(
120        [NotNull] this DatabaseFacade databaseFacade,
121        RawSqlString sql,
122        [NotNull] IEnumerable<object> parameters)
123    {
124        Check.NotNull(databaseFacade, nameof(databaseFacade));
125        Check.NotNull(sql, nameof(sql));
126        Check.NotNull(parameters, nameof(parameters));
127
128        var concurrencyDetector = databaseFacade.GetService<IConcurrencyDetector>();
129
130        using (concurrencyDetector.EnterCriticalSection())
131        {
132            var rawSqlCommand = databaseFacade
133                .GetRelationalService<IRawSqlCommandBuilder>()
134                .Build(sql.Format, parameters);
135
136            return rawSqlCommand
137                .RelationalCommand
138                .ExecuteNonQuery(
139                    databaseFacade.GetRelationalService<IRelationalConnection>(),
140                    rawSqlCommand.ParameterValues);
141        }
```

The same implementation is available in an asynchronous way as well, which instructs us to perform two implementations if we are planning to have an extension of our requirement. The following screenshot will have asynchronous implementation:

```
154        RawSqlString sql,
155        CancellationToken cancellationToken = default(CancellationToken))
156        => ExecuteSqlCommandAsync(databaseFacade, sql, Enumerable.Empty<object>(), cancellationToken);
157
158    // Note that this method doesn't start a transaction hence it doesn't use ExecutionStrategy
159    public static Task<int> ExecuteSqlCommandAsync(
160        [NotNull] this DatabaseFacade databaseFacade,
161        RawSqlString sql,
162        [NotNull] params object[] parameters)
163        => ExecuteSqlCommandAsync(databaseFacade, sql, (IEnumerable<object>)parameters);
164
165    // Note that this method doesn't start a transaction hence it doesn't use ExecutionStrategy
166    public static async Task<int> ExecuteSqlCommandAsync(
167        [NotNull] this DatabaseFacade databaseFacade,
168        RawSqlString sql,
169        [NotNull] IEnumerable<object> parameters,
170        CancellationToken cancellationToken = default(CancellationToken))
171    {
172        Check.NotNull(databaseFacade, nameof(databaseFacade));
173        Check.NotNull(sql, nameof(sql));
174        Check.NotNull(parameters, nameof(parameters));
175
176        var concurrencyDetector = databaseFacade.GetService<IConcurrencyDetector>();
177
178        using (await concurrencyDetector.EnterCriticalSectionAsync(cancellationToken))
179        {
180            var rawSqlCommand = databaseFacade
181                .GetRelationalService<IRawSqlCommandBuilder>()
182                .Build(sql.Format, parameters);
183
184            return await rawSqlCommand
185                .RelationalCommand
186                .ExecuteNonQueryAsync(
187                    databaseFacade.GetRelationalService<IRelationalConnection>(),
188                    rawSqlCommand.ParameterValues,
189                    cancellationToken);
190        }
```

The EF Core community has an open issue created with respect to our requirement, which is available at `https://github.com/aspnet/EntityFramework/issues/1862#issuecomment-220787464`.

In the preceding issue thread, a user `sirentek` provided us with a workaround until Microsoft fixes the same for us in the framework. Let's implement the extension methods required for the anonymous SQL query execution:

1. Create a `DatabaseExtensions` static class that holds the extension methods.

2. Implement `ExecuteSqlQuery` for an SQL query that returns a result set as opposed to `ExecuteSqlCommand`, which doesn't return anything.

3. Implement `ExecuteSqlQueryAsync` for asynchronous operations matching the `ExecuteSqlCommandAsync` implementation from Microsoft.

Microsoft has no plans to include them at the present time, not even in EF Core 2.0. It is similar to the earlier discussion we had for anonymous types support:

```
public static class DatabaseExtensions
{
  public static RelationalDataReader ExecuteSqlQuery(this
    DatabaseFacade databaseFacade, string sql, params
    object[] parameters)
  {
    var concurrencyDetector =
        databaseFacade.GetService<IConcurrencyDetector>();
      using (concurrencyDetector.EnterCriticalSection())
      {
        var rawSqlCommand = databaseFacade
        .GetService<IRawSqlCommandBuilder>()
        .Build(sql, parameters);

        return rawSqlCommand
         .RelationalCommand
         .ExecuteReader(
         databaseFacade.GetService<IRelationalConnection>(),
           parameterValues: rawSqlCommand.ParameterValues);
      }
  }

  public static async Task<RelationalDataReader>
     ExecuteSqlQueryAsync(this DatabaseFacade databaseFacade,
  string sql,
  CancellationToken cancellationToken = default(CancellationToken),
    params object[] parameters)
  {
    var concurrencyDetector =
      databaseFacade.GetService<IConcurrencyDetector>();
    using (concurrencyDetector.EnterCriticalSection())
    {
      var rawSqlCommand = databaseFacade
      .GetService<IRawSqlCommandBuilder>()
      .Build(sql, parameters);

      return await rawSqlCommand
      .RelationalCommand
```

```
            .ExecuteReaderAsync(
                databaseFacade.GetService<IRelationalConnection>(),
                parameterValues: rawSqlCommand.ParameterValues,
                cancellationToken: cancellationToken);
        }
    }
}
```

The following code usage is pretty simple; all it does is pass the SQL query required for the `ExecuteSqlQueryAsync` extension method and return a result set in the form of `DbDataReader`:

```
var results = await _context.Database
    .ExecuteSqlQueryAsync(@"select b.Title as BlogTitle, p.* from
            Post p join Blog b on b.Id = p.BlogId");
while (results.DbDataReader.Read())
{
    Console.Write(
        $"Blog Title: '{results.DbDataReader["BlogTitle"]}',
        Post Title: '{results.DbDataReader["Title"]}'");
}
```

We have iterated the `DbDataReader`, which prints the post along with its blog title. The following screenshot proves that anonymous types were returned from flat SQL queries from Entity Framework using our own extension method:

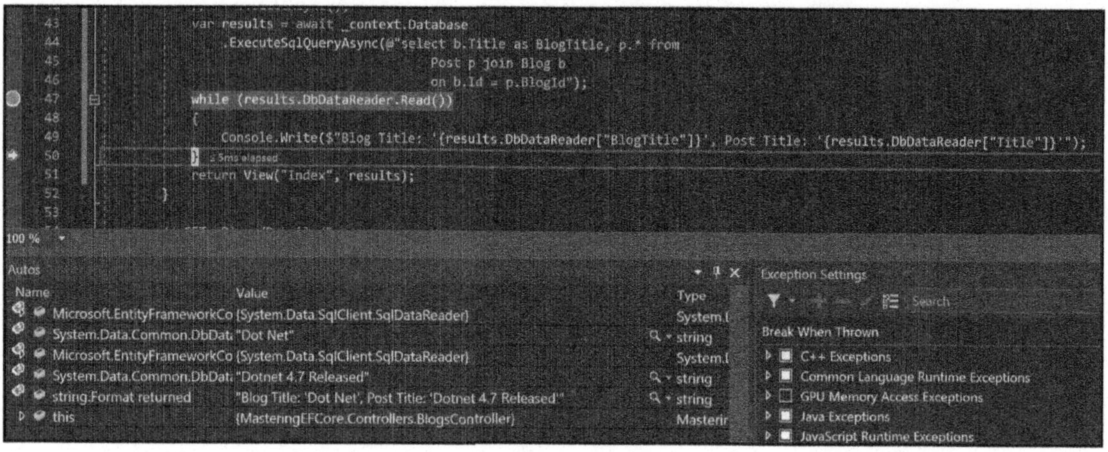

As an additional check, let us verify the second item being returned in the result set, and its matching with the .NET Core entry available in the **Post** table, the following screenshot confirms that the post entries were from .NET core blog only:

```
43        var results = await _context.Database
44            .ExecuteSqlQueryAsync(@"select b.Title as BlogTitle, p.* from
45                    Post p join Blog b
46                    on b.Id = p.BlogId");
47    while (results.DbDataReader.Read())
48    {
49        Console.Write($"Blog Title: '{results.DbDataReader["BlogTitle"]}', Post Title: '{results.DbDataReader["Title"]}'");
50    } ≤2ms elapsed
51    return View("Index", results);
52    }
53
```

We have investigated the availability of raw SQL execution without `DBSet` or POCO objects in Entity Framework. It was proven that Microsoft doesn't have any support at the present time. So, we had a workaround suggested by a user in the community to create an extension method to achieve the same. Then we were able to execute flat SQL queries directly on a database (without a `DBSet`) and return anonymous types (without a POCO object).

Summary

We have explored how to execute raw SQL queries in EF Core without providing direct ADO.NET implementation, and have a consistent implementation of the **Data Access** layer. We started with a simple SQL query, then looked at the security threats (SQL injection) it would expose us to. We have overcome those threats by using parameterized queries and stored procedures. We saw the ways available to marry (composing with LINQ) Entity Framework with raw SQL query execution, leveraging the same with `Include` functionality. Finally, we executed raw SQL queries without `DBSet` and the POCO model, even though there is no built-in support in EF Core.

So far, we have been accessing the data through LINQ to SQL or raw SQL queries without any pattern applied. In `Chapter 8`, *Query Is All We Need – Query Object Pattern*, we will figure out how to apply query-related patterns.

8

Query Is All We Need – Query Object Pattern

We have covered raw SQL query execution in **Entity Framework (EF)**, which might be required in a few valid scenarios to have control over queries or to improve performance. We have seen a simple SQL query, the security threat it could pose, and also a solution for this. Then we covered different ways of executing raw SQL queries in Entity Framework. Finally, we created an extension method to execute raw SQL queries without a DBSet and POCO model.

Let's discuss the repository pattern currently used in the **Object Relational Mapping (ORM)** layer, looking at its design issues, and we'll see how the query object pattern helps us in achieving this efficiently. The following design issues will be addressed in this chapter:

- The repository pattern started to abstract the ORM layer, but lately, the methods included in the repository were growing drastically, which defeats its purpose:
    - The necessity to simplify the data access layer led to the query object pattern
- We have been creating multiple methods in repositories that differ only by the nature of queries:
    - The query object pattern generalizes and improvises the repository methods
- Queries alone would not be sufficient in simplifying the data access layer:
    - Composing queries with generic commands extends the pattern to all CRUD operations

- The query object pattern still doesn't let the user extend the queries dynamically:
  - The simple query objects perform implementation inside queries, but expression trees delegate the implementation to the user, providing the required extendibility to the user

Ideally, we will be covering the following topics:

- Introduction to query objects
- Improving repositories with the query object pattern
- Composing queries with commands
- Enhancing queries with expression trees

Introduction to query objects

The query object pattern could be incorporated by introducing a query type and processing the query through the type, instead of processing it directly. Please perform the following approach we need to follow in order to incorporate the pattern in any application:

1. Create a query type with the fields required for the query, as follows:
   - Have a parameterized constructor that enforces the type instance to be created only if mandatory field values were provided
   - The mandatory fields required for the query must be included in the constructor

Let's create a query type that filters posts by Id; we need a query type that has an Id field and a constructor that populates the Id field:

```
public class PostDetailQuery
{
  public PostDetailQuery(int? id)
  {
    this.Id = id;
  }
  public int? Id { get; set; }
}
```

The query type is ready for implementation; let's proceed to the next step, creating handlers.

2. Create a query handler interface that enforces the type to handle queries, create `Handle()` in the interface that would enforces type to implement it.

The handler must be created in two folds; first, an interface should be created with the provision required for handling the execution:

```
public interface IPostDetailQueryHandler
{
    Task<Post> Handle(PostDetailQuery query);
}
```

The provision is in place; let's create the implementation with a concrete query handler type.

3. Create a query handler type that performs queries using data context, inject the database context using a constructor

The `BlogContext` database context is injected into the handler through the constructor, shown as follows:

```
public class PostDetailQueryHandler : IPostDetailQueryHandler
{
    private readonly BlogContext _context;
    public PostDetailQueryHandler(BlogContext context)
    {
        _context = context;
    }
}
```

The data context is now available; let's use the context of the query object to perform the query execution:

- Implement `Handle()` with actual queries using the data context

The query handler implementation consumes the query type created earlier, and the data context creates a filter using the data available in the query object and performs its execution:

```
public class PostDetailQueryHandler : IPostDetailQueryHandler
{
    // Code removed for brevity
    public async Task<Post> Handle(PostDetailQuery query)
    {
        return await _context.Posts
          .Include(p => p.Author)
```

```
        .Include(p => p.Blog)
        .Include(p => p.Category)
        .FirstOrDefaultAsync(x => x.Id == query.Id);
    }
}
```

Now the query handler implementation is complete, but it's still not consumed anywhere in the application. Let's see how it could be consumed in our controller.

4. Consume the query handler in the controller, inject the query handler using a constructor

The `PostDetailQueryHandler` type is injected through the constructor against the `IPostDetailQueryHandler` interface using the dependency injection (as we previously did for `BlogContext`) supported in .NET Core:

```
public class PostsController : Controller
{
  private readonly BlogContext _context;
  private readonly IPostDetailQueryHandler
  _postDetailQueryHandler;

  public PostsController(BlogContext context,
       IPostDetailQueryHandler postDetailQueryHandler)
  {
    _context = context;
    _postDetailQueryHandler = postDetailQueryHandler;
  }
  // Code removed for brevity
}
```

The query handler is available in the constructor now; let's consume this to perform the required execution in the action that requires it, identify the action (from the controller) that requires the query and consume the query handler to perform the execution

The `Details` action in the controller requires a query execution based on the post `Id`, so let's consume the query using `PostDetailQuery` created for this requirement. The following code would consume the query handler in the controller:

```
public async Task<IActionResult> Details(int? id)
{
  // Code removed for brevity
  var post = await _postDetailQueryHandler.Handle(new
    PostDetailQuery(id));
```

```
    // Code removed for brevity
  }
```

The preceding implementation would trigger a post filter based on the id passed on to the query object, thus wrapping the core implementation to the query type, satisfying the query object pattern:

- Finally, do not forget to support the constructor execution in the dependency injection in Startup.cs inside the ConfigureServices method:

```
services.AddScoped<IPostDetailQueryHandler,
PostDetailQueryHandler>();
```

We have seen how to create query objects and handlers, and how to consume them in controllers. In Chapter 9, *Fail Safe Mechanism – Transactions*, we'll see how to leverage or improvise the repositories by consuming query objects.

Improving repositories with the query object pattern

We need a provision to explain the necessity of a query object pattern, so let's create such a requirement and then we will look into query objects. We will create a repository for blogs in our system, we will see the advantages and disadvantages it brings to the application, and finally, we will see what are query objects and how they help us in improvising repositories.

Introduction to repositories

We have been performing CRUD operations in the controller directly with the data context; we could incorporate a repository in our application first, and later, query objects could be implemented in the repository.

Let us start with creating the interface required for the repository. It includes basic retrieval, business-specific retrievals, and the remaining CRUD operations. The following code contains the methods required for the IPostRepository:

```
public interface IPostRepository
{
    IEnumerable<Post> GetAllPosts();
```

```
    Task<IEnumerable<Post>> GetAllPostsAsync();
    Post GetPostById(int? id, bool includeData = true);
    Task<Post> GetPostByIdAsync(int? id, bool includeData = true);
    IEnumerable<Post> FindPostByTitle(string title);
    IEnumerable<Post> FindPostByAuthor(string author);
    IEnumerable<Post> FindPostByPublishedYear(int year);
    IEnumerable<Post> FindPostByHighestVisitors();
    IEnumerable<Post> FindPostByCategory(string category);
    IEnumerable<Post> FindPost(string keyword, int pageCount,
        int pageSize);
    int AddPost(Post item);
    Task<int> AddPostAsync(Post item);
    int UpdatePost(Post item);
    Task<int> UpdatePostAsync(Post item);
    int DeletePost(int? id);
    Task<int> DeletePostAsync(int? id);
}
```

The repository implementation starts with the database context injection, `BlogContext` in our case. Then the interface implementation starts with `FindPost`, which takes `keyword`, `pageCount`, and `pageSize`, which were consumed by the LINQ query in filtering posts using those parameters. The `keyword` was used as a wildcard search across all fields available in the `Post` entity:

```
public class PostRepository : IPostRepository
{
  private readonly BlogContext _context;
  public PostRepository(BlogContext context)
  {
    _context = context;
  }

  public IEnumerable<Post> FindPost(string keyword, int pageCount,
      int pageSize)
  {
    return _context.Posts
      .Where(x =>
      x.Title.ToLower().Contains(keyword.ToLower())
      || x.Blog.Title.ToLower().Contains(keyword.ToLower())
      || x.Blog.Subtitle.ToLower().Contains(keyword.ToLower())
      || x.Category.Name.ToLower().Contains(keyword.ToLower())
      || x.Content.ToLower().Contains(keyword.ToLower())
      || x.Summary.ToLower().Contains(keyword.ToLower())
      || x.Author.Username.ToLower().Contains(keyword.ToLower())
      || x.Url.ToLower().Contains(keyword.ToLower()))
      .Skip(pageCount-1).Take(pageSize);
  }
```

We could have the assignment to cover the remaining implementations (as well as new actions required to filter posts by category, author, and so on) required in the controller, as we mostly port the controller implementations into a repository method; for instance, the action implementation of the Get action gets into the GetAllPosts method of the repository. In this chapter, since we are working on an assignment that is required to proceed to the next section, we will have the solutions captured as well, just to ensure we have everything implemented before we move on to the next section.

Solution to the repository assignment

We could come up with the following URI that could be used in the application for filtering posts. We should definitely need provision to filter posts by category, author, visitor count, and so on, and these URIs should serve a response in a JSON format that will be consumed by AJAX calls. The following actions would server JSON data which could be consumed by the AJAX calls:

- Posts/FindPostsByAuthor
- Posts/FindPostByCategory
- Posts/FindPostByHighestVisitors
- Posts/FindPostByPublishedYear
- Posts/FindPostByTitle

Let's start building those JSON endpoints first, and then we will move on to porting existing actions into the repository.

The following steps need to be followed to implement JSON-driven HTTP action:

1. Set the appropriate HTTP verb, [HttpGet] in our case.
2. Set the return type as JSON using [Produces("application\json")].
3. The method implementation is straightforward:
    1. Define the controller action with the appropriate return type and an input parameter.
    2. Filter the data context using the input parameter and return the filtered data.
4. The code for the action is listed as follows:

```
[HttpGet]
[Produces("application/json")]
public IEnumerable<Post> FindPostByAuthor(string author)
{
```

```
        return _context.Posts
        .Where(x => x.Author.Username.ToLower().
            Contains(author.ToLower()));
}
```

This implementation alone would not be enough, as we are deviating from the regular MVC content negotiation. This action requires us to return JSON, so we need to configure the services to support this. Additionally, we will ignore the `ReferenceLoopHandling` to avoid unnecessary data included in the response.

In `startup.cs`, add the following configuration inside the `ConfigureServices` method:

```
services.AddMvc().AddJsonOptions(options =>
{
    options.SerializerSettings.ContractResolver =
        new DefaultContractResolver();
    options.SerializerSettings.ReferenceLoopHandling =

        Newtonsoft.Json.ReferenceLoophandling.Ignore;
});
```

Similar changes are required for the remaining URIs; let's take it up as an assignment:

- `Posts/FindPostByCategory`
- `Posts/FindPostByHighestVisitors`
- `Posts/FindPostByPublishedYear`
- `Posts/FindPostByTitle`

The same pattern should be followed for the remaining JSON actions and also for the remaining actions that need to be ported into a repository. The solution for this is available in the following Git repository: `https://goo.gl/DGBZMK`

The repository implementation is far more complete now. In the next section, we will start incorporating the query object pattern into the repository.

Incorporating the query object pattern into repositories

In the *Introduction to query objects* section of this chapter, the query object pattern we had explored need to be incorporated into the repository. Since we know the steps that need to be followed in creating query objects, let's start creating the required types.

List query object support in the repository

We have seen the `GetAllPosts` method, which includes related data for all implementations. Since we are creating a common query, which could be consumed in multiple places, we need to include this as a filter in the `GetAllPostsQuery` object:

```
public class GetAllPostsQuery
{
  public GetAllPostsQuery(bool includeData)
  {
    this.IncludeData = includeData;
  }
  public bool IncludeData { get; set; }
}
```

The `GetAllPostsQuery` consumes only the `IncludeData` filter in the type, which doesn't filter any data from the result set, but only excludes/includes related data. The following code would create a contract to enforce consumers to implement handle methods:

```
public interface IPostQueryHandler<T> where T : class
{
  IEnumerable<Post> Handle(T query);
  Task<IEnumerable<Post>> HandleAsync(T query);
}
```

The generic query handler interface now supports both synchronous and asynchronous operations, which returns a list of Posts. The `GetAllPostsQueryHandler` would perform the concrete implementation which will yield a list of Posts in synchronous and asynchronous manner as displayed in the following code:

```
public class GetAllPostsQueryHandler :
    IPostQueryHandler<GetAllPostsQuery>
{
  private readonly BlogContext _context;
  public GetAllPostsQueryHandler(BlogContext context)
  {
    this._context = context;
```

```
        }

        public IEnumerable<Post> Handle(GetAllPostsQuery query)
        {
           return query.IncludeData
             ? _context.Posts.Include(p =>
             p.Author).Include(p => p.Blog).Include(p => p.Category).ToList()
             : _context.Posts.ToList();
        }
        public async Task<IEnumerable<Post>>
            HandleAsync(GetAllPostsQuery query)
        {
         return query.IncludeData
           ? await _context.Posts.Include(p => p.Author).Include(p
             => p.Blog).Include(p => p.Category).ToListAsync()
           : await _context.Posts.ToListAsync();
        }
    }
```

The `GetAllPostsQuery` consumes the generic query handler to return all posts with or without including related data. The `IPostRepositoryWithQueries` will create a contract with `Get()` and `GetAsync()` method to retrieve list of Posts with the following code:

```
    public interface IPostRepositoryWithQueries
    {
      IEnumerable<Post> Get<T>(BlogContext context, T query)
         where T : class;
      Task<IEnumerable<Post>> GetAsync<T>(BlogContext context,
        T query) where T : class;
    }
```

The `PostRepositoryWithQueries` repository is created to accommodate the query objects with generic methods to accept any query type for its execution, thereby reducing the multiple methods created in the repository earlier. The concrete implementation of the repository is displayed below which delegates the query execution based on the query type:

```
    public class PostRepositoryWithQueries : IPostRepositoryWithQueries
    {
      private readonly BlogContext _context;

      public PostRepositoryWithQueries(BlogContext context)
      {
        _context = context;
      }

      public IEnumerable<Post> Get<T>(BlogContext context, T query)
        where T : class
```

```
  {
    switch(typeof(T).Name)
    {
      case "GetAllPostsQuery":
        var getAllPostsQueryHandler =
          new GetAllPostsQueryHandler(context);
        return getAllPostsQueryHandler.Handle(query
          as GetAllPostsQuery);
    }
  }

  public async Task<IEnumerable<Post>> GetAsync<T>(BlogContext
      context, T query)
    where T : class
  {
   switch (typeof(T).Name)
   {
      case "GetAllPostsQuery":
      var getAllPostsQueryHandler = new
        GetAllPostsQueryHandler(context);
        return await getAllPostsQueryHandler.HandleAsync(query
        as GetAllPostsQuery);
    }
  }
}
```

The repository's `Get` generic method changes its implementation based on the type passed during its invocation, and that reduces the repository implementation to one for all post list retrievals. The `PostRepositoryWithQueries` were consumed in the `PostsController` as shown in the following code:

```
public class PostsController : Controller
{
  private readonly BlogContext _context;
  private readonly IPostRepositoryWithQueries _repositoryWithQueries;

  public PostsController(BlogContext context,
    IPostRepositoryWithQueries repositoryWithQueries)
  {
    _context = context;
    _repositoryWithQueries = repositoryWithQueries;
  }

  // GET: Posts
  public async Task<IActionResult> Index()
  {
    return View(await _repositoryWithQueries.GetAsync(_context,
```

```
        new GetAllPostsQuery(true)));
}

// Code removed for brevity
}
```

We can see the controller started using the new repository through dependency injection and corresponding the `Get` action being called using the appropriate query object. In the preceding scenario, we have been using the `GetAllPostsQuery` object that was passed on to the `GetAsync` method of the new repository. In the next section, let's explore the implementation required to return an individual post object from the repository.

Single query object support in the repository

We have seen how a list of objects was returned from the repository in a generic fashion. Let's have a provision to return a single object from the repository:

```
public interface IPostRepositoryWithQueries
{
  // Code removed for brevity
  Post GetSingle<T>(T query) where T : class;
  Task<Post> GetSingleAsync<T>(T query) where T : class;
}
```

The preceding code adds synchronous and asynchronous methods to return a single `Post` object from the repository, still retaining the generic implementation since it could be used by multiple query objects that might return individual `Post` objects:

```
public class GetPostByIdQuery
{
  public GetPostByIdQuery(int? id, bool includeData)
  {
    this.Id = id;
    this.IncludeData = includeData;
  }

  public int? Id { get; set; }
  public bool IncludeData { get; set; }
}
```

The query type we have created now has one more filter by `Id`, apart from retaining `IncludeData` from the previous query type. The handler interface required to return single `Post` type is defined below:

```
public interface IPostQuerySingleHandler<T> where T : class
{
    Post Handle(T query);
    Task<Post> HandleAsync(T query);
}
```

We have a corresponding generic query handler to handle a single object from the handler implementation, which has synchronous and asynchronous support as well. The following code provides concrete implementation required for the `GetPostByIdQueryHandler` to filter Posts by identifier:

```
public class GetPostByIdQueryHandler :
    IPostQuerySingleHandler<GetPostByIdQuery>
{
    private readonly BlogContext _context;

    public GetPostByIdQueryHandler(BlogContext context)
    {
        this._context = context;
    }

    public Post Handle(GetPostByIdQuery query)
    {
        return query.IncludeData
            ? _context.Posts.Include(p => p.Author)
                .Include(p => p.Blog)
                .Include(p => p.Category).SingleOrDefault(x =>
                    x.Id.Equals(query.Id))
            : _context.Posts
                .SingleOrDefault(x => x.Id.Equals(query.Id));
    }

    public async Task<Post> HandleAsync(GetPostByIdQuery query)
    {
        return query.IncludeData
          ? await _context.Posts.Include(p => p.Author)
            .Include(p => p.Blog)
            .Include(p => p.Category).SingleOrDefaultAsync(x =>
              x.Id.Equals(query.Id))
            : await _context.Posts
                .SingleOrDefaultAsync(x => x.Id.Equals(query.Id));
    }
}
```

The query handler now ports the filter by `id` implementation to the handler; additionally, it includes/excludes related data based on the `IncludeData` filter:

```
public class PostRepositoryWithQueries :
  IPostRepositoryWithQueries
{
 private readonly BlogContext _context;

 public PostRepositoryWithQueries(BlogContext context)
 {
    _context = context;
 }

 public Post GetSingle<T>(BlogContext context, T query)
    where T : class
 {
    //switch (typeof(T).Name)
    //{
    // case "GetPostByIdQuery":
    // var getPostByIdQueryHandler = new
    GetPostByIdQueryHandler(context);
    // return getPostByIdQueryHandler.Handle(query as
    GetPostByIdQuery);
    //}

    var getPostByIdQueryHandler = new
        GetPostByIdQueryHandler(context);
    return getPostByIdQueryHandler.Handle(query
        as GetPostByIdQuery);
 }

 public async Task<Post> GetSingleAsync<T>(BlogContext
     context, T query)
 where T : class
 {
    //switch (typeof(T).Name)
    //{
    // case "GetPostByIdQuery":
    // var getPostByIdQueryHandler =
       new GetPostByIdQueryHandler(context);
    // return await getPostByIdQueryHandler.HandleAsync(query
       as GetPostByIdQuery);
    //}

    var getPostByIdQueryHandler =
        new GetPostByIdQueryHandler(context);
    return await getPostByIdQueryHandler.HandleAsync(query
```

```
          as GetPostByIdQuery);
    }
  }
```

We have commented code in the repository implementations since, currently, it supports only one query handler for returning a single object and having a switch case doesn't make any sense. Once we start adding new implementations for handling single objects, we will be using commented code instead, which supports multiple queries through a single action:

```
public class PostsController : Controller
{
  // Code removed for brevity

  // GET: Posts/Details/5
  public async Task<IActionResult> Details(int? id)
  {
    if (id == null)
    {
     return NotFound();
    }

    var post = await _repositoryWithQueries.GetSingleAsync(_context,
        new GetPostByIdQuery(id, true));
    if (post == null)
    {
      return NotFound();
    }

    return View(post);
  }

  // GET: Posts/Edit/5
  public async Task<IActionResult> Edit(int? id)
  {
    if (id == null)
    {
      return NotFound();
    }

    var post = await _repositoryWithQueries.GetSingleAsync(_context,
      new GetPostByIdQuery(id, false));

    // Code removed for brevity
  }
}
```

In the controller code, it is obvious that `GetSingleAsync` is used in multiple actions, but in the preceding highlighted usages one was including related data and the other was excluding it. We can also see the following code which provides the `Delete` action implementation along with include related data as it will be rendered in the `Delete` confirmation screen:

```
// GET: Posts/Delete/5
public async Task<IActionResult> Delete(int? id)
{
  if (id == null)
  {
    return NotFound();
  }

  var post = await _repositoryWithQueries.GetSingleAsync(_context,
      new GetPostByIdQuery(id, true));
  if (post == null)
  {
    return NotFound();
  }

  return View(post);
}
```

We have explored how query objects need to be incorporated inside the repository and implemented this for one single and list operation. Let's again take the remaining implementations as an assignment and complete the repository incorporation.

Solution to the repository with the queries assignment

The solution to the query objects' implementation to the remaining modules is available in the following Git repository path:

`https://goo.gl/iZb1Pg`

The solution to the query handler implementations to the remaining modules is available in the following Git repository path:

`https://goo.gl/XbXCM6`

The controller implementation with the remaining queries from the repository is listed as follows:

`https://goo.gl/yV474G`

In this section, we have incorporated query objects inside the repository. In the next section, we will see how we can compose queries with commands.

Composing queries with commands

We will streamline the implementation while implementing commands in our repository. The following code will allow us to create an interface which enforces `IncludeData` to be set for all queries:

```
public interface IQueryRoot
{
    bool IncludeData { get; set; }
}
```

We will use `IQueryRoot` as a base interface for the query handler, which returns generic return typed data. The following code extends the `IQueryRoot` and provide two interfaces to support synchronous and asynchronous operations:

```
public interface IQueryHandler<out TReturn> : IQueryRoot
{
  TReturn Handle();
}
public interface IQueryHandlerAsync<TReturn> : IQueryRoot
{
  Task<TReturn> HandleAsync();
}
```

Let's keep creating multiple generic interfaces required for different queries that inherit the query handler with a configured return type, and additionally define the fields required in each query type.

 We will be using **Variant Generic Interfaces**. Even though they are out of scope, let's discuss them briefly to understand the code. The **covariant** generic interface expects the type to implement methods that have a return type specified in the generic type parameters using the `out` keyword. The **contravariant** generic interface expects the type to accept method arguments as the type specified in the generic type parameters using the `in` keyword.

We will be using the contravariant generic interface in the following example, whereas the covariant generic interfaces were used widely in this chapter:

```
public interface IGetAllPostsQuery<in T> :
    IQueryHandler<IEnumerable<Post>>,
    IQueryHandlerAsync<IEnumerable<Post>>
{
}
public interface IGetPaginatedPostByKeywordQuery<in T> :
   IQueryHandler<IEnumerable<Post>>,
   IQueryHandlerAsync<IEnumerable<Post>>
{
  string Keyword { get; set; }
  int PageNumber { get; set; }
  int PageCount { get; set; }
}
public interface IGetPostByAuthorQuery<T> :
   IQueryHandler<IEnumerable<Post>>,
     IQueryHandlerAsync<IEnumerable<Post>>
{
  string Author { get; set; }
}
public interface IGetPostByCategoryQuery<T> :
   IQueryHandler<IEnumerable<Post>>,
   IQueryHandlerAsync<IEnumerable<Post>>
{
  string Category { get; set; }
}
public interface IGetPostByHighestVisitorsQuery<T> :
  IQueryHandler<IEnumerable<Post>>,
  IQueryHandlerAsync<IEnumerable<Post>>
{
}
public interface IGetPostByIdQuery<T> :
 IQueryHandler<Post>, IQueryHandlerAsync<Post>
{
  int? Id { get; set; }
}
public interface IGetPostByPublishedYearQuery<T> :
 IQueryHandler<IEnumerable<Post>>,
 IQueryHandlerAsync<IEnumerable<Post>>
{
 int Year { get; set; }
}
public interface IGetPostByTitleQuery<T> :
 IQueryHandler<IEnumerable<Post>>,
 IQueryHandlerAsync<IEnumerable<Post>>
```

```
{
  string Title { get; set; }
}
```

Let's create a command handler that would handle a command execution similar to the query handler interface that orchestrates the query execution. The following command handler code will create a generic interface which provides handle mechanism with generic return type:

```
public interface ICommandHandler<out TReturn>
{
  TReturn Handle();
}
public interface ICommandHandlerAsync<TReturn>
{
  Task<TReturn> HandleAsync();
}
```

Let's keep creating multiple generic interfaces required for different commands that inherit the command handlers. The following code will create interfaces required the Post CRUD operation using commands:

```
public interface ICreatePostCommand<TReturn> :
  ICommandHandler<TReturn>, ICommandHandlerAsync<TReturn>
{
}
public interface IDeletePostCommand<TReturn> :
  ICommandHandler<TReturn>, ICommandHandlerAsync<TReturn>
{
}
public interface IUpdatePostCommand<TReturn> :
  ICommandHandler<TReturn>, ICommandHandlerAsync<TReturn>
{
}
```

We need a QueryBase, which allows database context to be injected through the constructor, and this will be used by all queries that inherit QueryBase. The following code will create QueryBase which consumes BlogContext used by all queries accessing the data context:

```
public class QueryBase
{
  internal readonly BlogContext Context;
  public QueryBase(BlogContext context)
  {
    this.Context = context;
```

```
        }
    }
```

The GetAllPostsQuery inherits QueryBase and IGetAllPostsQuery, it enforces the developer to define IncludeData field and implement the Handle and HandleAsync methods that consume data context from the QueryBase type. The following code provides the concrete implementation of GetAllPostsQuery consuming QueryBase type:

```csharp
public class GetAllPostsQuery : QueryBase,
   IGetAllPostsQuery<GetAllPostsQuery>
{
    public GetAllPostsQuery(BlogContext context) : base(context)
    {
    }

    public bool IncludeData { get; set; }
    public IEnumerable<Post> Handle()
    {
      return IncludeData
        ? Context.Posts
        .Include(p => p.Author).Include(p =>
           p.Blog).Include(p => p.Category)
        .ToList()
        : Context.Posts
        .ToList();
    }
    public async Task<IEnumerable<Post>> HandleAsync()
    {
      return IncludeData
        ? await Context.Posts
        .Include(p => p.Author).Include(p =>
           p.Blog).Include(p => p.Category)
        .ToListAsync()
        : await Context.Posts
        .ToListAsync();
    }
}
```

We could take up an assignment to implement the remaining queries we had earlier using the new approach.

Similar to `QueryBase`, `CommandBase` is a base required for all commands that expose the data context for all consumers. The following code will create `CommandBase` which consumes `BlogContext` consumed by all command objects:

```
public class CommandBase
{
    internal readonly BlogContext Context;
    public CommandBase(BlogContext context)
    {
      Context = context;
    }
}
```

The `CreatePostCommand` inherits `CommandBase` and `ICreatePostCommand`, it enforces developers to define all the fields necessary to create a `Post` object and implement the `Handle` and `HandleAsync` methods that consume the data context from the `CommandBase` type. The following code creates concrete implementation of `CreatePostCommand` consuming `CommandBase` type:

```
public class CreatePostCommand : CommandBase,
    ICreatePostCommand<int>
{
 public CreatePostCommand(BlogContext context) : base(context)
 {
 }
 public string Title { get; set; }
 public string Content { get; set; }
 public string Summary { get; set; }
 public int BlogId { get; set; }
 public int AuthorId { get; set; }
 public int CategoryId { get; set; }
 public DateTime PublishedDateTime { get; set; }
 public int Handle()
 {
   Context.Add(new Post
   {
     Title = Title,
     Content = Content,
     Summary = Summary,
     BlogId = BlogId,
     AuthorId = AuthorId,
     CategoryId = CategoryId,
     PublishedDateTime = PublishedDateTime,
     CreatedAt = DateTime.Now,
     CreatedBy = AuthorId,
     Url = Title.Generate()
```

```
    });
    return Context.SaveChanges();
}
public async Task<int> HandleAsync()
{
  Context.Add(new Post
  {
    Title = Title,
    Content = Content,
    Summary = Summary,
    BlogId = BlogId,
    AuthorId = AuthorId,
    CategoryId = CategoryId,
    PublishedDateTime = PublishedDateTime,
    CreatedAt = DateTime.Now,
    CreatedBy = AuthorId,
    Url = Title.Generate()
  });
  return await Context.SaveChangesAsync();
}
}
```

We could take up an assignment to implement the Update and Delete commands and proceed with configuring the queries and commands in the new repository. The interface code required for the repository is listed below, which has provisions to query single or a list of data and also to execute any commands; every one of them is implemented in a generic fashion:

```
public interface IPostRepositoryWithCommandsQueries
{
  IEnumerable<Post> Get<T>(T query) where T :
        IQueryHandler<IEnumerable<Post>>;
  Task<IEnumerable<Post>> GetAsync<T>(T query) where T :
        IQueryHandlerAsync<IEnumerable<Post>>;
  Post GetSingle<T>(T query) where T : IQueryHandler<Post>;
  Task<Post> GetSingleAsync<T>(T query)
        where T : IQueryHandlerAsync<Post>;
  int Execute<T>(T command) where T : ICommandHandler<int>;
  Task<int> ExecuteAsync<T>(T command) where T :
        ICommandHandlerAsync<int>;
}
```

The generic implementation of the new repository is listed as follows as well. At this point, the repository doesn't know which query or command it's executing as it's resolved at runtime, the following code would create concrete implementation of `PostRepositoryWithCommandQueries` consuming command handling statements as well:

```
public class PostRepositoryWithCommandsQueries :
  IPostRepositoryWithCommandsQueries
{
    private readonly BlogContext _context;
    public PostRepositoryWithCommandsQueries(BlogContext context)
    {
      _context = context;
    }
    public IEnumerable<Post> Get<T>(T query)
        where T : IQueryHandler<IEnumerable<Post>>
    {
        return query.Handle();
    }
    public async Task<IEnumerable<Post>> GetAsync<T>(T query)
        where T : IQueryHandlerAsync<IEnumerable<Post>>
    {
        return await query.HandleAsync();
    }
    public Post GetSingle<T>(T query)
        where T : IQueryHandler<Post>
    {
        return query.Handle();
    }
    public async Task<Post> GetSingleAsync<T>(T query)
        where T : IQueryHandlerAsync<Post>
    {
        return await query.HandleAsync();
    }
    public int Execute<T>(T command) where T : ICommandHandler<int>
    {
        return command.Handle();
    }
    public async Task<int> ExecuteAsync<T>(T command) where T :
      ICommandHandlerAsync<int>
    {
      return await command.HandleAsync();
    }
}
```

The controller update to accommodate the new repository is listed as follows:

```
public class PostsController : Controller
{
  private readonly BlogContext _context;
  private readonly IPostRepositoryWithCommandsQueries
    _postRepositoryWithCommandsQueries;
  public PostsController(BlogContext context,
    IPostRepositoryWithCommandsQueries repositoryWithCommandsQueries)
  {
    _context = context;
    _postRepositoryWithCommandsQueries = repositoryWithCommandsQueries;
  }
}
```

The `Index` method that executes `GetAllPostsQuery` is updated, as follows:

```
// GET: Posts
public async Task<IActionResult> Index()
{
  return View(await _postRepositoryWithCommandsQueries.GetAsync(
    new GetAllPostsQuery(_context)
    {
      IncludeData = true
    }));
}
```

The `Create` command replaces the data context manipulation, as follows:

```
public async Task<IActionResult> Create([Bind("Id,Title,
    Content,Summary,PublishedDateTime,Url,VisitorCount,CreatedAt,
    ModifiedAt,BlogId,AuthorId,CategoryId")] Post post)
{
  // code removed for brevity
  await _postRepositoryWithCommandsQueries.ExecuteAsync(
  new CreatePostCommand(_context)
  {
    Title = post.Title,
    Summary = post.Summary,
    Content = post.Content,
    PublishedDateTime = post.PublishedDateTime,
    AuthorId = post.AuthorId,
    BlogId = post.BlogId,
    CategoryId = post.CategoryId
  });
  // code removed for brevity
}
```

We have covered exhaustively how commands are created and consumed along with queries in repositories and controllers. Let's visit the solution required for the previous assignment in the next section to proceed with the missing implementations.

Solution to the command queries assignment

The solution to the command queries assignment starts with the implementation of query objects, and is available in the following Git repository path:

```
https://goo.gl/RFKed5
```

The solution to the implementation of the remaining commands is available in the following Git repository path:

```
https://goo.gl/6aW15n
```

The solution to the controller implementation for the commands and queries is available in the following Git repository path:

```
https://goo.gl/ysNyc7
```

We have seen the exhaustive coverage of composing commands with queries. In the next section, let's explore enhancing the queries using expression trees.

Enhancing queries with expression trees

An expression tree is a mechanism that allows developers to create expressions that are necessary for the filters in the queries. In .NET, we have Func<T, TResult> to wrap a Where predicate and use it in multiple occurrences. We could use the same mechanism to create expression trees and leverage them in query objects.

The generic IQueryExpression interface has a provision to create an expression through Func, the following code creates contract for AsExpression().

```
public interface IQueryExpression<T>
{
  Expression<Func<T, bool>> AsExpression();
}
```

The concrete expression class implements `IQueryExpression` with concrete methods and their interface counterpart and wraps the `Where` predicate inside the `AsExpression` method, which returns a `Func` object. The following code provides a wildcard search on all fields from the `Post` entity using the expression approach:

```
public class GetPaginatedPostByKeywordQueryExpression :
  IQueryExpression<Post>
{
  public string Keyword { get; set; }
  public Expression<Func<Post, bool>> AsExpression()
  {
    return (x => x.Title.ToLower().Contains(Keyword.ToLower())
      || x.Blog.Title.ToLower().Contains(Keyword.ToLower())
      || x.Blog.Subtitle.ToLower().Contains(Keyword.ToLower())
      || x.Category.Name.ToLower().Contains(Keyword.ToLower())
      || x.Content.ToLower().Contains(Keyword.ToLower())
      || x.Summary.ToLower().Contains(Keyword.ToLower())
      || x.Author.Username.ToLower().Contains(Keyword.ToLower())
      || x.Url.ToLower().Contains(Keyword.ToLower()));
  }
}
```

The expression tree is used in the query object, as shown. It is obvious that the expression object is constructed and used as a parameter to the `Where` condition in the LINQ query. The below `GetPaginatedPostByKeywordQuery` implementation consumes the expression required for wild card search:

```
public class GetPaginatedPostByKeywordQuery : QueryBase,
  IGetPaginatedPostByKeywordQuery<GetPaginatedPostByKeywordQuery>
{
  // Code removed for brevity
  public IEnumerable<Post> Handle()
  {
    var expression = new GetPaginatedPostByKeywordQueryExpression
    {
     Keyword = Keyword
    };
    return IncludeData
      ? Context.Posts.Include(p => p.Author).Include(p =>
          p.Blog).Include(p => p.Category)
      .AsQueryable()
      .Where(expression.AsExpression())
      .Skip(PageNumber - 1).Take(PageCount)
      .ToList()
      : Context.Posts
      .AsQueryable()
```

```
        .Where(expression.AsExpression())
        .Skip(PageNumber - 1).Take(PageCount)
        .ToList();
    }
    public async Task<IEnumerable<Post>> HandleAsync()
    {
        var expression = new GetPaginatedPostByKeywordQueryExpression
        {
            Keyword = Keyword
        };
        return IncludeData
        ? await Context.Posts.Include(p => p.Author).Include(p
            => p.Blog).Include(p => p.Category)
         .AsQueryable()
         .Where(expression.AsExpression())
         .Skip(PageNumber - 1).Take(PageCount)
         .ToListAsync()
         : await Context.Posts
         .AsQueryable()
         .Where(expression.AsExpression())
         .Skip(PageNumber - 1).Take(PageCount)
         .ToListAsync();
    }
}
```

Here, the controller code remains intact as it has nothing to do with expression tree implementation, as it's the responsibility of the query object and the controller usage is not affected due to this change.

Solution to the expression trees assignment

The solution to the expression concrete classes required for the remaining queries is available in the following Git repository path:

```
https://goo.gl/gE6ZBK
```

The author, category, published year, and title-related query expressions are shared in the preceding repository path, as shown in the following screenshot:

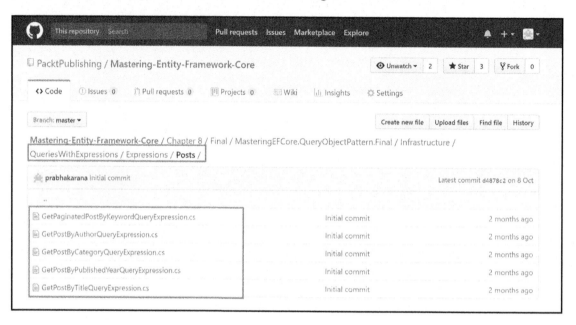

The solution to the remaining queries with expressions are available in the following Git repository path:

```
https://goo.gl/2tz9d9
```

The author, category, published year, and title-related query implementations using expressions are shared in the preceding repository path, which is shown in the following screenshot:

The expression trees were incorporated in commands and queries and we have seen the huge difference this brings up with respect to reusable code.

Summary

We have explored how to create query objects and applied patterns that would provide neat separation between queries and commands. We started with a simple query object, then created a repository that would wrap complete CRUD operations, followed by leveraging query objects in the repositories. Later, we created commands and objects, which were also incorporated into the repositories. Finally, we created expression trees to simplify and reuse the conditions and `Where` predicates in the query execution.

We have been working on an application that cannot be recovered from any failure. In `Chapter 9`, *Fail Safe Mechanism – Transactions*, we will revisit the application and handle code from any failures, using transactions.

9
Fail Safe Mechanism – Transactions

We have applied query object patterns to isolate query objects from the repository, which maintains query logic in one single place. We created a simple query object, then invented a repository to illustrate how query objects could be accommodated in the repositories. We then moved from queries to commands to perform real transactions using a similar pattern. Finally, we worked with expression trees to simplify and configure the conditions in a query execution.

Let's discuss how we could handle failure scenarios using transactions, how the transaction could be accessed between contexts, and also between different data access technologies:

- Is there any complex system that performs more than one data manipulation activity, then handles failures to maintain atomicity?
  - Transactions allow us to handle atomicity in failure scenarios.
- Do we need to handle transactions in simple applications?
  - Not required. The default behavior in EF would handle transactions only if all the changes were committed through `SaveChanges`.
- What if we need transactions to be maintained between multiple contexts in a complex system?
  - We do have provision to maintain transactions between multiple database contexts.

- What if we need transactions to be maintained between multiple technologies (EF and ADO.NET) in a complex system?
  - We do have provision to maintain transactions between EF and ADO.NET data manipulations.

The following topics will be covered to handle transactions in multiple scenarios:

- Default behavior of a transaction
- Creating a simple transaction
- Creating a cross-context transaction
- Leveraging transactions between multiple technologies

Default behavior of a transaction

EF supports transactions out of the box, all we need to do is perform `SaveChanges()` only once; it saves changes only if the transaction has been executed successfully, otherwise, the transactions will be rolled back automatically.

Let's investigate how we could practically leverage the default transactional behavior in our blogging system:

- We need two entities that need to be updated in a single web request
- Both the entities should be added/updated in the data context
- With a single `SaveChanges()`, both entities will be updated in the data store

In the blogging system, let's include support to add one or more tags in posts and learn about default transaction support in parallel with the `Tags` integration in posts.

Adding tags support in the blogging system

The fields required in the `Post` entity to incorporate `Tags` support in posts will be covered in this section. Let's start the activity by including the fields required to persist tag information in the `Post` model, as follows:

```
public class Post
{
    // Code removed for brevity
    [NotMapped]
    public ICollection<Tag> Tags { get; set; }
```

```
    [NotMapped]
    public ICollection<int> TagIds { get; set; }
    [NotMapped]
    public string TagNames { get; set; }
}
```

The tag information required in the Posts list view is listed as follows:

- Tags : This tag information is a filtered list of tags associated with the Post
- TagNames : This tag information is a filtered tag name in a comma-separated string

Let's incorporate the code required to expose the filtered Tag list flattened to a string named TagNames in the GetAllPostsQuery object. The flattened string value will be flattened using string.Join() as shown in the following code:

```
public class GetAllPostsQuery : QueryBase,
    IGetAllPostsQuery<GetAllPostsQuery>
{
  // Code removed for brevity
  public IEnumerable<Post> Handle()
  {
    // Code removed for brevity
    posts.ForEach(x =>
    {
      var tags = (from tag in Context.Tags
                  join tagPost in Context.TagPosts
                  on tag.Id equals tagPost.TagId
                  where tagPost.PostId == x.Id
                  select tag).ToList();
      x.TagNames = string.Join(", ",
        tags.Select(y => y.Name).ToArray());
        });
      return posts;
  }

  public async Task<IEnumerable<Post>> HandleAsync()
  {
    // Code removed for brevity
    posts.ForEach(x =>
    {
      var tags = (from tag in Context.Tags
                  join tagPost in Context.TagPosts
                  on tag.Id equals tagPost.TagId
                  where tagPost.PostId == x.Id
                  select tag).ToList();
```

```
        x.TagNames = string.Join(", ",
            tags.Select(y => y.Name).ToArray());
    });
    return posts;
    }
}
```

The tags will be listed in the `Posts` **Index** view, displayed as follows:

Title	Content	Summary	PublishedDateTime	Url	VisitorCount	CreatedAt	ModifiedAt	Author	Blog	Category	Tags	
Dotnet 4.7 Released	Dotnet 4.7 Released Contents	Dotnet 4.7 Released Contents Updated	14-08-2017 07:58:57 AM	dotnet-47-released	0	13-08-2017 08:26:57 AM	01-01-0001 12:00:00 AM	1	http://blogs.packtpub.com/dotnet	1	Dot Net	Edit	Details	Delete
.NET Core 1.1 Released	.NET Core 1.1 Released Contents		16-07-2017 07:58:57 AM		0	16-07-2017 07:58:57 AM	01-01-0001 12:00:00 AM	1	http://blogs.packtpub.com/dotnetcore	2	Dot Net Core	Edit	Details	Delete
EF Core 1.1 Released	EF Core 1.1 Released Contents		16-07-2017 07:58:57 AM		0	16-07-2017 07:58:57 AM	01-01-0001 12:00:00 AM	1	http://blogs.packtpub.com/dotnetcore	2	Dot Net Core	Edit	Details	Delete
Test	test	test	30-09-2017 11:00:00 PM	test	0	30-09-2017 09:30:33 PM	01-01-0001 12:00:00 AM	1	http://blogs.packtpub.com/dotnetcore	1	Dot Net, Dot Net Core	Edit	Details	Delete

We have seen the support provided for tags in the blogging system. In the next section, let's explore how the default transactional behavior works.

Leveraging default transaction behavior

We will be witnessing the default behavior of EF transactions in this section; let's continue in adding support to tags and see how transactions get involved on their own.

The changes required in the individual `Post` **Add/Edit** view are listed as follows:

- `Tags`: This tag information is a filtered list of tags associated with the `Post`
- `TagIds`: This tag information is a list of filtered tag IDs
- `TagNames`: This tag information is the filtered tag names in a comma-separated string

Let's incorporate the code required to expose the filtered tag list, tag ID list, and tag names flattened to a string in the `GetPostByIdQuery` object. These values will enable us to pre-select the tags while adding/editing `Post`:

```
public class GetPostByIdQuery : QueryBase,
   IGetPostByIdQuery<GetPostByIdQuery>
{
   // Code removed for brevity
   private Post IncludeTags(Post post)
   {
      int idValue = Id ?? 0;
      post.Tags = (from tag in Context.Tags
                   join tagPost in Context.TagPosts
                   on tag.Id equals tagPost.TagId
                   where tagPost.PostId == idValue
                   select tag).ToList();
      post.TagIds = post.Tags.Select(x => x.Id).ToList();
      post.TagNames = string.Join(", ",
         post.Tags.Select(x => x.Name).ToArray());
      return post;
   }
}
```

The tags that were selected while creating/editing the `Post` must be persisted in a different entity `Tag`. Let's see how this persistence occurs along with the `Post` persistence in the `CreatePostCommand` object. If we notice, there is no change to the `Post` persistence, but the `Tag` persistence consumes a concrete `Post` object in order to persist the tag. We need `PostId`, which will be available only after `SaveChanges()` is called, but we need this association before calling the `SaveChanges()`; let's get to that part shortly. After persisting both `Tag` and `Post`, we call `SaveChanges()` or `SaveChangesAsync()` only once; this ensures that the persistence occurs in a single transaction (default EF behavior).

Usually, we will perform SaveChanges() twice, one for Post and another for the Tag object. The first SaveChanges() will insert Post and allow us to fetch the auto-generated PostId that will be used in Tag row creation. We could leverage the default transaction by making only one SaveChanges() call and still fill the PostId data by passing the whole Post object to the Tag object, and EF ensures that it fills the PostId once the Post row is created.

EF ensures that even if any one of the transactions fails, the changes will be rolled back, as EF covers our back by default and we need to ensure that we make only one SaveChanges() to leverage this transaction behavior. The following implementation performs write operations in Post and Tag entities, yet having only one SaveChanges() ensures that transaction is maintained:

```
public class CreatePostCommand : CommandBase,
  ICreatePostCommand<int>
{
  // Code removed for brevity
  public ICollection<int> TagIds { get; set; }
  public int Handle()
  {
    Post post = new Post
    {
      // Code removed for brevity
    };
    Context.Add(post);
    foreach (int tagId in TagIds)
    {
      Context.Add(new TagPost
      {
        TagId = tagId,
        Post = post
      });
    }
    return Context.SaveChanges();
  }

  public async Task<int> HandleAsync()
  {
    Post post = new Post
    {
      // Code removed for brevity
    };
    Context.Add(post);
    foreach (int tagId in TagIds)
```

```
    {
      Context.Add(new TagPost
      {
        TagId = tagId,
        Post = post
      });
    }
    return await Context.SaveChangesAsync();
  }
}
```

The tags will be listed in the Posts **Add** view, displayed as follows:

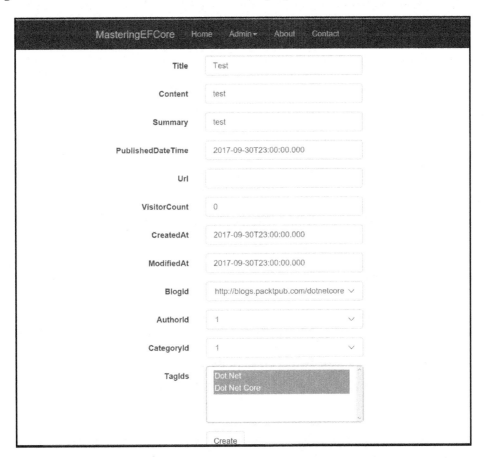

Similar changes are required for the UpdatePostCommand and DeletePostCommand objects; let's take it up as an assignment.

The solution to the assignment is available in the Git repository, at the following links:
`https://goo.gl/feBh9g`

`https://goo.gl/q5fXRi`

We haven't covered the updates required in the `Controller` and `View` for the previous functionality. Even though it seems out of scope, let's quickly cover the same. The view changes (including the `Tags` column) required for the `Posts` list view are displayed as follows:

```
// Code removed for brevity
<table class="table">
  <thead>
    <tr>
        // code removed for brevity
        <th>
            @Html.DisplayNameFor(model => model.Tags)
        </th>
        // Code removed for brevity
    </tr>
  </thead>
  <tbody>
    @foreach (var item in Model) {
    <tr>
        // Code removed for brevity
        <td>
            @Html.DisplayFor(modelItem => item.TagNames)
        </td>
        // Code removed for brevity
    </tr>
    }
  </tbody>
</table>
// Code removed for brevity
```

The `Tags` list required for the **Create** screen to populate tag drop-down is persisted in `ViewData` as a `MultiSelectList` object, which allows the user to map multiple tags to an individual post. The code which sets the `MultiSelectList` field with data is shown below:

```
public IActionResult Create()
{
  // Code removed for brevity
  ViewData["TagIds"] =
    new MultiSelectList(_context.Tags, "Id", "Name");
}
```

The tags were populated in the view as a `select` control assigning source from `ViewBag`. Also, we need to ensure the `multiple` attribute is enabled; otherwise, the control will not let the user select multiple tags, the `multiple` attribute is set as shown below:

```
<form asp-action="Create">
  <div class="form-horizontal">
  // Code removed for brevity
  <div class="form-group">
     <label asp-for="TagIds" class="col-md-2 control-label"></label>
     <div class="col-md-10">
        <select asp-for="TagIds" class="form-control"
        asp-items="ViewBag.TagIds" multiple="multiple"></select>
     </div>
  </div>
     // Code removed for brevity
  </div>
</form>
```

In the `Post` action, we still persist the `MultiSelectList`, but this time we pass on the selected `TagIds` along with the source data. This ensures that if there were any model errors while repopulating the view, the tags control will be pre-selected with the values from the model. The `TagIds` field should be included in the view model white-listing and finally the `MultiSelectList` is populated with the `TagIds` as shown in the following code:

```
public async Task<IActionResult>
Create([Bind("Id,Title,Content,Summary,PublishedDateTime,Url,
VisitorCount,CreatedAt,ModifiedAt,BlogId,AuthorId,
CategoryId,TagIds")] Post post)
{
    // Code removed for brevity
    ViewData["TagIds"] = new MultiSelectList(_context.Tags, "Id",
        "Name", post.TagIds);
    return View(post);
}
```

Similar changes are required for the `Update` and `Delete` operations of posts. Let's take it up as an assignment; the solution to the assignment is available in the Git repository. This concludes the default behavior of transactions in this section; let's explore creating a simple transaction in the next section.

Creating a simple transaction

We have seen the default behavior of a transaction if the multiple persistence occurs within a single `SaveChanges()`, what if we have a business requirement where multiple `SaveChanges()` are required and we still need to maintain the transaction scope? We have a provision to explicitly define a transaction and bring in the changes required inside this scope; EF exposes the `Database` type in `Context`, which has the `BeginTransaction()` functionality.

Let's try to achieve the aforementioned functionality in our `CreatePostCommand` type and still maintain the transaction scope. We could perform the same by retrieving the transaction object using the `BeginTransaction()` function; the retrieved object could be used either to commit or roll back the changes. The following code commits the changes after persisting the `Post` and `Tag` objects:

```
public class CreatePostCommand : CommandBase, ICreatePostCommand<int>
{
  // Code removed for brevity
  public int Handle()
  {
    int returnValue;
    using (var transaction = Context.Database.BeginTransaction())
    {
      // Code removed for brevity
      Context.Add(post);
      returnValue = Context.SaveChanges();
      foreach (int tagId in TagIds)
      {
        Context.Add(new TagPost
        {
          TagId = tagId,
          Post = post
        });
      }
      returnValue = Context.SaveChanges();

      transaction.Commit();
    }
    return returnValue;
  }
  public async Task<int> HandleAsync()
  {
    int returnValue;
    using (var transaction = Context.Database.BeginTransaction())
    {
```

```
    // Code removed for brevity
    Context.Add(post);
    returnValue = await Context.SaveChangesAsync();
    foreach (int tagId in TagIds)
    {
      Context.Add(new TagPost
      {
        TagId = tagId,
        Post = post
      });
    }
    returnValue = await Context.SaveChangesAsync();

    transaction.Commit();
  }
  return returnValue;
}
}
```

Similarly, the transaction was supported for the Update and Delete operations as well; the code for the same is listed as follows:

```
public class UpdatePostCommand : CommandBase, ICreatePostCommand<int>
{
  // Code removed for brevity
  public int Handle()
  {
    int returnValue;
    using (var transaction = Context.Database.BeginTransaction())
    {
      // Code removed for brevity
      returnValue = Context.SaveChanges();
      UpdateTags();
      returnValue = Context.SaveChanges();
      transaction.Commit();
    }
    return returnValue;
  }

  public async Task<int> HandleAsync()
  {
    int returnValue;
    using (var transaction = Context.Database.BeginTransaction())
    {
      // Code removed for brevity
      returnValue = await Context.SaveChangesAsync();
      UpdateTags();
```

```
      returnValue = await Context.SaveChangesAsync();
      transaction.Commit();
    }
    return returnValue;
  }
  // Code removed for brevity
}
```

The code required for the `Delete` operation is listed as follows:

```
public class DeletePostCommand : CommandBase, ICreatePostCommand<int>
{
  // Code removed for brevity
  public int Handle()
  {
    int returnValue;
    using (var transaction = Context.Database.BeginTransaction())
    {
      DeletePost();
      returnValue = Context.SaveChanges();
      DeleteTag();
      returnValue = Context.SaveChanges();
      transaction.Commit();
    }
    return returnValue;
  }

  public async Task<int> HandleAsync()
  {
    int returnValue;
    using (var transaction = Context.Database.BeginTransaction())
    {
      DeletePost();
      returnValue = await Context.SaveChangesAsync();
      DeleteTag();
      returnValue = await Context.SaveChangesAsync();
      transaction.Commit();
    }
    return returnValue;
  }
  // Code removed for brevity
}
```

We have seen how to create a simple transaction in this section. Let's dive deep in the coming sections. We will be exploring cross-context transactions in the next section.

Creating a cross-context transaction

We have seen transactions within a single context so far. Let's now explore how transactions could be maintained between different data contexts. We still have only one data context in the blogging system; let's introduce file upload functionality that will be maintained in a different database, thereby requiring us to create a different data context.

File upload support to the blogging system

The file upload functionality will be introduced in the `Posts` section, where we could upload an image against a post. To start with, let's create a `File` type, which is inherited from `IFormFile`. It will be used as a base type while uploading the file content to the controller action, the following code implementation would provide support for file upload functionality:

```csharp
public class File : IFormFile
{
  public Guid Id { get; set; }
  public string ContentType { get; set; }
  string ContentDisposition { get; set; }
  public byte[] Content { get; set; }
  [NotMapped]
  public IHeaderDictionary Headers { get; set; }
  public long Length { get; set; }
  public string Name { get; set; }
  public string FileName { get; set; }
  public void CopyTo(Stream target)
  {
    throw new NotImplementedException();
  }
  public Task CopyToAsync(Stream target, CancellationToken
    cancellationToken = default(CancellationToken))
  {
    throw new NotImplementedException();
  }
  public Stream OpenReadStream()
  {
    throw new NotImplementedException();
  }
```

```
        }
```

We need the command interface, `ICreateFileCommand`, to define handles required for `CreateFileCommand` execution. We will be consuming the existing `ICommandHandler` and `ICommandHandleAsync` as base types as shown below:

```
public interface ICreateFileCommand<TReturn> :
  ICommandHandler<TReturn>, ICommandHandlerAsync<TReturn>
{
}
```

We require a separate `CommandFileBase` with the blog file's data context since the `CommandBase` uses the blog context, the `BlogFilesContext` was consumed by the `CommandFileBase` as shown in the following code:

```
public class CommandFileBase
{
  internal readonly BlogFilesContext Context;
  public CommandFileBase(BlogFilesContext context)
  {
    Context = context;
  }
}
```

The `CreateFileCommand` type performs file persistence, which maintains the transaction and also consumes the transaction that was passed on to it through the constructor, the transaction shared through constructor and its usage is displayed in the following code:

```
public class CreateFileCommand : CommandFileBase,
  ICreateFileCommand<int>
{
  private readonly DbTransaction _dbTransaction;
  public CreateFileCommand(BlogFilesContext context) : base(context)
  {
  }
  public CreateFileCommand(BlogFilesContext context, DbTransaction
    dbTransaction)
  : this(context)
  {
    _dbTransaction = dbTransaction;
  }
  public Guid Id { get; set; }
  public string ContentType { get; set; }
  public string ContentDisposition { get; set; }
  public byte[] Content { get; set; }
  public long Length { get; set; }
  public string Name { get; set; }
```

```csharp
public string FileName { get; set; }
public int Handle()
{
  int returnValue = 0;
  using (var transaction = _dbTransaction != null
      ? Context.Database.UseTransaction(_dbTransaction)
      : Context.Database.BeginTransaction())
  {
    try
    {
      AddFile();
      returnValue = Context.SaveChanges();
      transaction.Commit();
    }
    catch (Exception exception)
    {
      transaction.Rollback();
      ExceptionDispatchInfo.Capture
        (exception.InnerException).Throw();
    }
  }
  return returnValue;
}
private void AddFile()
{
  File file = new File()
  {
    Id = Guid.NewGuid(),
    Name = Name,
    FileName = FileName,
    Content = Content,
    Length = Length,
    ContentType = ContentType
  };
  Context.Add(file);
}
public async Task<int> HandleAsync()
{
  int returnValue = 0;
  using (var transaction = _dbTransaction != null
    ? Context.Database.UseTransaction(_dbTransaction)
    : Context.Database.BeginTransaction())
  {
    try
    {
      AddFile();
      returnValue = await Context.SaveChangesAsync();
      transaction.Commit();
```

```
      }
    catch (Exception exception)
    {
      transaction.Rollback();
      ExceptionDispatchInfo.Capture(
        exception.InnerException).Throw();
    }
  }
  return returnValue;
}
}
```

Similar changes are required for the `Update` and `Delete` operations; let's take it up as an assignment.

 The solution to the assignment is available in the Git repository, and the core implementation of file persistence is available at `https://goo.gl/CUxFs9`.

The concrete implementation of file persistence is available at `https://goo.gl/1fEbCa`.

The `CreatePostCommand` receives the file along with the `Post` content. It creates a transaction and performs `Post` persistence, and passes on its transaction to the file command where the files get persisted and the transaction is reused as highlighted in the following code:

```
public class CreatePostCommand : CommandBase, ICreatePostCommand<int>
{
  // Code removed for brevity
  public CreatePostCommand(BlogContext context, BlogFilesContext
    blogFilesContext)
    : this(context)
  {
    _blogFilesContext = blogFilesContext;
  }
  // Code removed for brevity
  public ICollection<int> TagIds { get; set; }
  public File File { get; set; }
  public int Handle()
  {
    // Code removed for brevity
  }
  public async Task<int> HandleAsync()
  {
    int returnValue = 0;using (var transaction =
      Context.Database.BeginTransaction())
```

```
{
  try
  {
    CreateFileCommand createFileCommand =
    new CreateFileCommand(_blogFilesContext,
    transaction.GetDbTransaction())
    {
      Id = Guid.NewGuid(),
      Name = File.Name,
      FileName = File.FileName,
      Content = File.Content,
      Length = File.Length,
      ContentType = File.ContentType,
      ContentDisposition = File.ContentDisposition
    };
    returnValue = await createFileCommand.HandleAsync();
    Post post = new Post
    {
      // Code removed for brevity
      FileId = File.Id
    };
    // Code removed for brevity
    foreach (int tagId in TagIds)
    {
      Context.Add(new TagPost
      {
        TagId = tagId,
        Post = post
      });
    }
    returnValue = await Context.SaveChangesAsync();
    transaction.Commit();
  }
  catch (Exception exception)
  {
    transaction.Rollback();
    ExceptionDispatchInfo.
        Capture(exception.InnerException).Throw();
  }
}
return returnValue;
}
}
```

Similar changes are required for the `Update` and `Delete` operations; let's take it up as an assignment.

 The solution to the assignment is available in the Git repository at `https:/ /goo.gl/fDP1q4`.

The `Create` action supports the file upload functionality, where the file content is passed on to the `create` command to persist the file content to the file context. The following code provides file upload support in the controller `Create` action:

```
public async Task<IActionResult> Create([Bind("Id,Title,Content,
    Summary," + "PublishedDateTime,Url,VisitorCount,CreatedAt,
    ModifiedAt,BlogId," + "AuthorId,CategoryId,TagIds")] Post
    post, IFormFile headerImage)
{
  if (ModelState.IsValid)
  {
    Models.File file = null;
    if (headerImage != null ||
      headerImage.ContentType.ToLower().StartsWith("image/"))
    {
      MemoryStream ms = new MemoryStream();
      headerImage.OpenReadStream().CopyTo(ms);
      file = new Models.File()
      {
        Id = Guid.NewGuid(),
        Name = headerImage.Name,
        FileName = headerImage.FileName,
        Content = ms.ToArray(),
        Length = headerImage.Length,
        ContentType = headerImage.ContentType
      };
    }
    await _postRepository.ExecuteAsync(
      new CreatePostCommand(_context, _filesContext)
      {
        // Code removed for brevity
        TagIds = post.TagIds,
        File = file
      });
      return RedirectToAction("Index");
  }
  // Code removed for brevity
}
```

Similar changes are required for the `Update` and `Delete` operations; let's take it up as an assignment.

 The solution to the assignment is available in the Git repository at `https:/ /goo.gl/HWZXkC`.

We have seen the file upload functionality and shared the database transaction between context persistence; let's see whether it works as expected.

Limitations to the transaction scope

There is a limitation with EF Core with respect to multiple data contexts that work between two different connections. We will get the following error if we try to execute the current code, throwing the message, **"The specified transaction is not associated with the current connection. Only transactions associated with the current connection may be used"**:

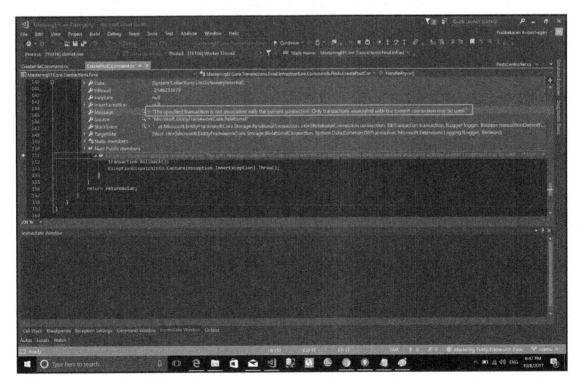

The explicit `TransactionScope` is required to support transactions between different data contexts (even between different connections); it is still not available in the current EF.

 The `TransactionScope` available in EF is yet to be supported by EF Core. It was initially planned to be shipped in EF Core 2.0 but was not released in the framework. Now the Microsoft EF team is currently targeting the first half of 2018 for the v2.1 framework, `System.Transactions` should be part of the release.

We have to closely watch the releases for the further updates:, the following screenshot confirms that the transactions will be supported in EF Core 2.1 release:

The schedule for EF Core is in-sync with the .NET Core and ASP.NET Core schedule which you can find here.

Next release: EF Core 2.1

Features we have committed to complete

- GroupBy translation
- System.Transactions support
- Cosmos DB provider
- Sample Oracle provider
- UWP testing
- Always Encrypted testing
- Initial column ordering in migrations and EnsureCreated
- Include for derived types
- Richer Application Insights integration

The limitation with the EF Core transaction scope should never stop us from the development. So, in the next section, let's create our own custom `TransactionScope`, which will perform the same functionality.

Custom transaction scope support

The transaction scope could be created by defining an interface, which requires us to either `Commit()` or `Rollback()`. The contract required for the custom transaction interface code is shown in the following code:

```
public interface ITransactionScope
{
  void Commit();
  void Rollback();
}
```

The database transactions were maintained/logged in a transaction list, which is then used to either `Commit()` or `Rollback()` for the entire set of transaction objects. In order to use `TransactionScope` within a `using` statement, we need to inherit and implement `IDisposable` as well. The custom `TransactionScope` implementation which maintains the `Commit()` and `Rollback()` is shown in the following code:

```
public class TransactionScope : ITransactionScope, IDisposable
{
  // Flag: Has Dispose already been called?
  private bool disposed = false;
  public TransactionScope()
  {
    Transactions = new List<IDbContextTransaction>();
  }
  ~TransactionScope()
  {
    Dispose(false);
  }
  public List<IDbContextTransaction> Transactions { get; set; }
  public void Commit()
  {
    Transactions.ForEach(item =>
    {
      item.Commit();
    });
  }
  public void Rollback()
  {
    Transactions.ForEach(item =>
    {
      item.Rollback();
    });
  }
  public void Dispose()
```

```
    {
      Dispose(true);
      GC.SuppressFinalize(this);
    }
    protected virtual void Dispose(bool disposing)
    {
      if (disposed)
          return;
      if (disposing)
      {
        // Free any other managed objects here.
        //
      }
      // Free any unmanaged objects here.
      //
      disposed = true;
    }
  }
}
```

We have seen the `Files` implementation/support for the blogging system, and we could start creating a repository that will allow us to perform persistence. For now, let's support `Execute()` and `ExecuteAsync()` in the repository, the contract required for the interface is defined in the following code:

```
public interface IFileRepository
{
    int Execute<T>(T command) where T : ICommandHandler<int>;
    Task<int> ExecuteAsync<T>(T command)
      where T : ICommandHandlerAsync<int>;
}
```

The concrete implementation of the `FileRepository` will consume the blog file context and invoke file commands created for the persistence operation, and the controller consumes the repository to achieve the functionality as shown in the following code:

```
public class FileRepository : IFileRepository
{
  private readonly BlogFilesContext _context;
  public FileRepository(BlogFilesContext context)
  {
      _context = context;
  }
  public int Execute<T>(T command) where T : ICommandHandler<int>
  {
      return command.Handle();
  }
  public async Task<int> ExecuteAsync<T>(T command)
```

```
            where T : ICommandHandlerAsync<int>
        {
            return await command.HandleAsync();
        }
    }
```

The repository injection could happen only if we provide support for the `FileRepository` in the `ConfigureServices()`, which injects the concrete object wherever required. The following configuration would inject the concrete object wherever the type is required:

```
public void ConfigureServices(IServiceCollection services)
{
    // Code removed for brevity
    services.AddScoped<IFileRepository, FileRepository>();
}
```

We can see the code implementation in the below `PostsController`, which consumes the `FileRepository` through the dependency injection using contructor:

```
public class PostsController : Controller
{
    // Code removed for brevity
    private readonly IFileRepository _fileRepository;
    public PostsController(BlogContext context, BlogFilesContext
filesContext,
        IPostRepository repository, IFileRepository fileRepository)
    {
        // Code removed for brevity
        _fileRepository = fileRepository;
    }
}
```

The injected repository will then be used in the post CRUD operations. The main focus for us is the custom `TransactionScope` usage to which multiple transactions were added. On successful execution of both the files and posts repositories, we commit the transaction scope, otherwise we roll back the changes. The code required for the custom transaction scope implementation is highlighted in the following code:

```
public async Task<IActionResult> Create([Bind("Id,Title,
 Content,Summary," + "PublishedDateTime,Url,VisitorCount,
 CreatedAt, ModifiedAt,BlogId," + "AuthorId,CategoryId,TagIds")]
 Post post, IFormFile headerImage)
{
    if (ModelState.IsValid)
    {
        // Code removed for brevity
        var transactions = new TransactionScope();
```

```
try
{
  transactions.Transactions.Add
    (_filesContext.Database.BeginTransaction());
  await _fileRepository.ExecuteAsync(
  new CreateFileCommand(_filesContext)
  {
    // Code removed for brevity
    Id = file.Id
  });
  transactions.Transactions.Add(
  _context.Database.BeginTransaction());
  await _postRepository.ExecuteAsync(
  new CreatePostCommand(_context)
  {
    // Code removed fore brevity
    FileId = file.Id
  });
  transactions.Commit();
}
catch (Exception exception)
{
  transactions.Rollback();
  ExceptionDispatchInfo.Capture(
    exception.InnerException).Throw();
}
return RedirectToAction("Index");
}
// Code removed for brevity
}
```

Similar changes are required for the Update and Delete operations; let's take it up as an assignment.

 The solution to the assignment is available in the following Git repository commit:
https://goo.gl/yLubPh

We have seen the transaction scope between different contexts and looked at, its limitations, and we created our own custom transaction scope as well. In the next section, we will add something we should have done long ago. Let's add a date picker to the solution, without which it's always difficult for us to perform repeated testing.

Adding date picker support to the blogging system

We can add the date picker to the system by importing `moment` and `datetimepicker`, which requires style sheets and JavaScript. The required libraries were included in the `_Layout.cshtml` as displayed below:

```
// Code removed for brevity
<head>
// Code removed for brevity
<environment names="Development">
    // Code removed for brevity
    <link rel="stylesheet" href="~/lib/eonasdan-bootstrap-
    datetimepicker/build/css/bootstrap-datetimepicker.css" />
</environment>
<environment names="Staging,Production">
    // Code removed for brevity
    <link rel="stylesheet" href="~/lib/eonasdan-bootstrap-
    datetimepicker/build/css/bootstrap-datetimepicker.min.css" />
</head>
<body>
  // Code removed for brevity
  <environment names="Development">
    // Code removed for brevity
    <script src="~/lib/moment/moment.js"></script>
    <script src="~/lib/eonasdan-bootstrap-datetimepicker/src/
    js/bootstrap-datetimepicker.js"></script>
  </environment>
  <environment names="Staging,Production">
    // Code removed for brevity
    <script src="~/lib/moment/min/moment.min.js"></script>
    <script src="~/lib/eonasdan-bootstrap-datetimepicker/build/
    js/bootstrap-datetimepicker.min.js"></script>
  </environment>
</body>
```

The `datepicker` class is added to the input control, which requires `datepicker` to be implemented, and the `datepicker` initialization is performed in the JavaScript code. With respect to this section, dealing with file uploading functionality, we have included the input file type, which allows us to upload the file content from UI to the controller action:

```
// Code removed for brevity
<form asp-action="Create" enctype="multipart/form-data">
<div class="form-horizontal">
  // Code removed for brevity
```

```
<div class="form-group">
  <label class="col-md-2 control-label">Header Image</label>
  <div class="col-md-10">
    <input type="file" id="headerImage" name="headerImage" />
  </div>
</div>
// Code removed for brevity
<div class="form-group">
  <label asp-for="PublishedDateTime" class="col-md-2
    control-label"></label>
  <div class="col-md-10">
      <input asp-for="PublishedDateTime"
       class="form-control datepicker" />
      <span asp-validation-for="PublishedDateTime"
         class="text-danger"></span>
  </div>
</div>
// Code removed for brevity
<div class="form-group">
    <label asp-for="TagIds" class="col-md-2 control-label"></label>
    <div class="col-md-10">
       <select asp-for="TagIds" class="form-control"
       asp-items="ViewBag.TagIds" multiple="multiple"></select>
    </div>
</div>
// Code removed for brevity
</div>
</form>
// Code removed for brevity
@section Scripts {
  // Code removed for brevity
  <script>
  // Code removed for brevity
  $('.datepicker').datetimepicker();
  </script>
}
```

We have seen the `datepicker` incorporation and the file upload input type included in the `Post` view. In the next section, we will see how transactions could be maintained between multiple technologies.

Leveraging transactions between multiple technologies

To illustrate the transactions between multiple technologies, let's implement a few of the missing features in the blogging system. In that way, we will have a mature, deployable blogging system towards the end of the book, and at the same time we will learn the concepts along the way. The features that we could consider for this section are:

- Recent `Posts` (anonymous)
- `Post` **View** (anonymous)
- Comments list to a blog post
- Adding comments to a blog post

Let's see how we will be using these features in the current section.

Recent posts support to the blogging system

The recent posts feature could be added to the system by performing the following steps:

1. Create an `IGetRecentPostQuery` query object interface.
2. Create a `GetRecentPostQuery` concrete query object.
3. Create a `RecentPostsViewComponent` **View** component.
4. Create a `Default.cshtml` view under **Shared** | **Components** | **RecentPosts.**
5. Perform a component invoke using the **View** component name and its parameter.

To reduce more code footprint where we just add features to the blogging system, let's maintain and share the code from Git repository commits. The previously listed implementation is performed and available in the following Git repository commit:

`https://goo.gl/kcWD3P`

We will be using **View** components to render the recent posts. It is a new concept that replaces the child actions in ASP.NET MVC Core, and it would be out of scope to explain them in detail, so kindly refer to the following official documentation for more information:

`https://docs.microsoft.com/en-us/aspnet/core/mvc/views/view-components`

The following screenshot will render the **Recent Posts** as a view component:

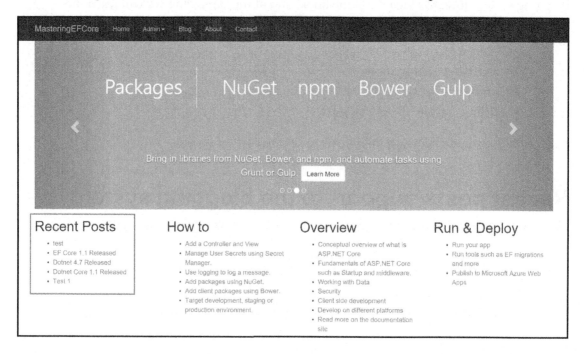

We have seen the changes required to include recent posts to the system. In the next section, let's focus on how anonymous posts were listed and an individual anonymous post was displayed.

Anonymous posts list and individual blog post

The anonymous posts list and individual blog post **View** feature could be added to the system by performing the following steps:

1. Change the current posts listing route to admin route.
2. Change the current display post route to admin route as well.

3. Create an `IGetPaginatedPostQuery` query object interface.

4. Create a `GetPaginatedPostQuery` concrete query object.

5. Create an action to list blogs anonymously, `GetPostsBlogHome()`.

6. Create an action to display blog anonymously, `Display()`.

7. Create a layout exclusively for a blog, since most of the sites have different layouts between landing pages and blogs.

8. Create a view, `GetPostsBlogHome.cshtml`, under the `Posts View` folder.

9. Create a view, `Display.cshtml`, under the `Posts View` folder as well.

10. Provide an appropriate hyperlink and its updates.

The preceding listed implementation is performed and available in the following Git repository commit:

`https://goo.gl/VPVJBg`

We have to show the posts to the anonymous users and let only authorized users see the administrator view of editing posts. In order to achieve this functionality, we have modified the route of the posts controller to wrap inside `Admin`, and the anonymous post listing was moved to the root (the tilde ~ symbol is used to redefine the API route) using attribute routing, as shown in the following screenshot:

```
26  +    [Route("Admin/Posts")]
26  27       public class PostsController : Controller
37  28       {
28  29           private readonly BlogContext _context;

@@ -62,6 +63,19 @@ public class PostsController : Controller
62  63              return View(posts);
63  64          }
64  65

66  +        [Route("~/blog")]
67  +        public async Task<IActionResult> GetPostsBlogHome(int pageNumber, int pageCount)
68  +        {
69  +            var results = await _postRepository.GetAsync(
70  +                new GetPaginatedPostQuery(_context)
71  +                {
72  +                    IncludeData = true,
73  +                    PageCount = pageCount,
74  +                    PageNumber = pageNumber
75  +                });
76  +            return View(results);
77  +        }
78  +
```

The anonymous post listing view would consume the preceding listed action, which would be rendered, as shown in the following screenshot, in the highlighted configured `~/blog` route:

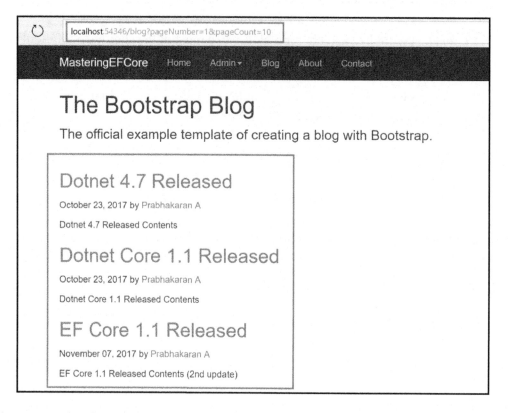

We have seen the changes required to include the anonymous posts list, and similar changes required for displaying an individual blog post are also available in the same repository commit page. In the next section, let's focus on how comments are listed.

Listing comments

The comments list feature could be added to the system by performing the following steps:

1. Create a repository interface, `ICommentRepository`.
2. Create a repository object, `CommentRepository`.

3. Create a query object interface, `IGetCommentsByPostQuery`.

4. Create a concrete query object, `GetCommentsByPostQuery`.

5. Configure the `CommentRepository` injection in the `Startup` file.

6. Create a **View** component, `CommentsListViewComponent`.

7. Create a **View**, `Default.cshtml`, under
   Shared | Components | CommentsList.

8. Include the current library in the `_ViewImports.cshtml` to support the custom tag helper.

9. Add components using the custom tag helper, `<vc:comments>`.

The preceding listed implementation is performed and available in the following Git repository commit:

`https://goo.gl/HqznNF`

The **View** component rendering of the comments list is displayed in the following screenshot:

The comments list that gets rendered using the **View** component in the anonymous blog is displayed in the following screenshot:

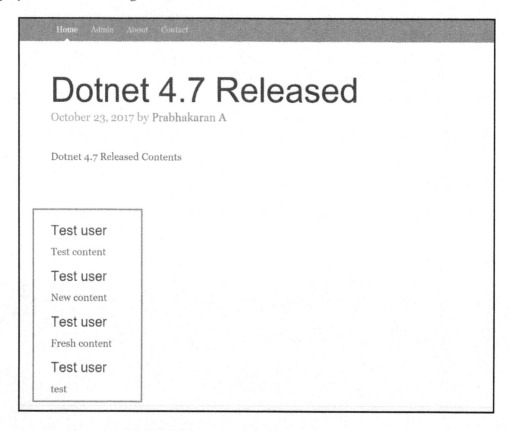

We have seen the changes required to include `Post` comments to the system. In the next section, let's focus on how comments are added.

Adding comments using external database transactions

The comments list feature could be added to the system by performing the following steps:

1. Inject the `IConfigurationRoot` from the `Startup` file.
2. Add `Execute` methods in the `ICommentRepository` interface.
3. Add `Execute` methods in the `CommentRepository` concrete type.

4. Create a query object interface, `ICreateCommentCommand`.

5. Create a concrete query object, `CreateCommentCommand`.

6. Inject `ICommentRepository` and `IConfigurationRoot` in the comments controller.

7. Create a **View** model, `CommentViewModel`.

8. Create an action to add comments anonymously, `CreatePostComment()`, to a blog post.

9. Create an action to display or add comments to the **View** component anonymously, `GetCommentsListViewComponent()`.

10. Create a **View** component, `AddCommentViewComponent`.

11. Create a `Default.cshtm` view under **Shared | Components | AddComment**.

12. Update the `Display.cshtml` view under the `Posts View` folder:
    - Add components using the `<vc:add-comment>` custom tag helper.

13. Add jQuery and other JavaScript-based libraries that were missed in the blog layout.

In step 5, while implementing `Handle()`, we will be implementing a transaction between multiple technologies, but it *should be executed in the same connection*.

The transaction was created between an ADO.NET implementation and an EF context implementation. It was made possible due to two things:

- Sharing connections between technologies
- Sharing transactions between technologies

The connection is passed to `SqlCommand` (for ADO.NET) and `DbContextOptionsBuilder` (for EF). The transaction is assigned to the `SqlCommand` `Transaction` field (for ADO.NET) and consumed using `Database.UseTransaction`(for EF). The connection shared between different technologies and maintaining the transaction scope is highlighted in the following implementation:

```
public class CreateCommentCommand: CommandBase,
  ICreateCommentCommand<int>
{
  // Code removed for brevity
  public int Handle()
  {
    int returnValue = 0;
    using (SqlConnection connection = new
    SqlConnection(_configuration.GetConnectionString("
    DefaultConnection")))
```

```
{
    connection.Open();
    using (var transaction = connection.BeginTransaction())
    {
      try
      {
      using (SqlCommand sqlCommand = new SqlCommand(
          "INSERT INTO Person(Nickname) " +
          "output INSERTED.ID VALUES(@Nickname)", connection))
          {
            sqlCommand.Parameters.AddWithValue("@FirstName",
              Nickname);
            sqlCommand.Transaction = transaction;
            int personId = (int)sqlCommand.ExecuteScalar();

            var options = new DbContextOptionsBuilder<BlogContext>()
              .UseSqlServer(connection)
              .Options;
            using (var context = new BlogContext(options))
            {
              Comment comment = new Comment
              {
                Content = Content,
                PostId = PostId,
                CreatedAt = DateTime.Now,
                ModifiedAt = DateTime.Now,
                CommentedAt = DateTime.Now,
                PersonId = personId,
                CreatedBy = personId,
                ModifiedBy = personId
              };

              context.Database.UseTransaction(transaction);
              context.Comments.Add(comment);
              returnValue = context.SaveChanges();
            }
            transaction.Commit();
            if (connection.State == System.Data.ConnectionState.Open)
              connection.Close();
              return returnValue;
          }
      }
      catch (Exception exception)
      {
       transaction.Rollback();
       ExceptionDispatchInfo.Capture(
         exception.InnerException).Throw();
      }
```

```
        }
      }
    return returnValue;
    }
  // Code removed for brevity
  }
```

The preceding listed implementation is performed and available in the following Git repository commit:

```
https://goo.gl/1CJDLv
```

The implementation required to add comments to the blog post is available in the preceding shared Git repository commit, and the **View** component rendering of the **Add Comment** view is displayed in the following screenshot:

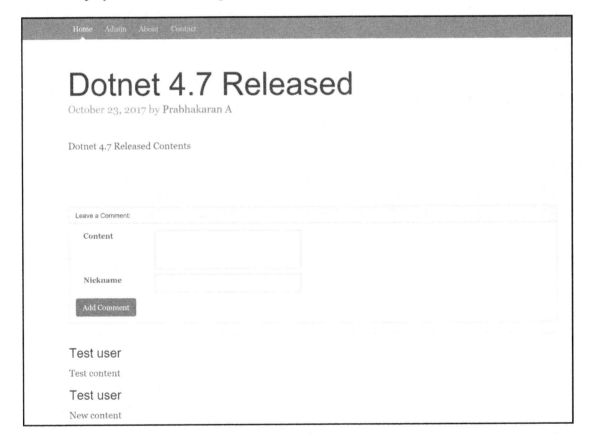

We have seen the transaction created and maintained between multiple technologies in this section, which wraps up the implementation of transactions between multiple technologies.

Summary

We have explored how to leverage the default transaction behavior in EF, which could be leveraged only if multiple operations are performed using a single `SaveChanges()`. Then we created a simple transaction, which allowed us to maintain transactions between multiple `SaveChanges()` commits. Later, we created cross-context transactions, identified their limitations, and overcame them with the custom `TransactionScope` that we built in this chapter. Finally, we created a transaction that was maintained between multiple technologies, provided it shares the connection and transaction objects. The different ways of handling transactions ensure that if anything goes wrong, they will be handled, ensuring we have built a fail-safe mechanism within single or between different data contexts, even between different technologies.

So far, we have been working with a single user and haven't factored in what will happen if we have concurrent users. In Chapter 10, *Make It Real – Handling Concurrencies*, we will revisit the application and handle concurrencies in all the transactions we have performed so far.

10
Make It Real – Handling Concurrencies

We have explored transactions, without which real-world transactions are not possible. We started with the default behavior and then went on to creating a transaction. Later, we learned about how a transaction could be shared between contexts, and finally we concluded by learning how external transactions were handled.

Let's identify the real-world problems available with respect to concurrencies, and we will see how we could handle them using the EF Core Framework:

- In a real-world application, the same data store might be accessed by different modules at the same time. How does EF Core handle those persistences?
  - EF Core has a few concurrency techniques that help us in creating a fail-safe mechanism.
- In which mechanism does EF Core expose concurrency techniques?
  - It exposes them using the usual techniques—data annotation and Fluent API.
- Do we need to add anything to the design to support concurrency?
  - It's a paradox; yes and no. If we are marking a column for concurrency checks then no schema change is required; otherwise, we need to introduce a timestamp/date row version column.

- Do we have any provision in not having such a column in a data model but still support concurrency tokens?
  - Yeah, it's quite possible. In the *No foreign key property* section of `Chapter 3`, *Relationships - Terminology and Conventions*, we discussed shadow properties. The same concept could be applied here where EF Core does internal concurrency checks without exposing them in the data model in a context.
- Nothing is fail-safe. Even if we build the mechanism to handle concurrencies, what control do we have if we face this conflict? What would be the action item and how do we ensure that the application is really fail-safe?
  - We could capture concurrency issues, and deal with current, original, and database values to resolve them.

The sections we will be including in this chapter are:

- Handling concurrency in EF
- Introducing concurrency tokens
- Concurrency tokens through shadow properties
- Concurrency tokens based on timestamp/row version
- Handling concurrency conflicts

Handling concurrency in EF

Imagine we were the developers assigned to develop/handle concurrency in the blogging system, what would be the starting point for us? The analysis would provide us with an answer for what is required to handle concurrency. Most importantly, it would help us understand the concurrency conflict and how it needs to be handled.

We will explore how concurrency conflict occurs and what needs to be done to handle it. Finally, we will see how it has been handled by the EF Core team.

Understanding the concurrency conflicts

We need to visualize where we would be facing this issue, in general, when the user tries to update data that is stale, which means the underlying data in the database has changed since the object was filled. Then we have a problem that needs to be addressed before we go live. If we don't handle concurrency, then the user who updates it last would retain his change, overwriting the data updated by other users.

In a real-world application, no single user accesses the application at a single point in time, multiple users use the application and it complicates the persistence of the data store.

Let's look at some scenarios that occur in such an application:

- Two users try to update the same entity at the same time
- If one of the users succeeds in the first persistence, then we end up overwriting the same entity by the second user

This is our point of interest, which could be coined as **concurrency conflict**. To replicate the issue, open the **Edit Post** page in two tabs. Assume the first user in the first tab is updating the post information, such as editing a blog post's **Title** and **Content**:

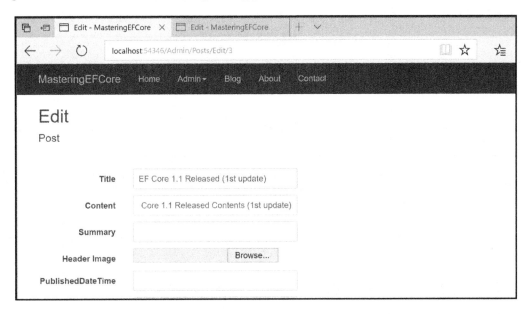

Another user in the second tab tries to modify the **Post Content**, who is unaware of the change performed in the **Post Title** and content by the other user (from the first tab):

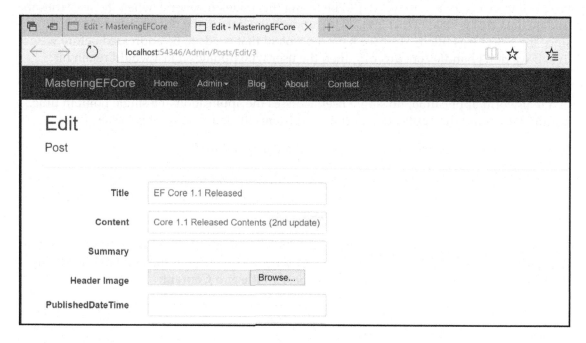

The change committed by the first user is no longer available in the model, which overwrites the data from the second user. Further execution with the highlighted data in the below screenshot would overwrite the data from second user:

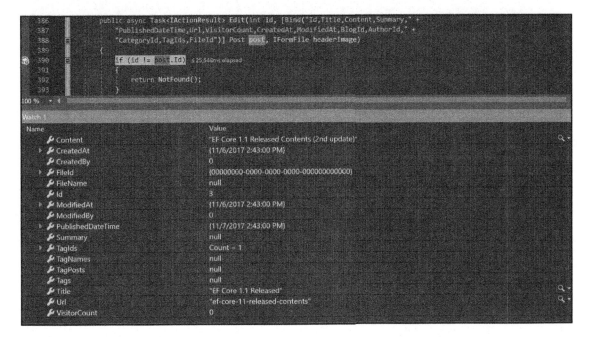

The **Post** list displays that the changes performed by the first user are overwritten by the second user:

The change committed by the first user should not be removed/overwritten with the new data without considering the data updated in the database. This is a concurrency issue that we will be discussing further in the next section.

Optimistic concurrency

Optimistic concurrency allows the concurrency conflict to occur and the application should respond appropriately, as mentioned in the following list:

- Tracking the changes on every property/column of an entity, which allows us to persist changes without affecting the stale data in the database, provided both the changes were performed in different properties

- Prevents the changes from being updated, by highlighting the current value from the data store and allowing the user to revisit his data for further persistence
- Overwrite the changes with the latest ones, and ignore the updated data in the data store

Optimistic concurrency could be adopted in an application that is more focused on performance and only during conflicts; the user would be spending additional time. This ensures that the time is spent wisely on most occasions, since we do not have any overhead for regular operations. The trade-off in the optimistic concurrency approach is that we are leaving the developers and the users to handle conflicts and store appropriate data stored in the database.

We have learnt about optimistic concurrency; let's look into pessimistic concurrency in the next section.

Pessimistic concurrency

As the name suggests, we perform locks at the data store that prevent users from updating stale data at the cost of performance. Yes, managing those locks by a data store consumes more resources, which in turn affects the performance. This could be achieved in the following way:

- While reading/updating the data from/into the data store, we will request a lock for other read-only or update access:
    - Locking a row for read-only access will allow other users to gain a lock for read-only but not for update
    - Locking a row for an update access will not let any other users either lock for read-only or update

Pessimistic concurrency could be adopted in the application where the users were too specific with the data and they do not compromise how the data was dealt with against the performance. The persisted data will always be valid, or in other words, we might never run into conflicts, but with a huge cost, performance. Every persistence will involve an overhead that ensures that we never run into conflicts with data persistence. In most scenarios, we will never compromise performance, and taking this approach would be very rare.

The ASP.NET Core Microsoft documentation (`https://docs.microsoft.com/en-us/aspnet/core/data/ef-mvc/concurrency`) highlights the disadvantages of pessimistic concurrency:

"Managing locks has disadvantages. It can be complex to program. It requires significant database management resources, and it can cause performance problems as the number of users of an application increases. For these reasons, not all database management systems support pessimistic concurrency. Entity Framework Core provides no built-in support for it, and this tutorial doesn't show you how to implement it."

Even though EF Core does not support pessimistic lock, we could leverage the same using flat SQL queries. We have learnt about pessimistic concurrency in this section; let's move on to start applying these concurrency tokens in the next section.

Introducing concurrency tokens

The concurrency token would be the benchmark value used by EF to identify whether the transaction has a conflict or not. We will be exploring different types of concurrency tokens available and, if modified, how they stop the other user from updating the same.

The concept should be pretty simple, and we will keep ourselves in the shoes of the Microsoft developers and see what algorithm should be adopted for the implementation.

The following algorithm is required at the higher level:

- The entity should identify at least one column (concurrency check column) to let's validate whether the row is updated or not
- The identified column will be used in any update operation performed by the framework to check whether the update is valid or not:
    - The column is concluded as valid if the previous value in the updating model and the original value fed to the data store match, otherwise it would be marked as invalid
- If the concurrency column has invalid data then an exception should be thrown:
    - A new concurrency exception should be created that will allow users to handle them
    - We should give a provision to the user to handle concurrency issues, and that's the reason we should throw an exception instead of a graceful exit

- If the concurrency column has valid data, then the update could be performed

The algorithm could be visualized using the following flow chart:

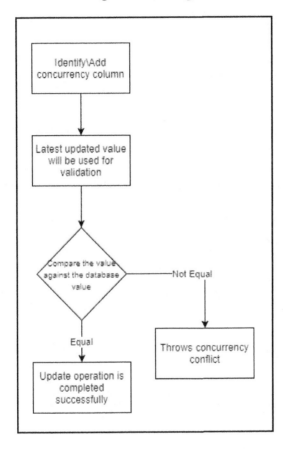

Let's visualize the preceding algorithm to resolve the concurrency conflict we faced while updating the post:

- The **Post** entity identifies and configures the `Timestamp` column as a concurrency check column
- The concurrency implementation expects the `Timestamp` column to be valid:
    - The **Post** model, which we send to the framework to update, will have:
        - Current `Timestamp` value as a byte array
        - Original `Timestamp` value fetched from the database before presenting to the update screen

- The Timestamp value's original value should match with the existing database value in the Timestamp value for the given row
- If the value doesn't match, concurrency exception should be thrown
- If the value matches, then the update is considered as valid and the framework allows the data store to be updated

We will explore the way in which the Microsoft team actually implemented the concurrency token mechanism:

- EF Core introduced a custom Timestamp attribute. Developers should mark one of the columns as the concurrency column
- The framework treats this column especially by marking the data loaded on the concurrency column in the context as the original value of the concurrency token
- When the user tries to update the record, it would check the original value against the value available in the database
- If the values don't match, then the framework throws a concurrency exception
- If both the values match, then the update is allowed by the framework

The concurrency token mechanism previously discussed matches with the flow diagram we used in this section. The concurrency is handled using the Timestamp property of the Post model, displayed as follows:

```
public class Post
{
  // Code removed for brevity
  [Timestamp]
  public string Timestamp { get; set; }
}
```

We have exhaustively learnt about what is a concurrency conflict, how it could be handled, and how Microsoft has supported concurrency in EF Core. In the next section, we will learn how to configure and use them in applications.

Non-timestamp based concurrency tokens

The knowledge we gained about concurrency tokens and how the implementation was performed in the EF Core Framework would be useful in introducing concurrency tokens in this section.

Introducing the usages of concurrency tokens would be a meager topic, so we will implement them in the blogging system and see them in action. After all, talking about algorithms and scenarios would not be sufficient. In order to understand and grasp the topic, we need to handle them in action, so let's do it.

The concurrency token could be configured in the following ways:

- Data annotations
- Fluent API

We will see how the configurations were performed using both the approaches in our blogging system in the next two sections.

Configuring non-timestamp tokens through data annotation

The data annotation configuration is straightforward; we have already seen the annotation in the *Introducing concurrency tokens* section of this chapter and it is not something new to us. Let's see how the ConcurrencyCheck attribute is configured:

```
public class Post
{
    // Code removed for brevity
    [ConcurrencyCheck]
    public string Url { get; set; }
    // Code removed for brevity
}
```

The preceding configuration will let EF Core consider the **Url** column as the concurrency check column, and any further update to this column will restrict users from performing parallel updates.

We have already seen the concurrency conflicts while trying to edit posts in different tabs, which is kind of a simulation of a real-time concurrency conflict. Since we have handled the concurrency, let's now see how it stops the user from persisting values into the data store.

The post highlighted in the following screenshot will have a **Url** value of **test-1**, and if the value is changed, then any other new persistence will be rejected by the framework:

MasteringEFCore	Home	Admin▾	Blog	About	Contact							

Index
Create New

Title	Content	Summary	PublishedDateTime	Url	VisitorCount	CreatedAt	ModifiedAt	Author	Blog	Catego
Dotnet 4.7 Released	Dotnet 4.7 Released Contents		10/23/2017 10:33:09 PM	dotnet-47-released	0	10/23/2017 10:33:09 PM	1/1/0001 12:00:00 AM	1	http://blogs.packtpub.com/dotnet	1
Dotnet Core 1.1 Released	Dotnet Core 1.1 Released Contents		10/23/2017 10:33:09 PM	dotnet-core-11-released-contents	0	10/23/2017 10:33:09 PM	1/1/0001 12:00:00 AM	1	http://blogs.packtpub.com/dotnetcore	2
EF Core 1.1 Released	EF Core 1.1 Released Contents (2nd update)		11/8/2017 1:14:00 AM	ef-core-11-released	0	11/7/2017 1:14:13 AM	11/7/2017 1:14:13 AM	1	http://blogs.packtpub.com/dotnetcore	2
Test 1	Test content 1		11/8/2017 10:12:00 AM	test-1	0	1/1/0001 12:00:00 AM	11/7/2017 10:12:19 AM	1	http://blogs.packtpub.com/dotnetcore	1

© 2017 - MasteringEFCore

Again, we were following the same simulation of having two tabs of the same blog **Edit** page; the first tab updates the post data with the same URL, which will allow the persistence. The following screenshot is the data populated and updated from the first user:

If the second tab retains the **Url** value, EF Core will persist the updated post data into the data store:

We can see from the following screenshot that the **Url** value is unchanged. This ensures that the record we were searching for of an update exists, thereby allowing EF to persist the entity:

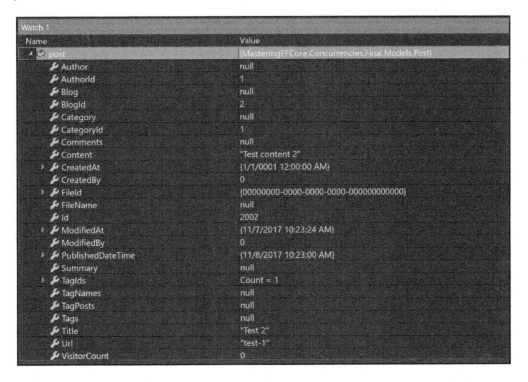

The second tab will try to change the **Url** value, which causes EF Core to stop the persistence of post data into the data store, which throws the error **Database operation expected to affect 1 row(s) but actually affected 0 row(s)**:

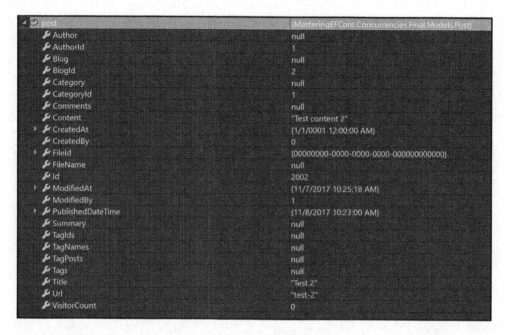

We can see that the error is thrown as explained, which says that the records don't exist anymore, which is supposed to update one row(s):

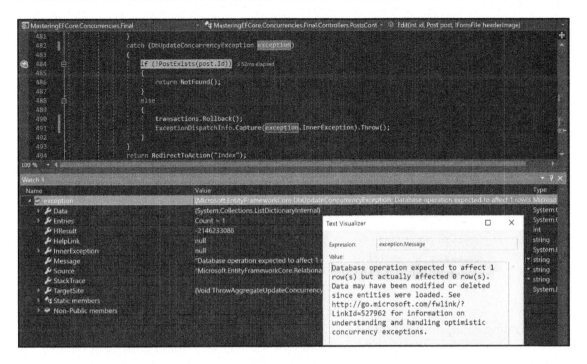

There is an internal operation carried out by EF to finalize whether the update is valid or not; that's the reason it says **1 row(s) is expected but 0 row(s) affected**.

EF will translate the update into an SQL query that will contain the `where` clause, including the identity column and the concurrency check column. If the value is changed, then obviously no record would be available for the update operation (which was supposed to exist), and that's the reason it simply responds back saying it **expected 1 row(s) to be updated but 0 row(s)** were affected.

We have seen how non-timestamp concurrency works, along with annotation configuration. In the next section, let's see how the same concurrency token could be configured through Fluent API.

Configuring non-timestamp tokens through Fluent API

The Fluent API configuration is made possible because Microsoft has exposed a series of extension methods, which allows us to execute appropriate functionality against the property of the model that supports it. In our blogging system, we will configure the `Url` of the `Post` entity as the concurrency token by enabling the property using `IsConcurrencyToken()` as shown in the following code:

```
protected override void OnModelCreating(ModelBuilder modelBuilder)
{
  // Code removed for brevity
  modelBuilder.Entity<Post>()
    .ToTable("Post")
    .Property(x=>x.Url)
    .IsConcurrencyToken();
  // Code removed for brevity
}
```

The preceding configuration will let EF Core consider the `Url` column as the concurrency token, and any further update to this column will restrict users from performing parallel updates, as it did in the data annotation configuration.

We have exhaustively seen how this concurrency token works, so let's move on to the next section that explores timestamp-based concurrency tokens.

Timestamp-based concurrency tokens

We have already explored `Timestamp`-based concurrency tokens in the *Introducing concurrency tokens* section. We can jump directly into the configuration, consider the same scenario and see how the conflicts were handled using the `Timestamp` concurrency token.

As we did with the non-timestamp based concurrency token, timestamp-based concurrency tokens could also be configured in the following ways:

- Data annotations
- Fluent API

We will see how the configurations were performed using both the approaches in our blogging system, and later we will see them in action.

Configuring timestamp tokens through data annotation

We have already seen how data annotation configuration works. For timestamp-based tokens, we need a property that will have a byte array, and it should be marked using the `Timestamp` data annotation. This is the only configuration required from our end; EF will take care of the rest:

```
public class Post
{
  // Code removed for brevity
  [Timestamp]
  public byte[] Timestamp { get; set; }
}
```

The preceding configuration will let EF Core consider the `Timestamp` column as the concurrency column, and any further update to this column will restrict users from performing parallel updates.

Since we are introducing a new column to the entity, related commands should be updated as well. In our scenario, we need to update the `UpdatePostCommand` type with new byte array `Timestamp` property and its usage as shown in the following code:

```
public class UpdatePostCommand : CommandBase, ICreatePostCommand<int>
{
  // Code removed for brevity
  public byte[] Timestamp { get; set; }
  // Code removed for brevity
  public async Task<int> HandleAsync()
  {
    var post = new Post
    {
      // Code removed for brevity
      Timestamp = Timestamp
    };
    // Code removed for brevity
  }
}
```

The new column should be included in the `Edit` method of `PostController`:

```
public async Task<IActionResult> Edit(
  int id, [Bind("Id,Title,Content,Summary," + "PublishedDateTime,
  Url,VisitorCount,CreatedAt,ModifiedAt,BlogId,AuthorId, "
  + "CategoryId,TagIds,FileId,Timestamp")] Post post,
   IFormFile headerImage)
{
  // Code removed for brevity
  if (ModelState.IsValid)
  {
    var transactions = new TransactionScope();
    try
    {
      Models.File file = null;
      if (headerImage == null || (headerImage != null
        && !headerImage.ContentType.ToLower().StartsWith("image/")))
      {
        await _postRepository.ExecuteAsync(
           new UpdatePostCommand(_context)
          {
            // Code removed for brevity
            Timestamp = post.Timestamp
          });
        return RedirectToAction("Index");
      }
      // Code removed for brevity
      transactions.Transactions.Add
        (_context.Database.BeginTransaction());
      await _postRepository.ExecuteAsync(
        new UpdatePostCommand(_context)
        {
          // Code removed for brevity
          Timestamp = post.Timestamp
        });
      transactions.Commit();
    }
    catch (DbUpdateConcurrencyException exception)
    {
      // Code removed for brevity
    }
     return RedirectToAction("Index");
  }
  // Code removed for brevity
}
```

Finally, the `Timestamp` column should be configured as a hidden column, just like we would perform for an identity column. This is required since the UI should retain the timestamp value on the `Post`:

```
// Code removed for brevity
<form asp-action="Edit">
  <div class="form-horizontal">
    <// Code removed for brevity
    <input type="hidden" asp-for="Timestamp" />
    // Code removed for brevity
  </div>
</form>
// Code removed for brevity
```

We are not there yet; we have updated the entity, but we are supposed to update the database. So, we need to update the schema as shown in the following screenshot, by adding migration and updating the database:

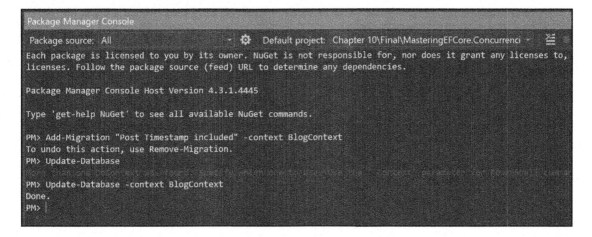

Let's get back to the same scenario, which will have two tabs and will try to perform the update at the same time. The following **Post** list page screenshot is highlighted with the existing values which will be modified by users for testing:

Title	Content	Summary	PublishedDateTime	Url	VisitorCount	CreatedAt	ModifiedAt	Author	Blog	Cate
Dotnet 4.7 Released	Dotnet 4.7 Released Contents		10/23/2017 10:33:09 PM	dotnet-47-released	0	10/23/2017 10:33:09 PM	1/1/0001 12:00:00 AM	1	http://blogs.packtpub.com/dotnet	1
Dotnet Core 1.1 Released	Dotnet Core 1.1 Released Contents		10/23/2017 10:33:09 PM	dotnet-core-11-released-contents	0	10/23/2017 10:33:09 PM	1/1/0001 12:00:00 AM	1	http://blogs.packtpub.com/dotnetcore	2
EF Core 1.1 Released	EF Core 1.1 Released Contents (2nd update)		11/8/2017 1:14:00 AM	ef-core-11-released	0	11/7/2017 1:14:13 AM	11/7/2017 1:14:13 AM	1	http://blogs.packtpub.com/dotnetcore	2
Test 1	Test content 1		11/8/2017 10:22:00 AM	test-1	0	1/1/0001 12:00:00 AM	11/7/2017 10:23:24 AM	1	http://blogs.packtpub.com/dotnetcore	1

In the first tab, we are retaining the value and performing an update that will update the values, since EF will allow one update to happen irrespective of the values updated in any of the columns (except Timestamp, which should not be updated by the user):

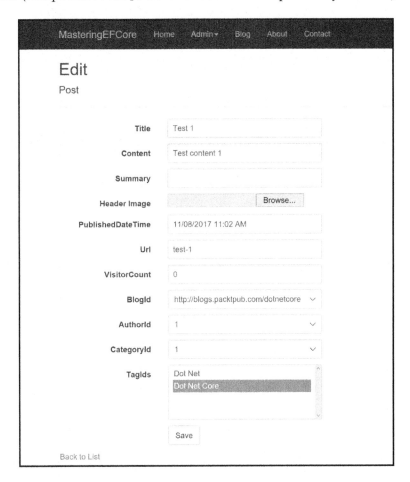

The **Post** entity data will be persisted without any issues since the Timestamp value doesn't change and it matches the value from the database.

The non-timestamp based concurrency token stops the update from happening if the concurrency check column value is changed, whereas the timestamp-based concurrency token will track the changes performed in the entity and will allow the change to be persisted if the timestamp value matches with the database value. Before persisting, it will increment the timestamp value.

The first tab operation works fine as expected; we can see the modified column was updated with the new value, confirming that the data was updated properly in the following screenshot:

MasteringEFCore	Home	Admin▾	Blog	About	Contact					

Index

Create New

Title	Content	Summary	PublishedDateTime	Url	VisitorCount	CreatedAt	ModifiedAt	Author	Blog	Cate
Dotnet 4.7 Released	Dotnet 4.7 Released Contents		10/23/2017 10:33:09 PM	dotnet-47-released	0	10/23/2017 10:33:09 PM	1/1/0001 12:00:00 AM	1	http://blogs.packtpub.com/dotnet	1
Dotnet Core 1.1 Released	Dotnet Core 1.1 Released Contents		10/23/2017 10:33:09 PM	dotnet-core-11-released-contents	0	10/23/2017 10:33:09 PM	1/1/0001 12:00:00 AM	1	http://blogs.packtpub.com/dotnetcore	2
EF Core 1.1 Released	EF Core 1.1 Released Contents (2nd update)		11/8/2017 1:14:00 AM	ef-core-11-released	0	11/7/2017 1:14:13 AM	11/7/2017 1:14:13 AM	1	http://blogs.packtpub.com/dotnetcore	2
Test 1	Test content 1		11/8/2017 10:59:00 AM	test-1	0	1/1/0001 12:00:00 AM	11/7/2017 10:59:36 AM	1	http://blogs.packtpub.com/dotnetcore	1

The second tab will try to update the `Post` entity, but it will fail irrespective of the column that was updated during this `Edit` operation. This behavior is expected since the `Timestamp` value was changed during the previous update, which makes the `Timestamp` value stale. The data in the following screenshot is updated by the second user which will be posted to the service:

We can see from the following error that the concurrency conflict has occurred and EF has thrown the error, which restricts the user from persisting the stale record. The data update is restricted due to stale data and the same is highlighted in the following image:

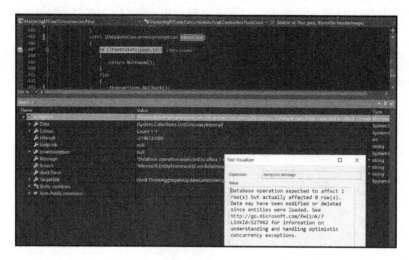

We have exhaustively seen how the timestamp-based concurrency token works and how it can be configured using data annotation. In the next section, let's see how we can configure the same token using Fluent API.

Configuring timestamp tokens through Fluent API

The Fluent API configuration is made possible because Microsoft has exposed such functionality against any property in the model. In our blogging system, we will configure the `Timestamp` of the `Post` entity as a concurrency token by enabling the property using `IsConcurrencyToken()` along with `ValueGeneratedOnAddOrUpdate()`. The following code would add a new property Timestamp as discussed in this section:

```
public class Post
{
    // Code removed for brevity
    public byte[] Timestamp { get; set; }
}
```

We have revisited the `Post` type and included the byte array timestamp property that will be used in the Fluent API configuration. The following configuration code would enforce the property value to be added or updated during persistence and marked as a concurrency token:

```
protected override void OnModelCreating(ModelBuilder modelBuilder)
{
  // Code removed for brevity
  modelBuilder.Entity<Post>()
    .ToTable("Post")
    .Property(x=>x.Timestamp)
    .ValueGeneratedOnAddOrUpdate()
    .IsConcurrencyToken();
  // Code removed for brevity
}
```

The preceding configuration will let EF Core consider the `Timestamp` column as the concurrency token, and any further update to this column will restrict users from performing parallel updates, as it did in the data annotation configuration.

We have exhaustively seen how this concurrency token works, so let's move on to the next section, which explores how concurrency conflicts were handled.

Handling concurrency conflicts

We have seen how to configure concurrency tokens and the errors it throws whenever there is a concurrency conflict. In this section, we will discuss different approaches available for handling concurrency conflicts.

The preceding configuration will let EF Core consider the `ModifiedAt` column as the concurrency check column, and any further update to this column will restrict users from performing parallel updates.

We have seen the approaches available for handling conflicts, let's discuss them in detail.

Applying optimistic concurrency

The optimistic concurrency will let the user try to update the entity. EF handles the overhead operations to ensure whether there is any concurrency conflict or not. This operation does not hurt performance, as pessimistic concurrency hurts, but it does handle concurrency in different ways.

The different approaches for handling optimistic concurrency are:

- Database wins
- Client wins
- User-specific custom resolution

We will be investigating further each of the approaches, one by one, in the next section.

Database wins

The **database wins** approach would allow the system/application to discard the client/UI changes and override the update operation using the latest data loaded from the database.

The following code shows how the concurrency conflicts are handled in the database wins approach. It reloads the entries from the database using `Reload()`, discards the client data in favor of the database, and performs the `SaveChanges()` operation to persist the updated changes from the database. The following code performs handles database first concurrency in the `Post` persistence:

```
public async Task<IActionResult> Edit(int id, [Bind("Id,Title,Content,
    Summary," + "PublishedDateTime,Url,VisitorCount,CreatedAt,
    ModifiedAt, BlogId,AuthorId," + "CategoryId,TagIds,FileId,
    Timestamp")] Post post, IFormFile headerImage)
{
  if (id != post.Id)
  {
    return NotFound();
  }
  if (ModelState.IsValid)
  {
    var transactions = new TransactionScope();
    try
    {
      // Code removed for brevity
    }
    catch (DbUpdateConcurrencyException dbUpdateConcurrencyException)
    {
      if (!PostExists(post.Id))
      {
        return NotFound();
      }
      else
      {
        try
```

```
                    {
                        dbUpdateConcurrencyException.Entries.Single().Reload();
                        await _context.SaveChangesAsync();
                        return RedirectToAction("Index");
                    }
                    catch (Exception exception)
                    {
                        ExceptionDispatchInfo.Capture
                          (exception.InnerException).Throw();
                    }
                }
            }
        }
        // Code removed for brevity
    }
```

We have seen how the database wins approach handles the concurrency conflict. In the next section, let's explore how the client wins approach handles the concurrency conflict.

Client wins

The **client wins** approach allows the system/application to override the database changes with the client/UI changes and update the data into the database.

The following code shows how the concurrency conflicts are handled in the client wins approach. It just updates the original values from the database, which will avoid concurrency conflict. It also allows the system/application to persist the changes from client/UI to be updated in the database without any issues:

```
public async Task<IActionResult> Edit(int id, [Bind("Id,Title,Content,
    Summary," + "PublishedDateTime,Url,VisitorCount,CreatedAt,ModifiedAt,
    BlogId,AuthorId," + "CategoryId,TagIds,FileId,Timestamp")] Post post,
        IFormFile headerImage)
{
    if (id != post.Id)
    {
        return NotFound();
    }
    if (ModelState.IsValid)
    {
        var transactions = new TransactionScope();
        try
        {
            // Code removed for brevity
        }
        catch (DbUpdateConcurrencyException dbUpdateConcurrencyException)
```

```
    {
      if (!PostExists(post.Id))
      {
        return NotFound();
      }
      else
      {
        try
        {
            var entry = dbUpdateConcurrencyException.Entries.Single();
            entry.OriginalValues.SetValues(entry.GetDatabaseValues());
            await _context.SaveChangesAsync();
            return RedirectToAction("Index");
        }
        catch (Exception exception)
        {
          ExceptionDispatchInfo.Capture
            (exception.InnerException).Throw();
        }
      }
    }
  }
  // Code removed for brevity
}
```

We have seen how the client wins approach handles the concurrency conflict. In the next section, let's explore how the user-specific custom resolution approach handles the concurrency conflict.

 It would be helpful to read Client Wins and Database Wins as Last In Wins and First In Wins respectively. This is a metaphor of the warehousing practices of **FIFO (First in First out)** and **LIFO (Last in First out)**.

User-specific custom resolution

The **user-specific custom resolution** highlights the latest changes from the database in the client/UI changes and updates the timestamp value so that on next SaveChanges(), the user could either consider the latest changes from the database and update them in client/UI, or just ignore them and proceed with saving the changes from the client/UI.

The following code shows how the concurrency conflicts are handled in the user-specific custom resolution approach. It just adds the model state error on to the conflicting fields with the current value, which gets displayed in the client/UI. The following code would handle concurrency and update the model state errors based on validation errors:

```
public async Task<IActionResult> Edit(int id, [Bind("Id,Title,
    Content,Summary," + "PublishedDateTime,Url,VisitorCount,
    CreatedAt,ModifiedAt, BlogId,AuthorId," +"CategoryId,TagIds,
    FileId,Timestamp")] Post post, IFormFile headerImage)
{
    if (id != post.Id)
    {
        return NotFound();
    }
    if (ModelState.IsValid)
    {
        var transactions = new TransactionScope();
        try
        {
            // Code removed for brevity
        }
        catch (DbUpdateConcurrencyException dbUpdateConcurrencyException)
        {
            if (!PostExists(post.Id))
            {
                return NotFound();
            }
            else
            {
                try
                {
                    foreach (var entry in dbUpdateConcurrencyException.Entries)
                    {
                        if (entry.Entity is Post)
                        {
                            var postEntry = entry.GetDatabaseValues();
                            var postFromDatabase = (Post)postEntry.ToObject();
                            var postToBeUpdated = (Post)entry.Entity;
                            if (postFromDatabase.Title != postToBeUpdated.Title)
                            {
                                ModelState.AddModelError("Title", $"Current value:
                                {postFromDatabase.Title}");
                            }
                            if (postFromDatabase.Content !=
                                postToBeUpdated.Content)
                            {
                                ModelState.AddModelError("Content", $"Current value:
```

```
                    {postFromDatabase.Content}");
                }
                ModelState.AddModelError(string.Empty, "The record was
                modified by another user" + " after the page
                was loaded.
                The save operation was canceled and the" + " updated
                database values were displayed. If you still want
                to edit" + " this record, click the Save button
                again.");
                post.Timestamp = (byte[])postFromDatabase.Timestamp;
                ModelState.Remove("Timestamp");
            }
            else
            {
                throw new NotSupportedException("Don't know how
                to handle concurrency conflicts for " +
                 entry.Metadata.Name);
            }
        }
    }
    catch (Exception exception)
    {
        ExceptionDispatchInfo.Capture
         (exception.InnerException).Throw();
    }
      }
     }
    }
   // Code removed for brevity
  }
```

The custom resolution will handle the conflict displayed as follows, which will highlight the issue in the validation summary, and also displays the current value against each conflicting field:

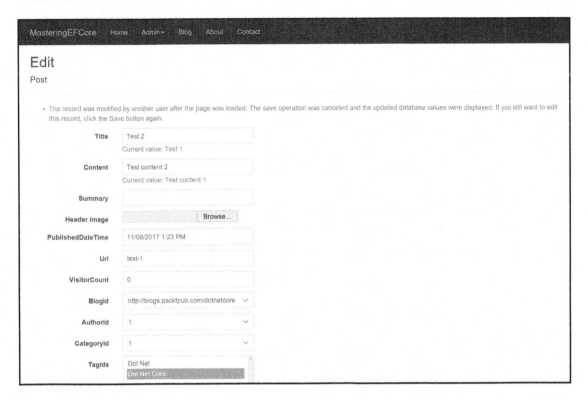

We have seen how the user-specific custom resolution approach handles the concurrency conflict. In the next section, let's explore how pessimistic concurrency handles the conflict.

Applying pessimistic concurrency

The pessimistic concurrency lets the user block everyone from accessing the entity until the read/write operation is complete. This might not give a good performance, but it ensures that nobody accesses the system with stale data. The following code would perform pessimistic lock which avoids conflict at the datastore itself:

```
public async Task<IActionResult> Edit(int id,
    [Bind("Id,Url,Title,Subtitle,Description,CategoryId")] Blog blog)
{
    // Code removed for brevity
    if (ModelState.IsValid)
    {
        try
        {
```

```csharp
using (var transaction = _context.Database.BeginTransaction())
{
  try
  {
    var blogToUpdate =
    await _context.Blogs.FromSql($"Select *
    from dbo.Blog with (xlock) where id={id}")
    .FirstOrDefaultAsync();

    if (blogToUpdate == null)
       return NotFound();

    blogToUpdate.Title = blog.Title;
    blogToUpdate.Subtitle = blog.Subtitle;
    blogToUpdate.Description = blog.Description;
    blogToUpdate.CategoryId = blog.CategoryId;
    blogToUpdate.Url = blog.Url;
    blogToUpdate.ModifiedAt = DateTime.Now;
    _context.Update(blogToUpdate);
    await _context.SaveChangesAsync();
    transaction.Commit();
  }
  catch (Exception)
  {
    transaction.Rollback();
  }
}
}
// Code removed for brevity
}
// Code removed for brevity
}
```

The `xlock` used in the preceding query will ensure that no other read/write operations can be performed against the entity. Let's test the functionality by refactoring the `Edit` method using transactions, which also uses `xlock` before performing the update:

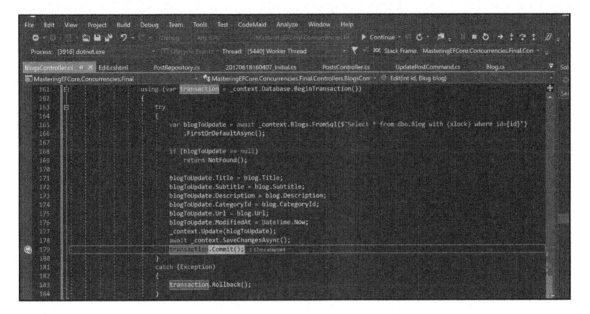

We can see that just before `transaction.commit()`, a breakpoint was set, which will still have an active `xlock` against the `Blog` entity. Meanwhile, if we try to fetch the records from the `Blog` entity, the operation will wait for the lock to be released, and that is why the following screenshot shows **Executing query...** until it gets access to the read operation:

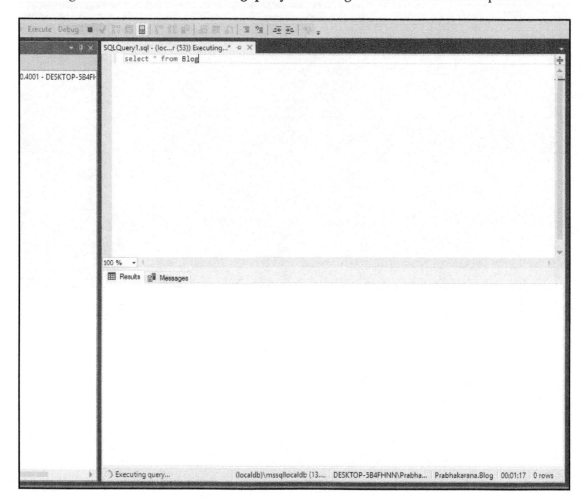

Once the transaction is committed, the select query executes as expected with the list of blogs as an outcome. This is the expected behavior in the pessimistic lock, and we have achieved the same using `xlock` in our code. In the following screenshot, the query which was loading during the persistence now executed completely as the lock is released after the persistence:

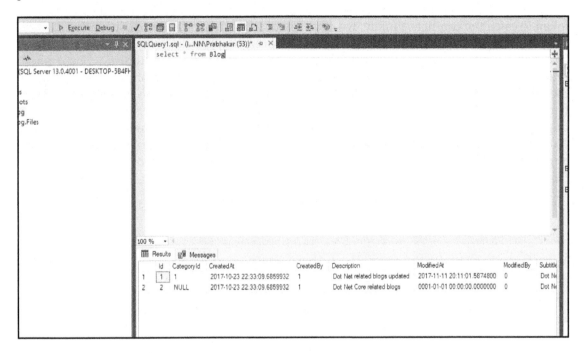

The pessimistic concurrency conflict was identified and resolved in this section, which concludes the concurrency handling in this chapter.

Summary

We started by exploring what is a concurrency conflict, and how Microsoft would have handled them in the Entity Framework implementation. We have seen how the concurrency token implementation would solve our issue, and then started with using concurrency tokens with the non-timestamp approach. Later, we used the timestamp-based concurrency token to catch the conflicts. Finally, we have found ways to handle those concurrency conflicts using both optimistic and pessimistic approaches. We can choose between the two based on our priority; if performance is vital to the project then pick optimistic concurrency, or if the business users are keen on data and are ready to have a trade-off with performance, then pick pessimistic concurrency. We have built the blogging system to illustrate certain features covered in the book, but it was not created to provide better performance. We might have used approaches that would yield better performance through muscle memory, but it's time to explore all possible options available in the framework to improve the application's performance. Let's explore them in Chapter 11, *Performance – It's All About Execution Time.*

11
Performance – It's All About Execution Time

We have created transactions to ensure every transaction will be committed only if all the transactions were successful. We have started with identifying conflicts, resolved them using the built-in/default transactions supported by **Entity Framework (EF)**, then worked with simple transactions. Then we covered handling transactions using timestamp and non-timestamp fields. Finally, we created transactions that could handle different data contexts and different technologies.

Let's discuss the performance issues we commonly face in EF, or any other data access layer implementation, and a way to address those performance concerns.

In this chapter, we will be covering the following:

- `AsNoTracking()` method
- Detecting changes
- Asynchronous operations
- Unnecessary volume returned
- `N + 1 Select` problem
- More data than required
- Mismatched datatypes
- Missing indexes

The AsNoTracking() method

EF's tracking behavior depends on the entry available in the change tracker; it is the default behavior. We could override this behavior to achieve performance improvements in certain scenarios where tracking is not required; for example, the read-only operations such as displaying a list of posts, displaying post information, and so on. This tracking is the key to EF in arriving at the changes required to be persisted during SaveChanges() execution.

How does tracking work?

As discussed in the previous section, any query that returns an entity (registered in data context) will be a part of tracking. Also as mentioned about how persistence occurs, the changes performed on those entities will be tracked and those changes will be persisted during SaveChanges() execution.

Let's look at the following code, which illustrates how tracking works in the framework:

```
public async Task<IActionResult> Edit(int id,
[Bind("Id,FirstName,
  LastName,NickName,Url,Biography,ImageUrl")] Person person)
  {
    // Code removed for brevity
    var personToUpdate = await
    _context.People.SingleOrDefaultAsync(
        item => item.Id.Equals(person.Id));
        // Code removed for brevity
        personToUpdate.Biography = person.Biography;
        personToUpdate.Comments = person.Comments;
        personToUpdate.FirstName = person.FirstName;
        personToUpdate.ImageUrl = person.ImageUrl;
        personToUpdate.LastName = person.LastName;
        personToUpdate.ModifiedAt = DateTime.Now;
        personToUpdate.NickName = person.NickName;
        personToUpdate.PhoneNumber = person.PhoneNumber;
        personToUpdate.Url = person.Url;
        personToUpdate.User = person.User;
        _context.Update(personToUpdate);
        await _context.SaveChangesAsync();
        // Code removed for brevity
    }
```

The `personToUpdate` retrieved from the data context will be part of tracking as it is returning the `Person` entity that is registered in the data context. The following code registers the `Person` entity to enable tracking in the framework:

```
public class BlogContext: DbContext
{
  // Code removed for brevity
  public DbSet<Person> People { get; set; }
  // Code removed for brevity
}
```

Since the entity is part of the data context, any changes performed in the returned item(s) will be tracked by EF Core irrespective of its usages, which could be read-only or might perform a write operation as well.

No-tracking queries

In the blogging system, the Person index screen will load a list of people available in the data store, which will not perform any write operation. In this use case, the code doesn't require any tracking as once the data is rendered in the View, the scope is complete. Having tracking over here is an overhead.

The following code would allow us to disable tracking in the executing query:

```
public async Task<IActionResult> Index()
{
    var people = await _context.People
    .AsNoTracking()
    .ToListAsync();
    // Code removed for brevity
}
```

The tracking could be disabled using `AsNoTracking()`, as used in the preceding query against the navigational property of data context in the LINQ query. This instructs EF Core that we do not require an overhead tracking operation as we are not intending to perform any changes with the result set.

TIP

The mock data should be generated to illustrate the performance impact in the application, the script we have used in this chapter to generate the mock data is available in the following Git commit:
https://goo.gl/Fg2YMF
Kindly use this script to mock thousands/millions of records in the tables, the file in the preceding commit contains script for the Person, User, and Post tables mocking. This has been included to help you evaluate performance in the DB.

The previous query, before optimization, took **170,294ms** to execute in a table with a million records, as illustrated in the following image:

```
// GET: People
public async Task<IActionResult> Index()
{
    var people = await _context.People
        .ToListAsync();
    var peopleViewModel = new List<PersonViewModel>();   ≤170,294ms elapsed
    people.ForEach(item =>
```

The LINQ query, after optimization, took only **59,017ms** to execute, which improved total execution time by 65%, as shown in following image:

```
// GET: People
public async Task<IActionResult> Index()
{
    var people = await _context.People
        .AsNoTracking()
        .ToListAsync();
    var peopleViewModel = new List<PersonViewModel>();   ≤59,017ms elapsed
```

This optimization is just a first step towards performance improvement; there is lot of scope to improve the application performance and we will visit each aspect of them in other sections of this chapter.

The million records we had inserted in the `Person` table would affect the preceding illustrated `Index()` action, which would return a list of people, it would throw a timeout error instead of rendering the list. We could avoid this issue by handling pagination implemented in Chapter 8, *Query Is All We Need – Query Object Pattern*, which is available in the `GetPaginatedPostByKeywordQuery.cs` of the following Git repository path:

`https://goo.gl/SwvVcC`.

The same approach of `Skip()` and `Take()` could be used here to avoid timeout issue, a quick fix would be limiting to 100 records as shown, which should be a paginated query in the future.

```
var people = await _context.People.Take(100)
.AsNoTracking()
.ToListAsync();
```

If the tracking is not required for the entire controller, we could disable it on a context level using `QueryTrackingBehavior` of the `ChangeTracker` type. Since the blogging system initializes the context on each request, we could disable tracking on the constructor using `QueryTrackingBehavior` as shown in the following code:

```
public PeopleController(BlogContext context)
{
  _context = context;
  _context.ChangeTracker.QueryTrackingBehavior =
    QueryTrackingBehavior.NoTracking;
}
```

We have seen how the tracking could be disabled at the query level or context level using two approaches. Kindly use them wisely to avoid running into updating/deletion issues, as those operations require tracking.

Projections

There is another built-in support from EF Core that provides tracking over projections (anonymous types or custom types that project the entity) as well. In the following example, we are projecting the `Person` model as `PersonViewModel`, which will contain both the type and an additional `NoOfComments` field. In this case, EF Core will track changes performed over the `Person` property of `PersonViewModel`, since it is part of the data context and the `NoOfComments` will not be tracked. The following code provides the above discussed projection:

```
public async Task<IActionResult> Index()
{
  return View(await _context.People
      .AsNoTracking()
      .Select(item =>
      new PersonViewModel
      {
        Person = item,
        NoOfComments = item.Comments.Count
      }).ToListAsync());
}
```

There is one more projection that will never perform any tracking. If the projection takes only the fields rather than the entity itself, then it will not track changes to the projected entity. Let's see them in action by introducing an **About** panel, which will be displayed across the public post that displays author information. A component is created to display author details, and its View implementation creates a projection that takes only `Name` and `Biography` from the `Person` entity. Since it's not projecting the entire entity, the `AboutViewModel` will not be tracked.

The following projection ensures that the data will never be tracked, as it does not contain any entities registered in the data context:

```
public class AboutViewComponent : ViewComponent
{
    private readonly BlogContext _context;
    private readonly IPersonRepository _repository;
    public AboutViewComponent(IPersonRepository repository,
        BlogContext context)
    {
        _repository = repository;
        _context = context;
    }

    public IViewComponentResult Invoke(int id)
```

```
    {
        var aboutViewModel = _context.People
          .Where(item => item.Id.Equals(id))
          .Select(item => new AboutViewModel
          {
              Name = item.FirstName,
              Biography = item.Biography
          }).SingleOrDefault();

        return View(aboutViewModel);
    }
}
```

We have seen how tracking works, ways to disable it, and also explored projections and their tracking behavior in EF Core. In the next section, let's investigate how detecting change behavior could be modified.

Detecting changes

We might run into performance issue while trying to perform bulk insertion that might be importing data from other sources or migrating content from another blogging system. In those scenarios, if we have AutoDetectChangesEnabled, then we might run into performance issues since EF Core's ObjectStateManager.DetectChanges() performs too costly operations on each insert operation.

For illustration, we could handle the bulk insert/update detect changes partly in our CreatePost code, which will perform a bulk tag insertion. We could handle this issue by disabling AutoDetectChangesEnabled just before adding the entities and enabling them back before calling SaveChanges(). The following little highlighted change would provide a huge performance improvement against the execution time:

```
public class CreatePostCommand : CommandBase,
  ICreatePostCommand<int>
  {
    // Code removed for brevity
    public int Handle()
    {
      // Code removed for brevity
      Context.ChangeTracker.AutoDetectChangesEnabled = false;
      foreach (int tagId in TagIds)
      {
        Context.Add(new TagPost
        {
          TagId = tagId,
```

```
        Post = post
      });
    }
    Context.ChangeTracker.AutoDetectChangesEnabled = true;
    // Code removed for brevity
  }
  // Code removed for brevity
}
```

We have seen how `DetectChanges()` affects the performance of bulk insert/update operations and the solution to the issue. In the next section, let's focus on asynchronous operations.

Asynchronous operations

We could call it a muscle memory, as we could notice that an asynchronous operation is already in place; we perform all operations in an asynchronous way. Even though it's been covered, let's reiterate how the asynchronous operations were handled in our blogging system and see the simplicity when we used `async/await` syntactic sugar implementations for asynchronous operations.

The asynchronous execution helps us in supporting multiple requests in parallel, without locking a thread against a long-running process. To understand how the threads should be managed properly, let's go through the following execution process:

- The request reaching the ASP.NET pipeline will be allocated to a thread, which takes care of the execution
- The thread will be occupied until the request is complete
- If the action consumes any long-running process in a synchronous way, then the thread will be blocked until the process execution is complete. If all the threads in the thread pool is occupied, then it cannot serve additional requests
- If the long-running process is implemented in an asynchronous way, then once the action is triggered, the thread will be released back to the thread pool, the released thread would be allocated to new request
- Once the long-running process is complete, a new thread will be allocated to complete the request execution

Since we already have an asynchronous implementation in place, we will start examining them right from the controller up to the data context execution. Let's take a look at the post controller `Index` action that is decorated with the `async` keyword, which also requires a return type to be wrapped inside the `Task<>` generic type. The asynchronous method should be invoked using the `await` keyword as shown in the following code:

```
public async Task<IActionResult> Index()
{
    var posts = await _postRepository.GetAsync(
    new GetAllPostsQuery(_context)
    {
      IncludeData = true
    });
    // Code removed for brevity
}
```

Let's dig in deep and investigate how this `GetAsync()` is implemented. It is a generic implementation that invokes `HandleAsync()` using the `async`/`await` keywords as shown here:

```
public async Task<IEnumerable<Post>> GetAsync<T>(T query)
    where T : IQueryHandlerAsync<IEnumerable<Post>>
    {
      return await query.HandleAsync();
    }
```

The `HandleAsync()` method is again implemented inside `GetAllPostsQuery` (in our scenario), which consumes the EF Core asynchronous `ToListAsync()` method, which wraps up our asynchronous implementation. This ensures that the database execution happens in an asynchronous way, and the operation continues after the data is returned from the data store. The following code performs asynchronous executions on `ToListAsync()` methods which will perform database operation:

```
public class GetAllPostsQuery : QueryBase,
  IGetAllPostsQuery<GetAllPostsQuery>
{
  // Code removed for brevity
  public async Task<IEnumerable<Post>> HandleAsync()
  {
    var posts = IncludeData
        ? await Context.Posts
        .Include(p => p.Author).Include(p => p.Blog)
        .Include(p => p.Category).Include(p=>p.TagPosts)
        .ToListAsync()
        : await Context.Posts
        .ToListAsync();
```

```
                    // Code removed for brevity
        }
    }
```

We have explored how asynchronous operations are implemented consuming EF Core `async` methods. In the next section, let's move on a little further and see how transactions are leveraged.

Transactions leveraging asynchronous operations

The transaction implementation still honors the asynchronous implementation; it doesn't bother even if the execution is performed using different threads, all it cares about is that the executions should happen within a given transaction. We can see that there is nothing in addition performed to support asynchronous operations for transactions; the `async` operation is simply performed within the transaction scope and it simply takes care of the rest.

Done. The asynchronous operations are still valid with the transactions we have created and used in the posts controller; the create action implements `ExecuteAsync()` using `async` and `await` keywords are highlighted as follows:

```
    public async Task<IActionResult> Create([Bind("Id,Title,
    Content,Summary," +
    "PublishedDateTime,Url,VisitorCount,CreatedAt,
    ModifiedAt,BlogId," + "AuthorId,CategoryId,TagIds")] Post post,
    IFormFile headerImage)
    {
      if (ModelState.IsValid)
      {
        // Code removed for brevity
        var transactions = new TransactionScope();
        try
        {
          if (file != null)
          {
            transactions.Transactions.Add(_filesContext.Database
            .BeginTransaction());
            await _fileRepository.ExecuteAsync(
            new CreateFileCommand(_filesContext)
            {
              Content = file.Content,
              ContentDisposition = file.ContentDisposition,
```

```
          ContentType = file.ContentType,
          FileName = file.FileName,
          Id = file.Id,
          Length = file.Length,
          Name = file.Name
       });
    }
    transactions.Transactions.Add(_context.
    Database.BeginTransaction());
    await _postRepository.ExecuteAsync(
    new CreatePostCommand(_context)
    {
      Title = post.Title,
      Summary = post.Summary,
      Content = post.Content,
      PublishedDateTime = post.PublishedDateTime,
      AuthorId = post.AuthorId,
      BlogId = post.BlogId,
      CategoryId = post.CategoryId,
      TagIds = post.TagIds,
      FileId = file.Id
    });
    transactions.Commit();
  }
  catch (Exception exception)
  {
    transactions.Rollback();
    ExceptionDispatchInfo.Capture
    (exception.InnerException).Throw();
  }
    return RedirectToAction("Index");
  }
  // Code removed for brevity
}
```

We have seen how `async` operations provide performance improvement for our application and its support in transactions. In the next section, let's focus on the volume of data returned.

Unnecessary volume returned

We have been using data luxuriously so far without keeping usage in mind. One fine example is the `delete` operation, which we can see in all the CRUD operations. If we take a look at the `Person delete` operation, we can see that the entire `Person` entity was returned from the context and it was used for the deletion. The following code retrieves the `Person` entity and uses the entity for delete operation:

```
public async Task<IActionResult> DeleteConfirmed(int id)
{
    var person =
    await _context.People.SingleOrDefaultAsync(m => m.Id == id);
    _context.People.Remove(person);
    await _context.SaveChangesAsync();
    return RedirectToAction("Index");
}
```

The pitfall for the preceding approach was, first a database call was made to retrieve the entire `Person` object, which is an overhead. After that, the required `delete` operation was performed using the `Id` of the person, which was available before the `Person` retrieval. The following screenshot is highlighted with the discussed two queries:

EventClass	TextData	Duration	Applicatio
Audit Logout		44027	Core .l
RPC:Completed	exec sp_reset_connection	0	Core .l
Audit Login	-- network protocol: Named Pipes s...		Core .l
RPC:Completed	exec sp_executesql N'SELECT TOP(2) ...	1	Core .l
Audit Logout		64444	Core .l
RPC:Completed	exec sp_reset_connection	0	Core .l
Audit Login	-- network protocol: Named Pipes s...		Core .l
RPC:Completed	exec sp_executesql N'SET NOCOUNT ON...	81	Core .l
Audit Logout		230	Core .l
RPC:Completed	exec sp_reset_connection	0	Core .l
Audit Login	-- network protocol: Named Pipes s...		Core .l
RPC:Completed	exec sp_executesql N'SELECT TOP(@__...	2	Core .l

```
exec sp_executesql N'SELECT TOP(2) [m].[Id], [m].[Biography], [m].[CreatedAt],
[m].[CreatedBy], [m].[FirstName], [m].[ImageUrl], [m].[LastName], [m].[ModifiedAt],
[m].[ModifiedBy], [m].[NickName], [m].[PhoneNumber], [m].[Url], [m].[UserId]
FROM [Person] AS [m]
WHERE [m].[Id] = @__id_0',N'@__id_0 int',@__id_0=1000002
```

We could simplify the approach by removing the `person` retrieval and creating a `Person` object using just the `Id` value, and updating the state of the entity as `Deleted` would instruct EF Core to perform a `delete` operation directly without retrieving the object from the data store. The following code reduces the query into one which performs delete operation alone:

```
[HttpPost, ActionName("Delete")]
[ValidateAntiForgeryToken]
public async Task<IActionResult> DeleteConfirmed(int id)
{
    Person person = new Person() { Id = id };
    _context.Entry(person).State = EntityState.Deleted;
    await _context.SaveChangesAsync();
    return RedirectToAction("Index");
}
```

We can see that the preceding approach does not make any `Person` retrievals yet. Still, the `delete` operation was performed successfully, as shown in the following screenshot:

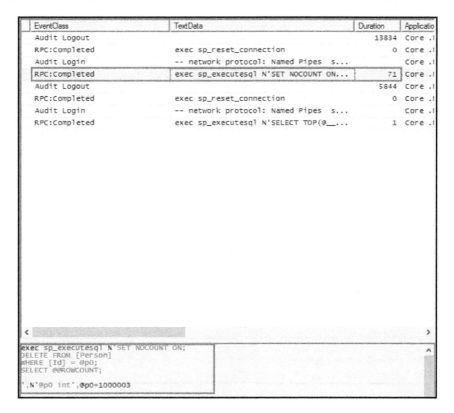

We have seen ways to avoid retrieving unnecessary data from the data store. In the next section, we will explore the `N + 1 Select` problem.

The N+1 Select problem

The `N + 1 Select` problem arises due to an internal data store call made by any ORM framework to perform a single operation. The problem could be outlined as follows:

1. A list of entities was returned that will be further iterated to perform some additional operation.
2. Assuming a navigational property is accessed inside the iteration:
   - Each time an iteration tries to access the navigational property, a database hit occurs
   - The hits will happen `N` times for `N` number of items returned in the first step
3. This makes the application perform `N+1 Select` (`N` for the iterations and `1` for the first call that retrieves the list), which should have been performed in a single database call.

This behavior is often termed as **lazy loading** in any ORM frameworks, which loads the subsequent/dependent data only when required. The lazy loading is yet to be supported by EF Core. This can be verified in the EF Core road map, which lists it as **Stretch goals**, as shown in the following screenshot:

Stretch goals

We will do our best to complete or at least make good progress on these:

- Lazy loading
- Read-only view types in the model
- Type conversions
- Data seeding
- Some lifecyle hooks (e.g. object materialized, connection opened)
- Reduce n+1 queries
- Consolidate navigation processing in query
- Update model from database

The issue (lazy loading support) created in the EF Core repository is also listed as follows:

`https://github.com/aspnet/EntityFrameworkCore/issues/3797`

Even though the framework currently does not support the feature, it would be ideal to analyze the issue and study the solutions for lazy loading. For discussion's sake, if EF Core supports lazy loading in the future, the following implementation will create the N + 1 Select issue, which will perform individual data store calls whenever the Comments navigational property is accessed.

The following highlighted code would trigger individual data store calls for populating the NoOfComments property:

```
var people = await _context.People
 .AsNoTracking()
 .ToListAsync();
var peopleViewModel = new List<PersonViewModel>();
people.ForEach(item =>
{
    peopleViewModel.Add(new PersonViewModel
    {
      Person = item,
      NoOfComments = item.Comments != null ?
        item.Comments.Count : 0
    });
});
```

In EF Core 2.0, the preceding code will return the navigational Comments property as NULL, assuming we were not accessing the property, since it is not eager-loaded. The following screenshot would highlight that the comment was not eager loaded:

```
37        //    }).ToListAsync();
38        var people = await _context.People
39            //.Include(item => item.Comments)
40            .AsNoTracking()
41            .ToListAsync();
42        var peopleViewModel = new List<PersonViewModel>();
43        people.ForEach(item =>
44        {
45            var comment = item.Comments;
46            peopleViewModel.Add(new PersonViewModel  ≤ 1ms elapsed
47            {
48                Person = item,
49                NoOfComments = item.Comments != null ? item.Comments.Count : 0
50            });
51        });
52        return View(peopleViewModel);
53    }
54
100 %  ▼
```

Watch 1		▼ ╨ ✕	Output
Name	Value	Type	Show output from: Debug
❤ comment	null	System.(	Application Insights Telemetry
			Application Insights Telemetry

It would strangely perform an additional database call to retrieve the count from the data store, even though the navigational property was returned as NULL:

When we include the Comments navigational property in the LINQ query, it would perform eager loading of the Comments entity to serve its request. The following code would let the EF Core to perform eager loading the comments:

```
var people = await _context.People
    .Include(item => item.Comments)
    .AsNoTracking()
    .ToListAsync();
var peopleViewModel = new List<PersonViewModel>();
people.ForEach(item =>
{
    var comment = item.Comments;
    peopleViewModel.Add(new PersonViewModel
    {
        Person = item,
        NoOfComments = item.Comments != null ?
        item.Comments.Count : 0
    });
});
```

We can see the execution made for the eager loading of the Comments entity in the following screenshot:

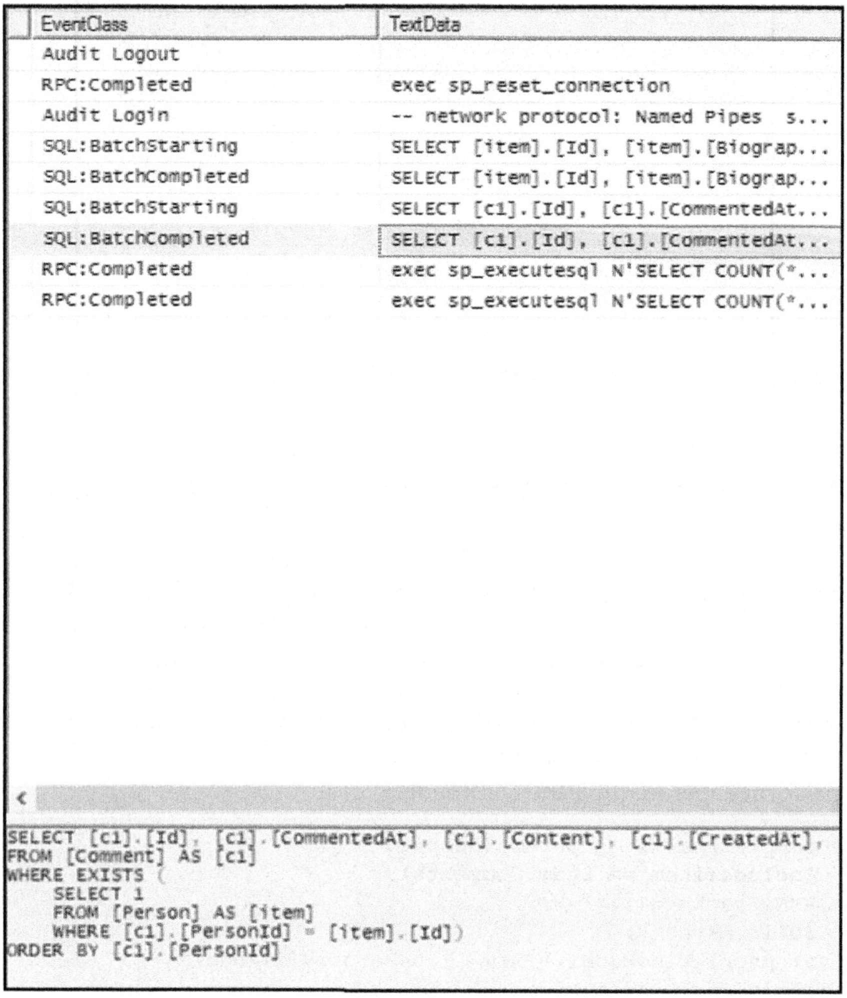

EventClass	TextData
Audit Logout	
RPC:Completed	exec sp_reset_connection
Audit Login	-- network protocol: Named Pipes s...
SQL:BatchStarting	SELECT [item].[Id], [item].[Biograp...
SQL:BatchCompleted	SELECT [item].[Id], [item].[Biograp...
SQL:BatchStarting	SELECT [c1].[Id], [c1].[CommentedAt...
SQL:BatchCompleted	SELECT [c1].[Id], [c1].[CommentedAt...
RPC:Completed	exec sp_executesql N'SELECT COUNT(*...
RPC:Completed	exec sp_executesql N'SELECT COUNT(*...

```
SELECT [c1].[Id], [c1].[CommentedAt], [c1].[Content], [c1].[CreatedAt],
FROM [Comment] AS [c1]
WHERE EXISTS (
    SELECT 1
    FROM [Person] AS [item]
    WHERE [c1].[PersonId] = [item].[Id])
ORDER BY [c1].[PersonId]
```

The eager loading will now return appropriate comments for the person who has commented on the blog posts. Now we can perform our operation of listing the number of comments the user has posted in the listing page as in the following highlighted image the comments were available:

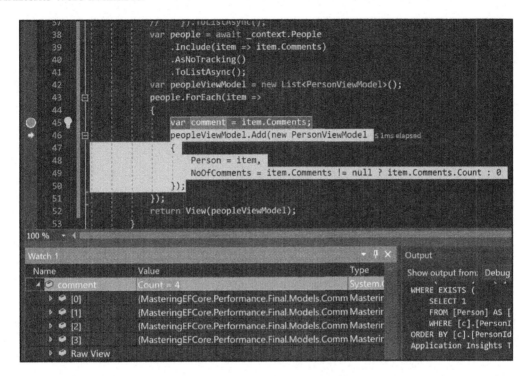

The number of comments is now listed as expected in the `People` list page, shown as in the following screenshot:

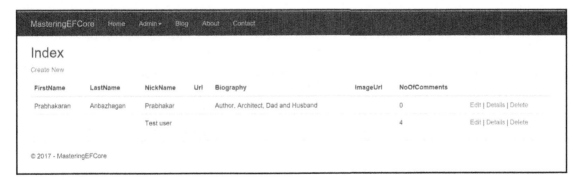

We have discussed the `N + 1 Select` problem, and then saw how the current EF Core Framework handles the scenario and the solution we could provide to resolve the issue. In the next section, we will explore how the data returned from the service or controller could be limited to only the fields that were consumed by the views.

More data than required

The **About** component we were creating consumes the `Person` entity, which contains a lot of information that is not necessary for the component, but still it is processed and returned to the `View`. We can see in the following code, the `AboutComponent` consumes the `GetPersonByIdQuery` and returns the entire `Person` entity to the `View`:

```
public IViewComponentResult Invoke(int id)
{
  var user = _repository.GetSingle(
  new GetPersonByIdQuery(_context)
  {
    IncludeData = true,
    Id = id
  });
  return View(user);
}
```

The preceding `View` component renders only the `Name` and `Biography` properties of the user entity. We can see them in the following view component code:

```
<h2>About @Model.Name</h2>
<p>
  @Model.Biography
</p>
```

The **View** component then consumes the data to render only the `FirstName` and `Biography` of the `Person` entity. It is obvious that we need to address this problem, as we are returning unnecessary data to the view.

We can visualize the rendered view from the following screenshot and see that it does not consume any other property from the user entity:

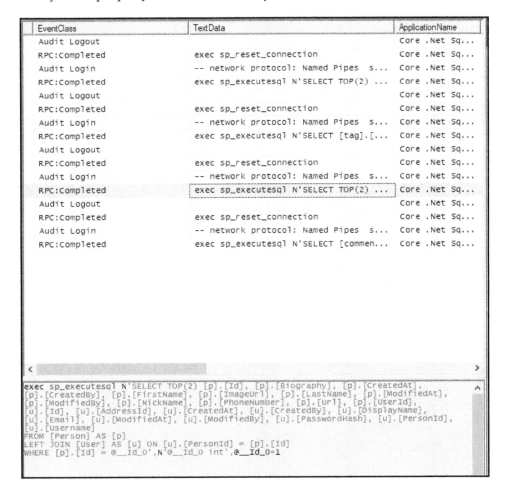

If we try to profile the data store call, we can see that there are a lot of columns included in the particular call, which consumes only two-column data:

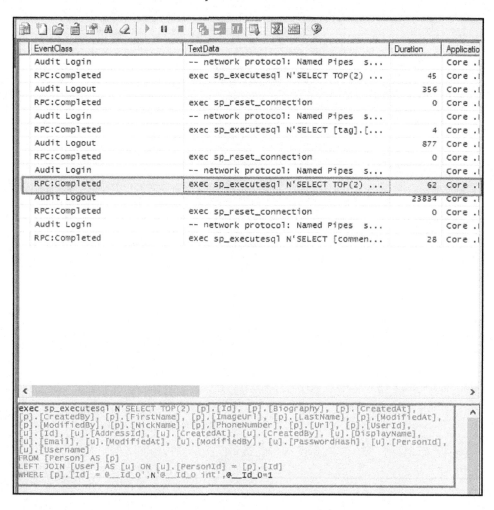

We can now narrow down the data returned using projection and a `View` model, which restricts the data only to `Name` and `Biography`:

```
public IViewComponentResult Invoke(int id)
{
  var aboutViewModel = _context.People
    .Where(item => item.Id.Equals(id))
    .Select(item => new AboutViewModel
      {
```

```
        Name = item.FirstName,
        Biography = item.Biography
    }).SingleOrDefault();

    return View(aboutViewModel);
}
```

Now, the profiler highlights the database call that contains only two columns required for the rendering of the database, thereby reducing the content that was retrieved from the database, as shown in the following screenshot:

EventClass	TextData	Duration
Audit Logout		71457
RPC:Completed	exec sp_reset_connection	0
Audit Login	-- network protocol: Named Pipes s...	
RPC:Completed	exec sp_executesql N'SELECT TOP(2) ...	22
Audit Logout		40
RPC:Completed	exec sp_reset_connection	0
Audit Login	-- network protocol: Named Pipes s...	
RPC:Completed	exec sp_executesql N'SELECT [tag].[...	5
Audit Logout		57
RPC:Completed	exec sp_reset_connection	0
Audit Login	-- network protocol: Named Pipes s...	
RPC:Completed	exec sp_executesql N'SELECT TOP(2) ...	1
Audit Logout		80
RPC:Completed	exec sp_reset_connection	0
Audit Login	-- network protocol: Named Pipes s...	
RPC:Completed	exec sp_executesql N'SELECT [commen...	6

```
exec sp_executesql N'SELECT TOP(2) [item].[FirstName], [item].[Biography]
FROM [Person] AS [item]
WHERE [item].[Id] = @__id_0',N'@__id_0 int',@__id_0=1
```

This addresses our problem of returning too much data from the data store. In the next section, let's look into mismatched data types.

Mismatched data types

The mismatched data type would hurt the performance. This might look obvious at first, but if we take a closer look, it is evident that we should be addressing the concern. The following tweaked `About` view component illustrates the retrieval of data using `PhoneNumber` rather than `Id`:

```
var aboutViewModel = _context.People
  .Where(item => item.PhoneNumber.Equals("9876543210"))
  //.Where(item => item.Id.Equals(id))
  .Select(item => new AboutViewModel
  {
    Name = item.FirstName,
    Biography = item.Biography
  }).SingleOrDefault();
```

The preceding LINQ query would be translated into the following SQL query: enable **Actual Execution plan** with the query execution, and it would be evident that something is wrong here. Whenever we have mismatched data types in a query, the data type conversion would enforce an index scan operation. In the following screenshot, we can see that the **Clustered Index Scan** is happening rather than performing a `seek` operation, which further affects the performance:

If we hover on the execution plan, we can see more information, such as the number of records, the cost of the operation, the number of execution, rows affected, and so on, which can be visualized in the following screenshot:

Clustered Index Scan (Clustered)	
Scanning a clustered index, entirely or only a range.	
Physical Operation	Clustered Index Scan
Logical Operation	Clustered Index Scan
Actual Execution Mode	Row
Estimated Execution Mode	Row
Storage	RowStore
Number of Rows Read	2
Actual Number of Rows	2
Actual Number of Batches	0
Estimated Operator Cost	0.0032842 (100%)
Estimated I/O Cost	0.003125
Estimated CPU Cost	0.0001592
Estimated Subtree Cost	0.0032842
Number of Executions	1
Estimated Number of Executions	1
Estimated Number of Rows to be Read	2
Estimated Number of Rows	2
Estimated Row Size	8131 B
Actual Rebinds	0
Actual Rewinds	0
Ordered	False
Node ID	2

Object
[Prabhakarana.Blog].[dbo].[Person].[PK_Person] [item]
Output List
[Prabhakarana.Blog].[dbo].[Person].Biography,
[Prabhakarana.Blog].[dbo].[Person].FirstName,
[Prabhakarana.Blog].[dbo].[Person].PhoneNumber

If we change the query to be based on Id, we can see that it magically uses seek instead of a scan operation. The following screenshot proves that the seeking operation is performed as expected:

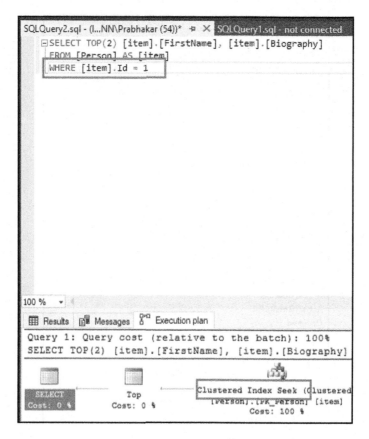

The following screenshot confirms our theory that the `seek` operation is faster than the `scan` operation, as the number of rows read was **1** in **seek** and **2** in the **scan** operation. The following screenshot performs seek operation confirms the discussion about row reads:

Clustered Index Seek (Clustered)	
Scanning a particular range of rows from a clustered index.	
Physical Operation	Clustered Index Seek
Logical Operation	Clustered Index Seek
Actual Execution Mode	Row
Estimated Execution Mode	Row
Storage	RowStore
Number of Rows Read	1
Actual Number of Rows	1
Actual Number of Batches	0
Estimated I/O Cost	0.003125
Estimated Operator Cost	0.0032831 (100%)
Estimated CPU Cost	0.0001581
Estimated Subtree Cost	0.0032831
Estimated Number of Executions	1
Number of Executions	1
Estimated Number of Rows	1
Estimated Number of Rows to be Read	1
Estimated Row Size	8061 B
Actual Rebinds	0
Actual Rewinds	0
Ordered	True
Node ID	1

Object
[Prabhakarana.Blog].[dbo].[Person].[PK_Person] [item]
Output List
[Prabhakarana.Blog].[dbo].[Person].Biography,
[Prabhakarana.Blog].[dbo].[Person].FirstName
Seek Predicates
Seek Keys[1]: Prefix: [Prabhakarana.Blog].[dbo].[Person].Id = Scalar
Operator((1))

So, fixing the data type of the model would avoid this data type conversion and would perform effective filtering of data. In the next section, let's analyze missing indexes.

Missing indexes

We will modify the **About** View component with FirstName and LastName filter, using which we should have an index in the data store. If we analyse the data store, we don't have such an index in the following screenshot; it would be wise to create one for better performance:

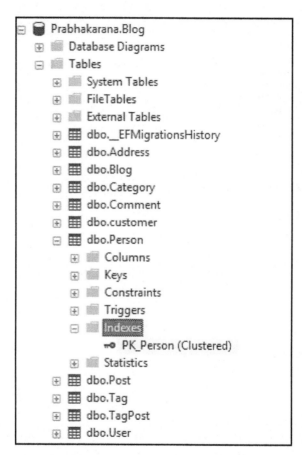

Let's start working on improvising SQL query performance, and the starting point would be tracing the query using a SQL profiler. So, copy the translated SQL query of translated **About** View component LINQ query from the right-click the SQL Server Profiler, paste it in the **SQL Query Analyzer** window, and select **Trace Query in SQL Server Profiler**, highlighted as shown in the following screenshot:

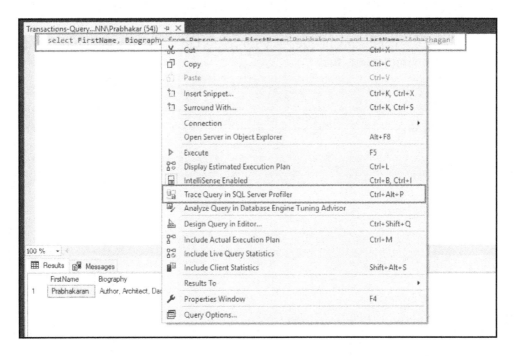

Once the profiler is attached, execute the query in the **Query Analyzer Window,** which should be displaying the following results, enable and see the actual execution plan as well:

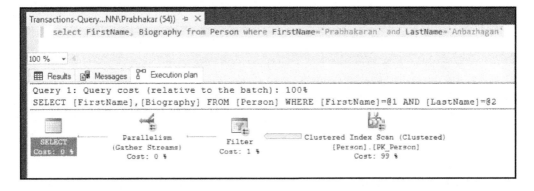

The SQL profiler will capture anything that occurs in the database. Since we are querying the Person entity, it is capturing all queries with respect to that entity operation, which is evident in the following screenshot:

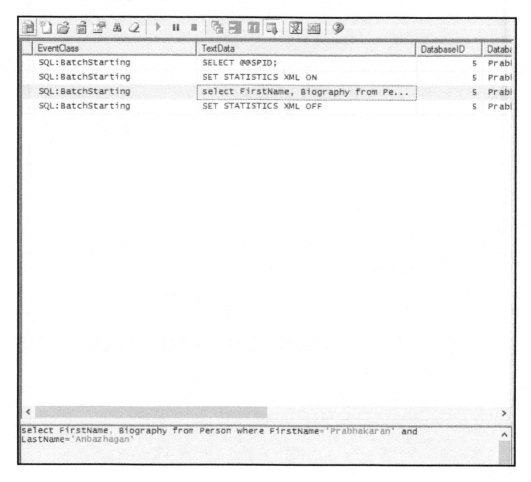

The query should be optimized using a tuning advisor and it requires the trace data to perform its analysis, so we need to save this profiler data for performance tuning analysis, as shown in the following screenshot:

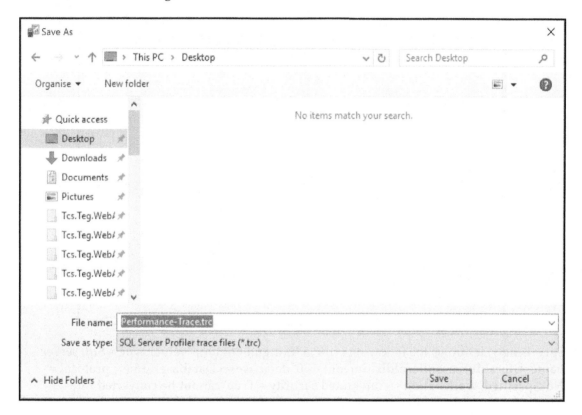

The data required for the performance tuning is now ready. The next step would be to consume it in a tuning advisor. Right-click the SQL query and select **Analyze Query in Database Engine Tuning Advisor** for further operations, as shown in the following screenshot:

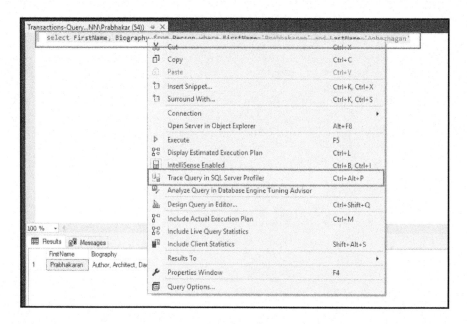

Surprisingly, it throws the following error: **The argument type 'server type = Sql, server name = (localdb)\mssqllocaldb, timeout = 30, database = <DatabaseName>, protocol = NotSpecified, workstation = , integrated security = True' cannot be converted into parameter type 'Microsoft.SqlServer.Management.Common.SqlConnectionInfo'. (mscorlib)**, which means that we are using a tuning advisor against the SQL Express Edition, and it is not supported:

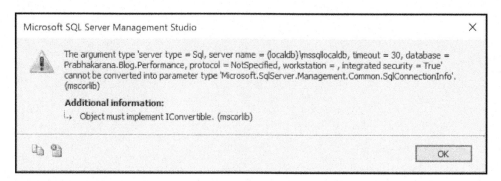

We need at least the Developer Edition to consume a tuning advisor; let's download the Developer Edition (`https://www.microsoft.com/en-in/sql-server/sql-server-downloads`), as shown in the following screenshot, configure it, and then proceed with the performance tuning:

Once the Developer Edition is installed and the database is configured, open the tuning advisor from the query window, and it should now open properly. Then, create a new session with the following details such as **Session name**, **Workload** as **File** type, and its location. Select the **Database for workload analysis**, and finally select the databases we need to tune, as shown in the following screenshot:

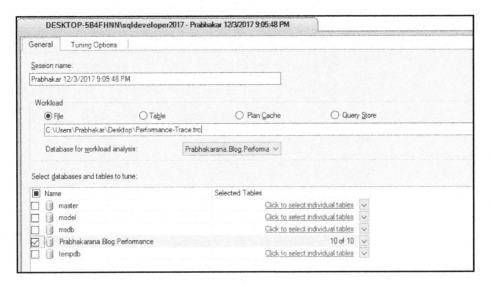

We are all set to initiate the analysis. Click the **Start Analysis** button, as shown in the following screenshot, to start the tuning analysis, which will perform tuning analysis within the selected parameters:

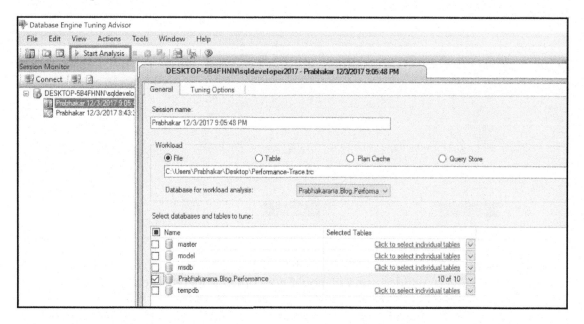

When the analysis is completed, we can see the success messages printed out in the **Progress** tab, as displayed in the following screenshot. Our point of interest would be in generating **Recommendations**:

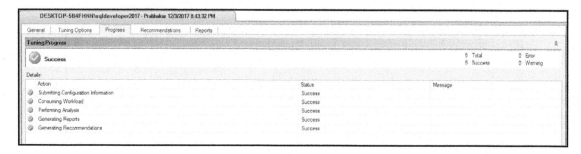

Open the **Recommendations** tab and it will list the recommendations, as shown in the following screenshot. It allows us to tune the performance of the database, which is a SQL query in our scenario:

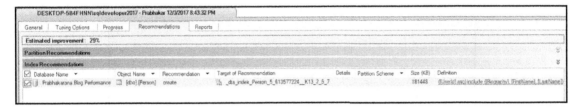

Click the definition entry inside the **Recommendations** tab, which opens the following **SQL Script Preview,** to fix the performance issue. In a regular application, we would be copying this query and executing it in the database. Since we are using the ORM framework, we need to perform the same task using the framework instead, and the crux of the message is that we need an index to fine-tune the SQL query:

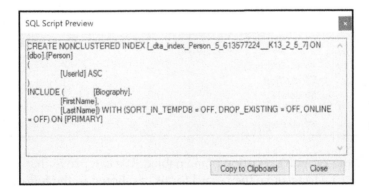

The `HasIndex()` Fluent API method would do the trick for us. It would use the marked column(s) and create a non-clustered index in the data store, and the code required for our example is shown as follows:

```
protected override void OnModelCreating(ModelBuilder
modelBuilder)
{
  // Code removed for brevity
  modelBuilder.Entity<Person>()
    .HasIndex(p => new { p.FirstName, p.LastName });
}
```

The migration added and updated to the database would create the required non-clustered index, as shown in the following screenshot:

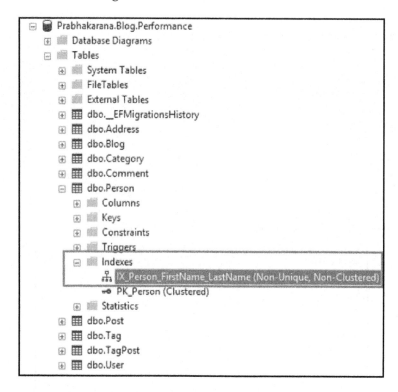

Let's run the same query with execution plan enabled. We can prove that the operation now consumes only one row to retrieve the record for us, as shown in the following screenshot:

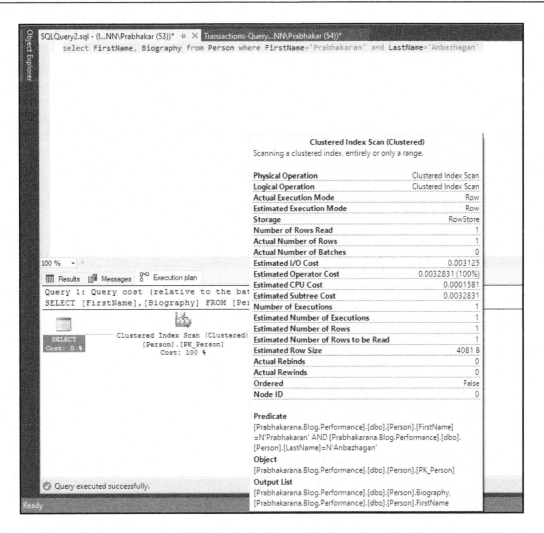

We have seen how to create an index required to optimize our retrieval query, which concludes our analysis and solution towards better performance.

Summary

We have explored multiple performance issues that we might run into, and the solutions required to tackle those issues. We started with the tracking behavior of EF Core and its projection behavior, then we explored detecting changes with bulk insert/updates, and how to handle them. We enhanced the application by supporting asynchronous operations, which allow us to handle threads effectively. Then we analyzed/fixed the data that was retrieved and transmitted over the network, right from volume, and columns until a number of database calls made to the data store. Finally, we saw how the data type mismatch affects us, also how the missing indexes affect our retrieval performance, and the way to improvise in those scenarios. The performance improvement measures we have been investigating in this chapter would help us in improving a system with worst performance (10,000ms+) to a system with best performance (<=1000 ms) which will be the performance **Service Level Agreement (SLA)** of most systems. So far, we have been dealing with only one tenant in the data store. In Chapter 12, *Isolation – Building a Multi-Tenant Database*, we will be dealing with a multi-tenant database and its row-level security.

12
Isolation – Building a Multi-Tenant Database

We explored multiple performance issues that we might run into, and the solution required to tackle those issues. We started with the tracking behavior of EF Core, its projection behavior, and then we explored detecting change issues with bulk insert/updates and how to handle them. We enhanced the application by supporting asynchronous operations that allow us to handle threads effectively. Then, we analyzed/fixed the data that was retrieved and transmitted over the network, right from volume and columns, up until the number of database calls made to the data store. Finally, we saw how the datatype mismatch affected us, also how the missing indexes affected our retrieval performance, and the way to improvise in those scenarios.

Let's discuss the authentication implementation required, and then row-level security, and later multi-tenancy in this chapter.

The sections we will be including in this chapter are as follows:

- Authentication in the blogging system
- Row-Level Security:
    - Filter predicate
    - Block predicate
- Multi-tenancy:
    - Standalone
    - Database-per-tenant
    - Shared multi-tenant
    - Dive into multi-tenancy

Authentication in the blogging system

The authentication mechanism is the foundation required to support row-level security or multi-tenancy in the system, so we have to start building authentication in our application. There are various forms of authentication available, but we will be implementing cookie-based authentication in our blogging system.

The following code block will add cookie-based authentication as a service inside the `ConfigureServices()` method of `Startup.cs`:

```
public void ConfigureServices(IServiceCollection services)
{
  // Code removed for brevity
  services.AddAuthentication(o =>
  {
    o.DefaultAuthenticateScheme =
    CookieAuthenticationDefaults.AuthenticationScheme;
    o.DefaultChallengeScheme =
    CookieAuthenticationDefaults.AuthenticationScheme;
  })
  .AddCookie();
}
```

The configuration required to use the cookie-based authentication service must be performed inside the `Configure()` method of `Startup.cs`, as shown here:

```
public void Configure(IApplicationBuilder app,
IHostingEnvironment env,
ILoggerFactory loggerFactory, BlogContext blogContext)
{
  // Code removed for brevity
  app.UseAuthentication();
}
```

The authentication could be applied globally to all controllers by adding `AuthorizeFilter` to the configuration `Filters` collection. The required configuration should be performed inside the `ConfigureServices()` method of `Startup.cs`, as shown here:

```
public void ConfigureServices(IServiceCollection services)
{
  // Code removed for brevity
  services.AddMvc(configuration =>
  {
    var authorizationPolicy = new AuthorizationPolicyBuilder()
      .RequireAuthenticatedUser()
```

```
        .Build();
    configuration.Filters.Add(new
    AuthorizeFilter(authorizationPolicy));
}).AddJsonOptions(options =>
    {
        options.SerializerSettings.ContractResolver = new
        DefaultContractResolver();
        options.SerializerSettings.ReferenceLoopHandling
          = Newtonsoft.Json.ReferenceLoopHandling.Ignore;
    });
}
```

Enabling authorization across the controllers would enforce the authentication API to redirect the user to `Account/Login`, which is the default route in authentication. Since the `Login` action also requires authorization, we may end up in an infinite redirect to the same action that would throw the following error message: **HTTP Error 404.15 - Not Found**. The request filtering module is configured to deny a request where the query string is too long. Please refer to the following screenshot:

We can solve this issue by enabling the anonymity using the following code snippet that includes the `AllowAnonymous` attribute to the `Login` action method:

```
[AllowAnonymous]
public IActionResult Login(string redirectUrl)
{
  ViewBag.RedirectUrl = redirectUrl;
  return View();
}
```

We will also need the `Login` `HttpPost` action to be anonymous since the user will not be authenticated while sending his login credentials to the server, so add `AllowAnonymous` to the following action as well:

```
[AllowAnonymous]
[HttpPost]
public async Task<IActionResult> Login(LoginViewModel
loginViewModel)
{
  // Code removed for brevity
  var claims = new List<Claim>
  {
    new Claim(ClaimTypes.Name, loginViewModel.Username)
  };

  var claimsIdentity = new ClaimsIdentity(
    claims,
    CookieAuthenticationDefaults.AuthenticationScheme);

  await HttpContext.SignInAsync(
    CookieAuthenticationDefaults.AuthenticationScheme,
    new ClaimsPrincipal(claimsIdentity));
  return RedirectToAction("Index", "Home");
}
```

The authentication-related implementation is committed to the Git repository and is available in the following URL:

`goo.gl/XudiqY`

We can run and see how the authentication and authorization works in the blogging system. From the following illustration, we can see that the **Register** and **Login** functionality is included, the other admin hyperlinks were hidden from the user, and, finally, Blog and **Recent Posts** were made anonymous so that any user could see the blog posts. Please refer to the following screenshot:

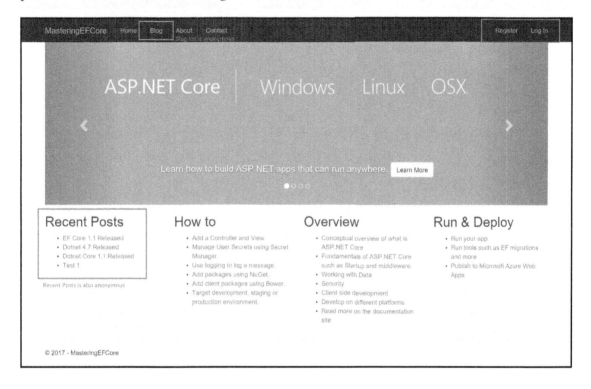

The **Blog** page displays the list of blog posts created in the system and is anonymously available to the user to read them. The following image shows the posts from different blogs listed on the same page anonymously, as expected:

Opening any one of the posts will show the following blog post display page, which displays a post with corresponding comments, a provision to add comments (even anonymously), and, finally, an **About** section that briefs us about the author:

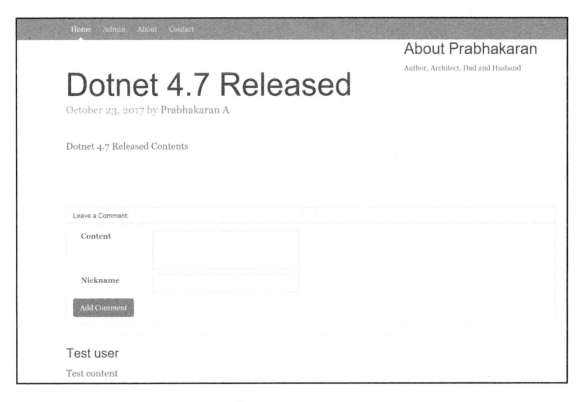

If we would like to access the **Admin** screens, we need to login to the system. Let's use the following **Login** screen to get authentication to access the authorized section of the system. On successful authentication, the system will generate a cookie for the user that will be used by the system to ensure that the user is authenticated in his concurrent requests:

On successful authentication, we will be seeing the following highlighted modules visible on the screen, the first one is the *Welcome* message of the user and the other is the admin links visible in the navigation bar:

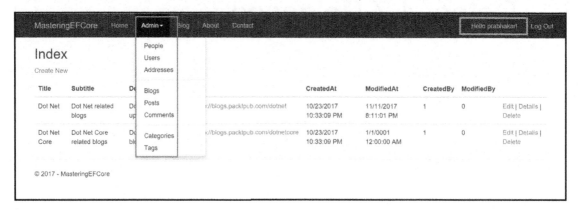

Now we are good to go, the system can now support row-level security, which is discussed in the next section.

Row-Level Security

The **Row-Level Security (RLS)** will allow us to maintain data from all users in a single database, but still ensure that only data related to the user is shared and the other user's content is kept hidden. The underlying logic could be implemented in any approach, which is left to the developer's creativity, but we will stick with tenants since we will be dealing with multi-tenancy in the system. Let's create a `Tenant` type using the following code snippet that can accommodate a person's information along with their tenant ID and name:

```
public class Tenant
{
    public Guid Id { get; set; }
    public string Name { get; set; }
    public Person Person { get; set; }
}
```

We have included two tenants to test the row-level security in our implementation, and we have used two people available in the system to have tenants mapped to them; now, configure the tenants as shown here:

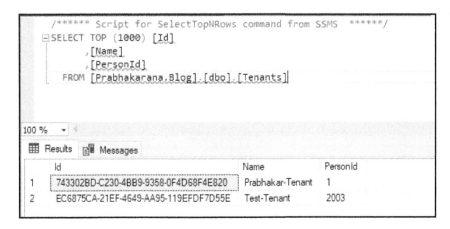

We had three entries in the Person entity, one was an anonymous user and the other two were registered users, the registered users having ids **1** and **2003** shown in the following screenshot were configured while creating tenants:

The Blog entity does not have a provision to segregate the contents based on the tenants. We need to support tenant in the Blog entity; include the following code lines to have `TenantId` property to have tenant support in the Blog entity:

```
public class Blog
{
    // Code removed for brevity
    public Guid TenantId { get; set; }
}
```

The migration should be added and the database should be updated to have the blog entity support tenants. Once you complete modifying the blog data to contain appropriate tenant IDs based on the author information, it should have the following data in the datastore:

The Post entity does not have tenant support either. We should follow the same approach of adding the following code snippet to support tenants in the `Post` entity:

```
public class Post
{
    // Code removed for brevity
    public Guid TenantId { get; set; }
}
```

Once migration is added and updated to the datastore, we should be performing the same data modification as we did to blogs that will have the following posts data in the datastore:

The system now supports tenants. Let's move on and perform the configuration required to ensure that tenant information was properly maintained.

Filter predicate

We will start with creating the tenant predicate using the following code that will allow the user to perform read operations based on the given tenant id or return all data if no tenant id is provided:

```
CREATE FUNCTION dbo.TenantPredicate (@TenantId
uniqueidentifier)
    RETURNS TABLE
    WITH SCHEMABINDING
AS
    RETURN SELECT 1 AS TenantPredicateResult
    WHERE (@TenantId = CAST(SESSION_CONTEXT(N'TenantId') AS
    uniqueidentifier))
OR
    (SESSION_CONTEXT(N'TenantId') =
    convert(nvarchar(50),cast(cast(0 as binary) as
    uniqueidentifier)))
```

The preceding `TenantPredicate` function will accept tenant id as an input parameter and returns a bit value as a table if the tenant id matches with the one from the session, or if it's empty. The tenant id will be matched for the authorized users and the empty tenant id will be used to display all posts for admins or anonymous users (anonymous user do not have a tenant id).

Once the predicate is created, we can use them in creating security policies, and, since we are dealing with filter predicate, let's create a tenant policy for `read` operations. The following piece of code will create a filter predicate on blogs and posts, and whenever a read operation is performed on those entities, the predicate kicks in and verifies and filters data based on the session value:

```
CREATE SECURITY POLICY dbo.TenantPolicy
ADD FILTER PREDICATE dbo.TenantPredicate(TenantId) ON dbo.Blog,
ADD FILTER PREDICATE dbo.TenantPredicate(TenantId) ON dbo.Post
GO
```

The session context of `TenantId` could be set using the following SQL query that passes key and value to the `sp_set_session_context` stored procedure. The code sets the `Prabhakar-Tenant` in the session context, which means it will serve data only specific to that tenant unless and until the session is changed or cleared:

```
EXEC sp_set_session_context @key=N'TenantId', @value='743302BD-
C230-4BB9-9358-0F4D68F4E820'
```

Once the session is set, any read operation will yield result based on the session tenant configuration. The following screen displays that the `Prabhakar-Tenant` is set in the session, then the posts retrieved were only related to that tenant which ensures that the filter predicate is working as expected:

If we change the tenant to a Test tenant, then the post related to Test tenant alone will be returned as shown here:

We explored the filter predicate right from configuration up until verifying it through a read operation. Now, we will explore the block predicate in the next section.

Block predicate

The block predicate is similar to the filter predicate with respect to configuration, only it restricts the user from performing write operations on other tenant's data. As mentioned, the configuration remains the same with a few changes, as shown in the following piece of code, instead of allowing anonymous users to access. We will restrict it only to the administrators, as highlighted here:

```
CREATE FUNCTION dbo.TenantPredicate (@TenantId uniqueidentifier)
    RETURNS TABLE
    WITH SCHEMABINDING
AS
    RETURN SELECT 1 AS TenantPredicateResult
    WHERE (@TenantId = CAST(SESSION_CONTEXT(N'TenantId') AS
uniqueidentifier))
OR
    -- Add administrator support once roles were implemented
```

The security policy creation is also similar, as displayed here. The only difference will be the predicate used in the policy, which will be the block predicate in our case:

```
CREATE SECURITY POLICY dbo.TenantPolicy
ADD BLOCK PREDICATE dbo.TenantPredicate(TenantId) ON dbo.Blog,
ADD BLOCK PREDICATE dbo.TenantPredicate(TenantId) ON dbo.Post
GO
```

The write operations should be performed in a similar way, where the session context should be set first with the tenant id, based on that the write operation should be performed. The following illustration shows that the session context is set to `Prabhakar-Tenant` and a write operation is performed:

We never discussed failure scenarios when a user tries to `write` record in another tenant. The following screenshot shows that an error, **The attempted operation failed because the target object 'Prabhakarana.Blog.dbo.Blog' has a block predicate that conflicts with this operation. If the operation is performed on a view, the block predicate might be enforced on the underlying table. Modify the operation to target only the rows that are allowed by the block predicate.**, would be returned if there is any violation to the predicate:

We explored row-level security using both filter and block predicates. Now, we will move on to the multi-tenant databases in the next section.

Multi-tenancy

The people living in a gated community could be easily related with the term multi-tenancy. We will be having multiple families living in their own flat/home (a user) within a building/phase (a tenant); together, they will form a gated community that is nothing but multi tenancy. In software terminology, a system supporting a set of users grouped together as a tenant (based on roles) would have their data stored in a single or shared database, and still serving data based on the tenant is called multi-tenancy.

The multi-tenancy application can be classified as follows:

- Standalone
- Database-per-tenant
- Shared multi-tenant

We will explore each one of the applications individually in the next sub-sections.

Standalone

The standalone model deals with an individual application and its own database, isolating everything from different tenants, right from database to the application. It helps the developers to customize the application and have different schema for different customers, which will be widely used in product-based companies. Nowadays, companies were drifting toward this approach due to microservices architecture. Also, the need arises based on the volume of the transactions and the sensitivity of data.

The following diagram explains the standalone model, where each application has its own database:

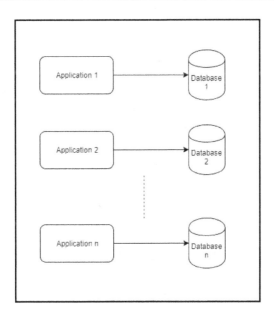

If we watch closely, there is one more thing: the application will never interact with each other. In the multi-tenancy terminology, each application instance is owned by a tenant and the tenant has ownership to the complete the database. The financial institutions will have the standalone model due to sensitivity and volume of data. It would be easy for the developers to provide access to the vendors if they want to customize, have control over their data, scale the application or database without affecting others, and more, yet, still, its a costly solution since it deals with multiple database from a software company's perspective.

We explored the standalone model in this section. Now, let's move on to database-per-tenant in the next section.

Database-per-tenant

The database-per-tenant model deals with a single/shared application, but with its own database (tenant, have their own database), isolating the database alone. It will help developers have a single code base for the application having customization kept in the database; if they do not move all their customization to the database, they end up affecting every vendor whenever any new features/product support is included in the system. The database isolation will help the companies have control over data, even though the code base is shared across the vendors.

The following diagram explains the database-per-tenant model where one application has its multiple databases (one per tenant):

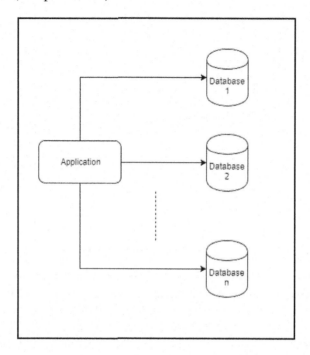

The main drawback in sharing a common application is that if any one of the vendor has more threshold, then the entire application has to be scaled-up. In the multi-tenancy terminology, one application instance is shared by all the tenants and the tenant has complete ownership to its own database. The insurance companies providing customized packages to vendor companies could be having this model, which would let them have control over functionality, yet still would let the vendors have control over their data. It would be easy to deploy any vendor customization, but any feature deployment would become difficult since the code base or the application has been shared across.

We explored the database-per-tenant model in this section. Now, let's move on to shared multi-tenant in the next section.

Shared multi-tenant

The shared multi-tenant model deals with a shared application and all the tenants shared the single database, isolating the application alone. It helps the developers to deploy features quickly, without affecting other vendors still maintaining the data in a single database. Any schema-related changes would be under much scrutiny as it affects all the other vendors as well as makes the database tightly coupled with other vendors.

The following diagram explains the multi-tenant model where each application shares the same database:

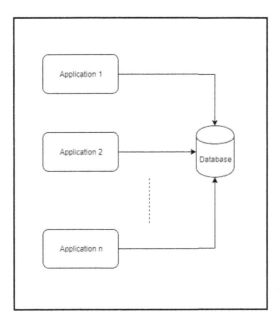

The main drawback in sharing a common database is that if any one of the vendor has more volume, it affects all the consuming vendors, forcing us to scale-up the database server. In the multi-tenancy terminology, multiple application instances of all the tenants share a single database. A company with different departments/modules sharing a single database will be a right candidate for this model. Each department will be considered as a tenant that will have its own users, yet it still shares the single database across the enterprise. It would be easy to deploy any feature quickly, but vendor customization would become difficult since the application shares a common database.

We explored the multi-tenant model in this section. Now, let's move on to the multi-tenancy implementation in the next section.

Dive into multi-tenancy

The multi-tenancy implementation is completely dependent on the tenant configuration that was built in the row-level security section in this chapter. The Entity Framework Core eradicates the necessity of any custom implementation or any third-party package to handle tenant handling in the system. EF Core 2.0 provides query-filtering features that allows us to filter the tenant based on the configured ID right in the data-context level.

The code required to implement the tenant configuration in the data context is highlighted here:

```
public class BlogContext: DbContext
{
  // Code removed for brevity
  public Guid TenantId { get; set; }
  protected override void OnModelCreating(ModelBuilder
  modelBuilder)
  {
    modelBuilder.Entity<Blog>()
     .ToTable("Blog")
     .HasQueryFilter(item => item.TenantId.Equals(TenantId));
    modelBuilder.Entity<Post>()
      .ToTable("Post")
      .HasQueryFilter(item => item.TenantId.Equals(TenantId));
    // Code removed for brevity
  }
}
```

The controller implementation required for tenant handling is pretty straightforward:

- The User identity name is used to retrive the Person information from the data store
- From the Person entity, the tenant id is retrieved
- The retrieved identity is then configured in the data context, which will be used in the corresponding data context operations

The preceding implementation steps were followed in this piece of code to configure tenants in the data context from a controller:

```
public class BlogsController : Controller
{
  // Code removed for brevity
  public async Task<IActionResult> Index()
  {
    SetTenantId();
```

```
      return View(await _context.Blogs.FromSql("Select * from
      dbo.Blog").ToListAsync());
    }

  private void SetTenantId()
  {
    if (this.User == null) return;
    var person = _context.People.FirstOrDefault(item =>
    item.User.Username.Equals(this.User.Identity.Name));
    if (person != null)
    {
        _context.TenantId = person.TenantId.HasValue ?
      person.TenantId.Value : Guid.Empty;
    }
    return;
  }
```

Do not forget to drop the predicates included in the previous section, otherwise, the application may not yield any results from the Blog or Post entities. Execute the following SQL query to remove predicates from the tenant policy:

```
ALTER SECURITY POLICY dbo.TenantPolicy
DROP FILTER PREDICATE ON dbo.Blog,
DROP FILTER PREDICATE ON dbo.Post,
DROP BLOCK PREDICATE ON dbo.Blog,
DROP BLOCK PREDICATE ON dbo.Post
GO
```

The **Blog** listing page looks like the following screenshot before the tenant configuration is in place, which contains all the blog information even though the user from Prabhakar-Tenant tenant is logged in:

MasteringEFCore	Home	Admin ▾	Blog	About	Contact			Hello prabhakar!	Log Out

Index

Create New

Title	Subtitle	Description	Url	CreatedAt	ModifiedAt	CreatedBy	ModifiedBy	
Dot Net	Dot Net related blogs	Dot Net related blogs updated	http://blogs.packtpub.com/dotnet	10/23/2017 10:33:09 PM	11/11/2017 8:11:01 PM	1	0	Edit	Details	Delete
Dot Net Core	Dot Net Core related blogs	Dot Net Core related blogs	http://blogs.packtpub.com/dotnetcore	10/23/2017 10:33:09 PM	1/1/0001 12:00:00 AM	1	0	Edit	Details	Delete
test	test	test	https://test	11/27/2017 12:00:00 AM	11/27/2017 12:00:00 AM	2003	0	Edit	Details	Delete

© 2017 - MasteringEFCore

Once the tenant implementation is completed, the following screenshot proves that the same user who logged in the preceding scenario will now have only two records from the database to which the user from Prabhakar-Tenant will have access to:

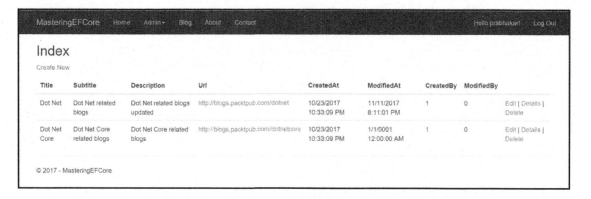

The user from `Test-Tenant` has logged in the following screenshot and the data is limited to only one to which the tenant user will have access to:

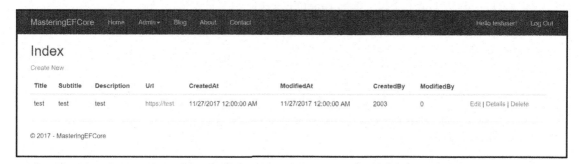

We explored the multi-tenancy and the different models available in them, and then we finally configured and used multi-tenancy in our blogging system.

Blocking cross-tenant write operation

The multi-tenant implementation does not restrict users from performing cross-tenant updates like we handled in the row-level security section. We should add this support in our blogging system through multi-tenant implementation. The current code base does not allow us to extend the behavior. So far, the information of tenants was stored only in the entities that do not let's validate them generically on data context. We have a strong requirement to get a taste of **Domain-driven design (DDD)** so we can start using EntityBase in our application. The following entity code has Id and TenantId fields that contain entity identifier and tenant identifier of the user who owns the entity:

```
public class EntityBase
{
  public int Id { get; set; }
  public Guid TenantId { get; set; }
}
```

The EntityBase class should be consumed by the entities that should be a part of a tenant implementation; this enforcement will help us in handling cross-tenant updates. This does not stop the user to implement tenants without inheriting from EntityBase, it just does not handle cross-tenant updates out of the box. The Blog entity should inherit EntityBase; this enforces us to remove the redundant Id and TenantId fields as shown here:

```
public class Blog : EntityBase
{
  // Remove the Id and TenantId fields
  // Code removed for brevity
}
```

The cross-tenant update should be handled in BlogContext, which will allow us to override the SaveChanges() method. The EntityBase type is the key in differentiating entities that support tenants from the others. The following piece of code filters ChangeTracker entries based on EntityBase and projects TenantId as a distinct list, which would allow us to validate and throw an exception if there are more than one tenants present in the filtered tenantIds:

```
public class BlogContext: DbContext
{
  public override int SaveChanges()
  {
    ValidateMultiTenantPersistence();
    return base.SaveChanges();
  }
  // Override other save changes as well
```

```
private void ValidateMultiTenantPersistence()
{
  var tenantIds = ChangeTracker.Entries()
      .Where(item => item.Entity is EntityBase)
      .Select(item => ((EntityBase)item.Entity).TenantId)
      .Distinct();
  if (!tenantIds.Any()) return;
  if (tenantIds.Count() > 1 ||
  !(tenantIds.Count().Equals(1) &&
  tenantIds.First().Equals(TenantId)))
  {
      throw new MultiTenantException("Invalid tenant id(s) found:
      " + string.Join(", ", tenantIds));
  }
 }
}
```

We have used a custom exception in the preceding implementation, but we haven't implemented it, so let's do it now. The custom exception is expected to inherit an Exception type, and it should also have a provision to contain the error message to pass it on or the data required to build the error message. In the following code snippet, we are receiving a custom error message injected by the consuming code that throws it:

```
public class MultiTenantException : Exception
{
  public string ErrorMessage { get; private set; }
  public MultiTenantException(string errorMessage)
  {
    ErrorMessage = errorMessage;
  }
}
```

The last piece of the puzzle, TenantId, must be set in the controller that consumes the data context, and the following piece of code will set the tenant information. The user information is retrieved using the logged in user's identity. Get TenantId from the data store and finally update it in the data context:

```
public async Task<IActionResult> Create(Blog blog)
{
  SetTenantId();
  blog.TenantId = _context.TenantId;
  // Code removed for brevity
}
private void SetTenantId()
{
  if (this.User == null) return;
  var person = _context.People.FirstOrDefault(item =>
```

```
      item.User.Username.Equals(this.User.Identity.Name));
      if (person != null)
      {
        _context.TenantId = person.TenantId.HasValue ?
        person.TenantId.Value : Guid.Empty;
      }

    return;
  }
```

We have completed our cross-tenant update handling, and the blog creation will let us see them in action. The blog create operation will set `TenantId` from the logged in user `prabhakar`, who is a part of the tenant, `Prabhakar-Tenant`, with the `{743302BD-C230-4BB9-9358-0F4D68F4E820}` identifier, as illustrated in this screenshot:

The tenant id could not be modified, but for illustration purpose, let's modify the tenant information and see how the update is handled in the data context. The `TenantId` that is modified in the **Immediate Window**, from `{743302BD-C230-4BB9-9358-0F4D68F4E820}` `(Prabhakar-Tenant)` to `{EC6875CA-21EF-4649-AA95-119EFDF7D55E}` `(Test-Tenant)`, is highlighted in the following screenshot:

```
129        [HttpPost]
130        [Route("Create")]
131        [ValidateAntiForgeryToken]
132        public async Task<IActionResult> Create(Blog blog)
133        {
134            SetTenantId();
135        ▶ blog.TenantId = context.TenantId;
136        if (ModelSt ▷ 🔍 blog.TenantId {ec6875ca-21ef-4649-aa95-119efdf7d55e} ⊟
```
```
Immediate Window
blog.TenantId = Guid.Parse("{ec6875ca-21ef-4649-aa95-119efdf7d55e}")
{ec6875ca-21ef-4649-aa95-119efdf7d55e}
```

If we further process with the updated `TenantId`, we will get the following highlighted exception since the `Blog` entity is marked with `EntityBase`. The exception is thrown as highlighted here, because `TenandId` retrieved from the change tracker does not match `TenantId` from the data context:

```
private void ValidateMultiTenantPersistence()
{
    var tenantIds = ChangeTracker.Entries()
                    .Where(item => item.Entity is EntityBase)
                    .Select(item => ((EntityBase)item.Entity).TenantId)
                    .Distinct();

    if (!tenantIds.Any()) return;
    if (tenantIds.Count() > 1 ||
        !(tenantIds.Count().Equals(1) && tenantIds.First().Equals(TenantId)))
    {
        throw new MultiTenantException("Invalid tenant id(s) found: " + string.Join(", ", tenantIds)); ≤1ms elapsed
    }
}
```

The exception thrown from the controller will be rendered as displayed in the following screenshot. This does not redirect to the custom error page since the ASPNETCORE_ENVIRONMENT is set to Development, the users from the other environment will view a custom error screen that will limit the information rendered to the user:

The anonymous pages would get affected due to the query filter, which could be handled using IgnoreQueryFilters() fluent api method. The RecentPosts module implementation could be fixed as shown in the following code:

```
public class GetRecentPostQuery : QueryBase,
IGetRecentPostQuery<GetRecentPostQuery>
    {
        // Code removed for brevity
        public IEnumerable<Post> Handle()
        {
            var posts = IncludeData
                        ? Context.Posts
                            .IgnoreQueryFilters()
                            // Code removed for brevity
                        : Context.Posts
                            .IgnoreQueryFilters()
                            // Code removed for brevity
            // Code removed for brevity
        }
        // Code removed for brevity
    }
```

The same approach could be applied on `GetPostByUrlQuery` and `GetPaginatedPostQuery` to render posts anonymously.

The cross-tenant update is handled using multi-tenant implementation with data context validation in this section. This makes the behavior consistent with the implementation we performed in the row-level security section as well.

Summary

We started with authentication implementation, which is the foundation for row-level security and multi-tenancy. Then, we explored row-level security and how we could manage them using filter and block predicates. Finally, we started exploring multi-tenancy and its different models and deep dived into the implementation in our blogging system. We have come to a conclusion in our EF Core journey, along with building a complete ecosystem for the blogging system.

We had explored Entity Framework Core by building a blogging system, the features were included in the system with the intention of covering topics. So ideally we could leverage the knowledge we had acquired so far to build a complete blogging ecosystem. We could develop our own .NET Core blogging system which could be deployed in any operating system, which saves our hosting cost a lot since we have a lot cheaper hosting options using Linux operating system. Glad I could help you in acquiring EF Core knowledge, the use case is not limited to blogging system but it is vast, you could now build any system you have in mind rapidly using EF Core ORM now. Happy coding!

Index

one-to-many relationship 90, 94
one-to-one relationship
  about 85
  building, with Fluent API 87, 90
optimistic concurrency
  about 266
  applying 287
  client wins 289
  database wins 288
  user-specific custom resolution 290

P

parameterized queries
  building 175, 177, 178, 180
pessimistic concurrency
  about 267
  applying 293, 297
  reference link 268
POrtable COmponents (POCO)
  about 169
  avoiding, for SQL query execution 188
post entity script
  about 36, 39
  reference link 36
post entity
  working with 45
principal entity 61
principal key 62
project
  creating 11, 40
  Entity Framework, installing 40
  File menu 12
  Start page 11
  Web App structure 15, 16

Q

queries
  composing, with commands 211, 216, 218
  enhancing, with expression trees 219
query object pattern
  about 196, 197, 199
  incorporating, into repositories 203
  used, for improving repositories 199

R

raw SQL queries
  about 170
  reference link 173
recent posts feature
  adding, to blogging system 251
RegularExpression field validation 138, 140
relational database facade extension
  reference link 188
relationship terms
  about 60
  alternate key 63
  Association 61
  Containment 62
  data models 60
  dependent entity 64, 65
  foreign key 65, 66
  navigation property 66
  principal entity 61
  principal key 62
relationships
  about 84
  building techniques 104
  building, with foreign key 104
  building, with principal key 105
  building, with required method 106
  many-to-many relationship 96, 98
  one-to-many relationship 90, 95
  one-to-one relationship 85
remote validation 161, 163, 166, 167
repositories
  about 199, 201
  assignment, solution 201, 202
  improving, with query object pattern 199
  list query object support 203, 206
  query object pattern, incorporating into 203
  single query object support 206, 210
  solution, with queries assignment 210
Required field validation
  about 115
  incorporating, in blogging system models 121
reverse engineering
  on database 42
Row-Level Security (RLS)